MW00577728

RISING ABOVE OFFICE CONFLICT

RISING ABOVE OFFICE CONFLICT

A Light-Hearted Guide for the Heavy-Hearted Employee

Clare E. Fowler

ROWMAN & LITTLEFIELD
Lanham • Boulder • New York • London

Published by Rowman & Littlefield
An imprint of The Rowman & Littlefield Publishing Group, Inc.
4501 Forbes Boulevard, Suite 200, Lanham, Maryland 20706
www.rowman.com

86-90 Paul Street, London EC2A 4NE

British Library Cataloguing in Publication Information Available

Library of Congress Cataloging-in-Publication Data

Names: Fowler, Clare E., author.
Title: Rising above office conflict : a light-hearted guide for the heavy-hearted employee / Clare E. Fowler.
Description: Lanham : Rowman & Littlefield Publishers, [2023] | Series: The acr practitioner's guide series | Includes bibliographical references and index.
Identifiers: LCCN 2022056445 (print) | LCCN 2022056446 (ebook) | ISBN 9781538171271 (cloth) | ISBN 9781538171288 (ebook)
Subjects: LCSH: Women—Employment—Psychological aspects. | Interpersonal conflict. | Interpersonal relations—Psychological aspects. | Conflict management—Psychological aspects. | Work environment.
Classification: LCC HD6053 .F69 2023 (print) | LCC HD6053 (ebook) | DDC 331.4—dc23/eng/20230216
LC record available at https://lccn.loc.gov/2022056445
LC ebook record available at https://lccn.loc.gov/2022056446

∞™ The paper used in this publication meets the minimum requirements of American National Standard for Information Sciences—Permanence of Paper for Printed Library Materials, ANSI/NISO Z39.48-1992.

Dedicated to my family, who gave me unlimited support. And mochas.

Thank you.

Because the ones I work for do not love me, because I have said too much and I haven't been sure of what is right and I've hated the people I've trusted, because I work in an office and we are lost and when I come home I say their lives are theirs and they don't know what they apologize for and none of it mended, because I let them beat me and I remember something of mine which not everyone has, and

because I lie to keep my self and my hands, my voice on the phone because I swallow what hurts me, because I hurt them—

I give them the hours I spend away from them and carry them, even in my sleep, at least as the nag of a misplaced shoe, for years after I have quit and gone on to another job where I hesitate in telling and I remember and I resent having had to spend more time with them than with the ones I love.

—Killarney Clary

CONTENTS

PREFACE

Years ago, some friends and I were having dinner. Cheryl and Leroy brought their crab dip, Kim and Shahalie brought perfect charcuterie boards with the little pepperoni roses, Paul and Junie brought a salad, and Willy and Becky brought smoked tri-tip. I was in a vegetarian phase, so I brought brownies.

We had a great night, but, as always, the conversation turned to work. And coworkers. And many, many complaints about their coworkers. "Backstabber," said Cheryl. "Micromanaging, idea-stealing, entitled egg-hole," said Alison. "%^&*," said Becky, who swears when she's frustrated.

I've studied this office conflict stuff for decades, so I should have been able to suggest a book or a resource, right? I scoured the hundreds of fantastic books written about workplace conflict—but they were all written for mediators and lawyers. I didn't have a single thing I could suggest that they would actually read. Trust me—I've tried handing hundreds of textbooks to my husband to point out how I think he should speak, and for some reason he never reads them. Clearly, I decided, there has to be a better book. Something that my husband and my friends, who have no interest in conflict resolution, would actually pick up. And heck, if I'm going to ask them to read something, why not make it something that they could actually enjoy?

By the way, my husband actually read this book, woo-hoo! He says to grab a beer and read the book; it works.

AUTHOR'S NOTE

FEMININE AND MASCULINE? STILL USING THOSE TERMS?

I've spent the last decade trying to find ways to resolve conflict that are empowering. And when I saw one that really worked, I would run it by some other mediators and then incorporate the idea and maybe some of their suggestions into this book. But one suggestion didn't sit right. A friend mentioned that I should avoid the terms *feminine*, *masculine*, any reference to gender or individual identity, and instead just say this is how all people responded. As if every person could be lumped into one group and that we all respond to conflict the same.

It felt like my friend was saying that instead of admiring the individual blue and pink and green Play-Doh, let's mush them all into one big ball. (Do your kids/nieces and nephews do that too? Mash all of the Play-Doh together and then it looks like a lump of refried beans?)

And I understand why my friend made that comment. Keeping all of the Play-Doh separate is hard. Squishing them together is easier—easier to study and to describe. Refried beans are just one color and consistency, which makes them easier to lump together.

It took me a few months of sitting with this to understand why I was resisting my friend's suggestion. Play-Doh is simply more interesting to look at when you can see the swirl of blues and greens and purples, and I don't want to squish all of these colors together as if each one wasn't beautiful, as if each one didn't deserve a spot of its own. Just like I don't want to squish feminine qualities and masculine qualities and nonbinary and trans qualities all together and act like they aren't wonderful all on their own. Even more, these gender roles have developed much different responses to conflict, which all have their own value, and by pretending that there are not any differences we are diminishing their uniqueness.

Sooooo instead of following my friend's advice and ignoring gender, I added a gender and culture analysis to each and every behavior chapter. There is just a lot of wisdom out there that works, and I want to describe it and pass it on to you. Some people can be so tender and warm and handle so many things with patience, in an amazingly stereotypical feminine response. Others can tune out distractions and bravely face a daunting conflict, with a stereotypical masculine response. Both responses have inherently beautiful qualities and are something to be proud of. My only request is that you don't choose a particular response because you are supposed to. Break out of your bucket! Look at all the different options and feel empowered to choose the blue or green or purple conflict resolution option that suits you.

Psychologist Mark Cummings tells us that we observed our parents'/guardians' fighting styles, the good and bad, the attack and the wait approach, and decided what to adopt for ourselves. What he realized was that children were drawn toward a particular approach based on their values or personality ("I want to be seen as caring," or "I want to be seen as brave") and then altered it later based on gender or culture. He encouraged people to return to the conflict resolution path that fit them best, saying that would be the most effective for them.

To choose which options are the most effective, I am keeping all of our different responses to conflict separated into lots of different buckets, feminine, masculine, LGBTQ+ when available, and even a few faith-based and political buckets. And I am sticking with the terms *feminine* and *masculine* to describe them for two reasons. First, many people can relate to the terms *feminine* and *masculine*. Also, incorporating the terms that have historically been used allows me to pull from the decades of research[1] analyzing feminine and masculine responses to conflict and share these with you.[2]

Many of the current feminine and masculine responses are based on research by Deborah Tannen,[3] who says:

- Men have a *report*-style approach to communication, and
- Women have a *rapport*-style approach.

I suggest reviewing the wins from both of these historical styles in this book, and then creating your own. So instead of limiting yourself to a report style or a rapport style, empower yourself and create your *resolve* style.

FIGHT LIKE A GIRL (OR BOY)

Most of my childhood was just me and my mom. And we had a blast. But a single mom, working, going to school in the evening, has no time for gender roles. She just did what had to be done. Chopped wood, painted my nails, fixed a tire, had a tea party, helped with my homework, and taught me how to throw a softball. I followed her approach of not worrying about gender roles and just doing what had to be done—and loving it.

I realized that I had grown up in a world where my mom taught me not to be confined by expectations. If I needed a tool from a pink bucket or a blue bucket, then I would grab it. If I needed to make up my own tie-dye bucket full of brand-new tools, that's exactly what I did.

I want to bring that mentality to conflict resolution. If there is an excellent approach to resolve a conflict, who cares if it is traditionally considered feminine or masculine? Reach deep into that bucket!

So how do we actually put that into practice? Well, as I describe these 20 different behaviors, I follow them up with a typical feminine and masculine response to that behavior, including thoughts on which one might be more effective for that situation and for different people. Learn about these cool options, and then design your own conflict adventure.[4]

EMPOWERMENT

Empowerment is such a buzzword right now that I am nervous to use it for fear it will be out of style or be turned into something offensive by the time this book is published. But there just isn't a better word.

When I was a little girl, I looked up to Princess Diana. She had the gentlest wave. With all the power of the monarchy at her fingertips, she still managed to acknowledge people so tenderly. I remember watching how she handled all the criticism and shade—with only a perfect smile. I thought this was how you handled difficult situations. Show them you hear their concerns with a demure smile. I used to think that her brief responses showed extreme self-discipline. Now I know differently: She didn't know what else to do.

When my husband was young, he looked up to Jack Lambert. Lambert was 6'4", so I guess most people looked up to him. He is known as the greatest linebacker of his era. Lambert was the Steelers Enforcer, Dracula in Cleats. He had lost his teeth, and he even decided not to replace them to make him look scary. See, he didn't weigh as much as many of the other linebackers, so scaring them was one way to get an initial edge. He wanted to be taken seriously, so he scared everyone around him: He didn't know what else to do.

This book is a story of empowerment when you don't know what else to do. It is learning how to handle controversy and criticism with something more than a gentle wave or scary dentistry. It is my own story, as I learned how to tackle things that scared me. It is my husband's story, as he created his own path for dealing with hardship. And it is the stories of thousands of employees who have walked through conflict and come out stronger and better for it.

INTRODUCTION

CONFLICT: AKA, HOW TO TURN A MESS INTO A BIGGER MESS

Let's face it—there are some really interesting characters in the workplace.

And some days it probably seems like all of those characters are in a story entitled *How Can We Annoy You Even More*.

Working with these very colorful characters has taught me three things:

- Conflict is in every workplace.[1]
- Conflict is probably going to be hard.[2]
- People want to get out of their conflicts but don't know how.

Most employees say they know conflict will hit their office someday, they know it is going to be hard, but they just don't know what to do about it and no one is helping. Imagine hearing a tornado warning for your area, and then hearing, "But we have no advice for you, folks, hope you make it through." Not the most hopeful outlook![3] No wonder we are facing a mental health crisis in our workforce.

People usually don't know how to get out of conflict because they don't understand how it started or how to find the exit. Imagine being dropped into the middle of a maze without knowing where the beginning or the end was but being expected to figure it out! Unless you are competing for the Goblet of Fire or on *The Amazing Race*, this can be really frustrating.

Conflict can come from two places: (1) the company structure (many companies are built on a competitive instead of a collaborative system—more on that later) or (2) from the people (most people want to communicate well with their coworkers, but sometimes it just feels like you are speaking a different language. Lots more on this throughout the book).

If people don't understand how the conflict started, how can they be expected to get out of it!? Instead, people resort to two completely different and very unhelpful tactics to end the conflict: (1) Ignore the entire conflict (turtling) or (2) attack everyone involved (thundering).[4]

There Is a Better Option!

The good news is that you are not the first person to argue with a coworker! Workplace fighting has happened before (think about Britney Spears's squabbles). So let's learn from what has worked for everyone else (we will also look at what has not worked for others—I'm looking at you, Cain and Abel) and then come up with your own plan of attack. Not like a literal, physical attack. Y'know, we will attack the problem metaphorically, not with fists.

Won't it be nice to find a better option and feel like you are finally in control, instead of the conflict controlling you? That you are empowered? That you have been given a guidebook that points you to your exit? To get out of a conflict, I often have my employees go through two steps, which is what we will do in this book: (1) Assessment: Determine what type of a behavior you are dealing with—some are wonderful, and some are Darth Vader reincarnated. (2) Action: Look at all of the options for getting out of the conflict and pick what will work best for you.

WHAT TO EXPECT WHEN YOU'RE READING

Why

Historic workplace studies used to just focus on money: making the company as efficient and profitable as possible. And many of these studies found that for a very short period of time, competition can increase profitability. Which means that many of our modern workplaces were founded on competitive principles.

However, recent studies have found that long-term competition is disastrous for the workplace. Great for the NFL, awful for office morale. Competition leads to increased depression, increased turnover, infighting, increased personal and sick days, and quiet quitting. Which all of course leads to decreased mental health and decreasing long-term company profits.

The current approach to company culture is collaboration. Even the National Institutes of Health is discouraging a competitive, critical office environment and instead encouraging companies to include employees in decisions and create a safe space for them to talk.[5] This culture is accepted in theory, but many offices still don't know how to put these collaborative practices into, well, practice. This means that many employees are stuck between a culture clash in management theory and employee culture, with zero training for navigating this perilous position. No wonder we needed a book on resolving office conflict!

What

Rising Above Office Conflict builds on thousands of mediations to show you what has worked for other companies and employees in all kinds of fields: hospitals and hospitality, tech and teaching, construction and commerce, faith and food. From these mediations, I listed the 20 most common behaviors people ask me about. Some are annoying behaviors because they are distracting (Chatty Patty, Inappropriate Ivan, The Hulk, etc.); some are annoying because you might be jealous of how effective they are (The Golden Child, People Pleaser, or Honey Badger). Then I list simple tips for what actually works with these behaviors—everything from ignoring it to talking about it to reporting it to quitting. Yes, many of these situations were taken from workplaces I have observed, but the facts, names, and places have, of course, all been changed.

But wait, there's more! There's a solutions explorer for trying out a few different options based on your identity or your values and deciding what makes sense for you.

Who

Rising Above Office Conflict is for every level of the workforce.

- Employees who are having a hard time with coworkers, customers, or management
- Managers who want to help their employees
- Everyone else (family, friends, HR, coworkers) who gets sucked into a conflict by proximity
- People who want control over their reactions to difficult situations
- People who just want to understand conflict a bit better

Format

These 20 behaviors are explained through stories, backed up by data, and then given a suggested response. There are 2 helpful behaviors and 18 difficult ones—see if you can figure out which is which!

I have given behaviors playful names to make it easier for us all to talk about them, but that doesn't mean that this isn't serious. Conflict can be really hard, and the toll it takes on our mental health is hard, and for some people just getting to work is really hard. But it is time that we figured out a way to talk about it, so I wanted to open the conversation by assigning names to the behaviors that we can all relate to.

Your Decision

The suggestions in this book are just that—suggestions. They are provided to give you advice about what has worked for other people. Pay attention to your "gut" reactions and decide which option is most in line with your values and your goals. I have included suggestions about gender, family, and faith-based values to jump-start your decision-making process. Whatever your role in the company, and whatever type of conflict you're facing, you should be able to turn to your specific type of conflict and find helpful tips.

You might be in the middle of the conflict maze, but you can use this guidebook to know where the maze started, and to find your exit.

1

CONFLICT

The Secret Playbook

So, you could spend $100K on a doctorate to learn some vocab about conflict.

But what if we saved you just a bit of time and money and reviewed the most important terms.

What causes conflict? Like my favorite In-N-Out burger, there's a quick and handy way to examine conflict:

THE 3 X 3 APPROACH

Three types of conflict:

1. **Internal**: When a *coworker* in your office is driving you nuts[1]
2. **External**: When a *customer* outside of your office is being really difficult[2]
3. **Systemic**: When your whole *office* is just messed up from top to bottom[3]

Three common causes of conflict:

1. **Communication**: When your coworker missed out on the drawing for *social skills*, this means they won't be winning any awards for kindness or clarity.[4]

2. **Scarcity**: When there just *isn't enough* of something you need, like resources for your job, time to do your job, or money for your pocket[5]
3. **Confusion**: When your boss explains something and you walk away *wondering* if you both speak the same language; not enough guidance on job and role definitions[6]

Three points of conflict:[7]

1. **Entrance**: When you realize that you are not on the same page with someone (conflict awareness—this stage is hard to avoid; it's going to happen)
2. **Escalation**: When someone has really crossed the line and it's time to tell them (conflict is starting to go uphill—hard to escape; you're in the thick of it)
3. **Exit**: When you figure out how to deal with each other going forward (conflict resolution—hard to achieve; until you found this book!)

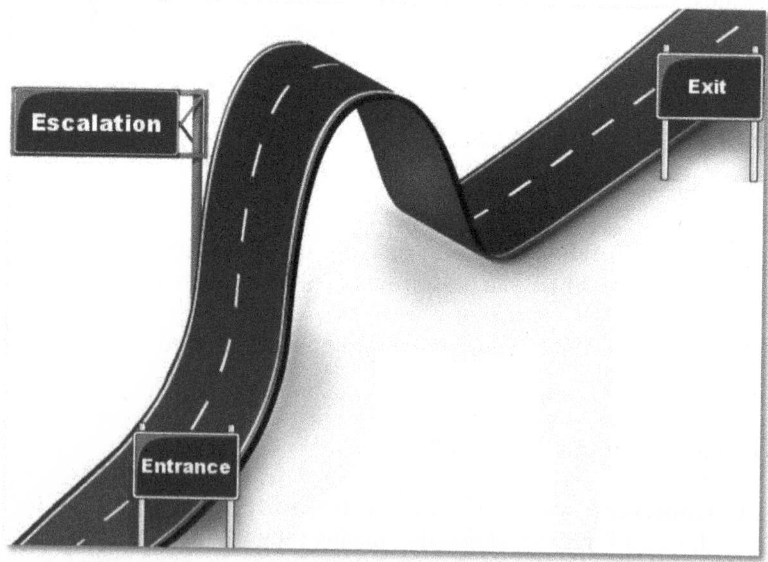

Source: Author

Everybody does conflict. What does this mean? It means conflict can and does happen everywhere, to everyone, in every aspect of your office (and your life).

Conflict is like a 3:00 a.m. salted caramel truffle ice cream craving—we all have them. (We do all have them, right? It's not just me?) Even the kindest, calmest person finds themselves in conflict. It's because we all have different values and different expectations, and when those bump into each other we end up in conflict. The key is to realize that these conflicts don't have to spiral out of control, you just need to learn a few new tools for dealing with your coworkers. Now that we understand the 3 x 3 theory to diagnose these conflicts, we can learn some of these new tools. First, read this book. Second, go out and tackle the conflicts in your life. Third, be excited about what you learn and how you grow. Fourth, celebrate with the salted caramel truffle ice cream.

2

POSITIVE CONFLICT

Choosing the Right Mindset for Wrongdoings

People say *you can always count on death and taxes*. But with Han Solo proving that cryogenics can help us avoid death, and with some of the crazy schemes that people go through to avoid taxes, perhaps it is more accurate to say *you can always count on conflict*. Every single relationship, given time, will experience a conflict. This doesn't mean there is something wrong with the relationship—it means it is deepening.

Once people move past the honeymoon phase of their workplace, they begin to see past the curtain. They realize that Sarah is a micromanager, Tom is vain, Shantara tells inappropriate jokes, Ralph is a pushover, and Leah is always late. This doesn't mean you need to quit—it means it is time for some difficult conversations.

This section provides a variety of choices you can make as you tackle conflict. You are not powerless. You are not stuck in your situation. But you do have a lot of decisions to make as you take back control. Choose your process and your outcome, and assess the effect on your mental health as well as the effect on your office. As you move through this chapter, take time to choose: What do you want from this conflict?

CHOOSING YOUR RESPONSE

So why are we looking at conflict from a gender viewpoint? (Please see earlier note about gender, and remember that means that a person of any gender is having a feminized or masculinized response.)[1] Think about how the royalty shamed Princess Diana. The Old Boys Club dismissed the new female hire. The chairman of the board would hit on his assistant after having a few drinks? What are we taught to do? Smile and wave, girls. Smile and wave.

So, some of us stuffed our frustration down, thinking we would just put up with it to keep our peace and keep our job. A study conducted by Alice Eagly and Steven Karau showed that given the same circumstances, women had to work harder than men to receive a promotion. This study also showed that when men and women occupied the same leadership position, women were perceived less favorably. We were seen as either too weak or too aggressive.[2] This made us look like babies, wimps who wouldn't stand up for themselves. Until some of us had more than we could bear, and then we exploded. We screamed and protested and shouted at the injustice—and rightly so! Now they call us bullies.

But shouldn't there be another option? Shouldn't there be a way to bring about change and respect without being a meek wallflower or an abrasive tyrant? Can't there be an option in between where we treat people with the respect we expect?

This requires two things:

1. Respect yourself. Realize that you deserve a healthy office environment. If your children were being mistreated at the office, wouldn't you stand up for them? Of course! But don't you deserve to be treated well in the office too? And don't you deserve someone to stand up for you? Absolutely! So, take that same Mama Bear energy you would use for your kids and use it to stand up for yourself!
2. Empower yourself. Once you identify your boundaries and your requirements for a healthy office, you will then need to protect those boundaries. And in order to protect those boundaries, you need the skills to be able to say "that is enough; it is time for change" in a way that people can hear you.

Realize that when you run into a conflict it is often indicative of a deeper issue with yourself or the other person. When members of the Boston Philharmonic Orchestra were getting into conflict, conductor Ben Zander told them that first they needed to look within themselves to find out why they were reacting this way.[3] In conflict, there is an unrecognized concern or an unvalidated value. Once we are at peace about those values, conflicts begin to lessen, which is why conflict is empowering—it is a signal to us that it is time to grow. Zander continually paused when members of his orchestra began to argue and told them to enjoy this opportunity to learn about themselves.

This book gives you the practical skills to move through conflict, and it also asks you to do some self-care and examine how you can grow through the conflict.

Going through conflict can be uncomfortable, but if handled appropriately it can be a positive experience. Yeah, right, you're thinking, the same way a root canal can be a positive experience, if we are able to focus on the outcome. But what you decide to do about conflict now will determine if this conflict will be a negative or a positive experience.

The reason most conflicts stink so much is that we don't know *how* to make them positive.

"Whoa, whoa, whoa," you're thinking. "That's taking it a little far. Conflict can't be a positive experience. The middle seat on the back row by the bathrooms of a bumpy plane would be a more positive experience." Just wait, keep reading. Let me try to make a believer out of you.

The key to a positive conflict outcome? Talk to each other.[4] I mean, that's it. To be totally honest, you could probably stop reading this book now, because you have the main point: Figure out ways to talk to each other. *We are taught how to do quadratic equations, invest in stock portfolios, change a tire—but we are not taught how to sit down and talk to each other.*

Choose to Talk to Each Other

One manager told me about an explosive argument with his team about the company website. A new hire was criticizing the website, calling it outdated and embarrassing. She addressed it at every staff meeting, she asked the IT department to redesign it, and she asked if time and funding could be allocated to work on the problem. "It was annoying—she kept nitpicking the website we designed," the owner said. "I remember she told me she felt excluded from the office, which was true, because we stopped inviting her to staff meetings. We were just so sick of her constant complaining!" People began to make fun of the new hire behind her back, saying that she would just disagree with any idea they had. They stopped telling her about meetings. People were putting notes on her office chair, "Hi, welcome to my office. Tell me your idea—so I can make fun of it." The manager was realizing he must have hired a critical, entitled millennial and it was probably time to just fire her. But, thank goodness, the manager (who was a millennial himself, by the way) wasn't a big fan of cancel culture. He wanted to see if they could work the problem out.

The manager asked her to come in and they just talked about what had been going on. And he listened. He was able to see where she was coming from. He called me later and said, "You know what? She was right. Our website *was* outdated and not useful. It was horrible having to fight with her about it for a year—it made the whole office uncomfortable. But now that I finally listened to her and did something about it, we have a much better website. Our sales are up and employees are happier. And we realized something: She will fight really stinking hard to make sure something is perfect. And our office is the better for it. We all apologized to her. She teases us about it now—good-naturedly. But we also learned that if we need something done right, we should take it to her."

Going through this conflict was hard because the team wasn't using the right communication tools. But in the end, it was positive—their website and their staff relationships improved.

Imagine if you went through life and everyone was like you. There wasn't any opportunity to learn anything new about anyone. I mean, actually imagine living with clones of yourself. (Okay, it does sound nice for a minute, we could always agree on dinner and what to watch!) But, could you think of a more boring way of life? Relationships would be so shallow! And what would you talk about? "So, I am still doing karate on Saturdays. And you? Oh, you are still doing karate on Saturdays? That's nice. Oh, you had gyros last night, so did I. So, uh yeah . . . still nothing new." Blech. We wouldn't learn anything. No richness or growth or diversity of thought.

If we spend our lives in an empty white room without any interaction, then we wouldn't learn anything new about anyone else. We also wouldn't have the opportunity to learn anything new about ourselves.

I picture a close relationship as two puzzle pieces. Over time they have pushed and pulled on each other and learned to lean on one's strengths and support the other's weaknesses. Every time we run into something new and different, there has to be a little push and pull on the relationship. This back-and-forth is what connects two puzzle pieces. The interlocking gives them strength.

If instead you put the flat edge of two side pieces next to each other, the two straight edges would just fall away from each other. Without any of the back-and-forth, there isn't anything holding these puzzle pieces together. And we are just like those puzzle pieces. The back-and-forth and push and pull of moving through conflict is what strengthens our relationships.[5]

Conflict is often a sign that we have run into something new, a new value or idea. And, this can feel scary if we don't know how to deal with it. But this book teaches you how to deal with new stuff so conflicts don't have to be scary. How exciting! You can be curious! You can learn all kinds of new things about people. I mean, let's be honest, some people are weird and you would probably rather not know all of these details. But a lot of people actually end up being pretty darn fascinating.

Conflict is also an opportunity to deepen relationships. You can grow, learn more about another, and forge a better bond when you run into a conflict, or you can hide in your hole and throw poison darts at each other with your eyes. Simply put, one reaction destroys relationships and one enhances them. The best relationships flourish when new data pours in, revealing the unexpected and expanding our acceptance of each other. In short, there is no way to have a meaningful relationship with someone without navigating a few conflicts.

Choose the Effect on You

Another hopeful aspect of modern conflict theory is that difficult conflicts can have positive effects on the office—and on you. Mediator Ken Sande says that conflict resolution is about more than just resolving the facts or numbers in a dispute, it should be an opportunity for growth.[6] Even when you decide that the best thing for you is to leave your current employment, this does not mean you have to see yourself as a victim or a failure. Instead, see it as an opportunity for growth. What have you learned from this experience? What will you take away from it so that you are not caught in this situation again? How has this empowered you to become stronger in the office? How will you help other people going through a similar situation?

Conflict might not be our first choice, but it forces us to grow.

Choose How to Enter into Conflict

Imagine you walk into a room and see two doors with signs that read:

Door A: Office Conflict Door B: Trip to Cancún

Most of us would probably choose Door B, because most of us avoid conflict when we can. It's uncomfortable. It's unpredictable. We could learn things about others or ourselves that we would rather not face.

Even if conflict is not exactly as fun as a trip to Cancún, you may still find yourself on the other side with the healthy glow of growth. For you . . . and those around you benefitting from your growth, conflict does not have to be awful or scary.

- Conflict forces us to learn more about other people.
- Conflict forces us to learn more about ourself.
- Conflict forces us to realize that we can have a difficult conversation with someone and not explode.

Choose to Protect Your Mental Health

Whenever I have an email that I don't know how to handle, I push it off. I spend my day handling all of the easy emails first. But the problem is that I still know I have to deal with that email. So, the entire day I have an extra bit of anxiety. I'm a bit shorter and terse in my responses, I can't fully relax or enjoy my day, because there is a looming uncertainty weighing on me.

The end of the day comes. Those dang Keebler elves didn't show up and take care of my email, so I guess I have to deal with it myself. And it is hard—figuring something out, finding a reference, or bringing up an awkward subject. But as soon as I send that email, there is an instant sense of relief. The cloud over my head gives way to blue skies. And I think, why didn't I just tackle this sooner?

Many workplaces are noticing deteriorating mental health. In 2020, Mental Health America surveyed 5,000 employees. Seventy-one percent said that the workplace had a strong effect on their mental health, and 83 percent said they were feeling emotionally drained from work.[7] And there can be many causes for that—changes from having been quarantined, international instability, chemical imbalances, past trauma. But I truly believe that a common cause of deteriorating mental health in workplaces is unaddressed coworker conflict. Just like that difficult email hanging over my head, an unaddressed conflict hangs in the air.

Some of the more common effects of unaddressed workplace conflict include:[8]

- Anxiety
- Trouble focusing
- Difficulty trusting coworkers
- Project failure
- Employees losing hope and motivation
- Absenteeism and turnover
- Termination

Mark Sinolak, MD, stated at the 2022 International Ombuds Association Conference (virtual) that office ombuds reported that 83 percent of workers' complaints involved relationship conflict. Simply put, relationship conflict exists in every workplace and it is draining employees. Dealing with it might not be the only way to improve one's mental health, but it definitely helps.

Many people try to ignore conflict and pretend it isn't that bad. They think maybe it will go away. Or that they can handle it. Or that they should be tough enough not to react to it. However, when we continually tell ourselves that the painful conflict isn't painful, we are gaslighting ourselves. We are telling ourselves that something isn't true, when our brain clearly knows it is. So listen to what your brain has been screaming at you! Take care of your mental health, avoid the therapy bills down the road, and let's go take care of your workplace conflict!

Choose the Effects on Your Office

Conflict can even help your office. Like the company website example earlier, staying with conflict can help to improve a product or a policy.

Imagine for a moment, what would happen if people decided to just avoid all difficult conversations. Imagine if Mother Teresa decided to just sit home, playing video games, eating Cheetos, and avoiding *any* difficult conversations. Nothing would ever change! Nothing would improve! So, even though it might be uncomfortable, change and improvements start with difficult conversations.

Your office can be improved. Every office can. There is a better way to order paper, respond to action items, celebrate successes, and so on. But nothing will change if no one is willing to talk about it.

THE PRICE OF CHANGE IS TALKING

> How far that little candle throws his beams! So shines a good deed in a weary world.
>
> —William Shakespeare, *The Merchant of Venice*

Have I convinced you yet? Let's tackle this conflict!

WORKPLACE COMMUNICATION CONFLICT THEORY

Choose Your Ingredients

Yes, I use a lot of food analogies. I often bake when I'm upset. I have spent a lot of time working out conflicts by mixing batter, so the two have just become intertwined for me. If this makes you hungry, I get it; it makes me hungry too.

Anyone who follows social media knows that people with similar values can end up with drastically different conclusions. Why? Simply put, people go through a different baking process.

Since I bake, a lot, my cupboards are eternally stocked with eggs, butter, sugar, flour, cocoa, vanilla, and baking soda. On a whim I can whip up a shortbread. After a rough day, I want to create a plate of brownies. Fine, two. Okay, three. All right? Three plates of brownies. If at the last minute I hear those cliché words, "Mom, you have to bring snacks for tomorrow's game," I excel in that moment—because I have the basic ingredients. These simple ingredients can morph into a variety of delectables depending on how you mix, match, and prepare them. You still with me? Or did you run to look for brownies?

Choose Your Outcomes

Let's translate those ingredients to values:

- Eggs for connection
- Butter for comfort
- Sugar for joy
- Flour for raising hope
- Cocoa for respect
- Vanilla for kindness
- Baking soda for lightening up difficult situations

We are all made up of these same basic ingredients. How in the world then do these common values yield such different outcomes?

What did you do with the ingredients? Did you make rich brownies or overdone sugar cookies? Perhaps pancakes or biscuits or doughnuts? Dang it, now I need a cookie. I'll be right back.

Most of us share the same fundamental collection of ingredients. We are born with similar sets of values: joy, respect, kindness. The amount measured out to us at birth, the proportions we add through experience, and the amount of heat applied is what changes the treat we serve up to the world.

Have you ever run into a childhood friend and realized that you went in a completely different direction? I recently saw a friend I had known through school, church camp, lots of Barbie play sessions, volunteer groups, and swim lessons. We left each other notes in our lockers, and we exchanged long letters after we moved away. But then I noticed we changed. She was tougher than I was—she could handle difficult things, she went on intense adventure hikes, and she had a tougher exterior. I know that we were fashioned out of the same ingredients—so how did we end up with such a different flavor?

ORGANIC PROCESSES ARE UNPREDICTABLE

You know what else is amazing about baking? It is rarely the same. I can use the same ingredients in the same way, but the flavor or the texture will always be a tiny bit different. I use the same recipe, but each batch of brownies is just a bit different. Okay, it is possible that I'm just not a very good cook, but I prefer to think the reason is simply: *Organic processes are unpredictable*. So even if two people with similar backgrounds and similar ingredients have been through similar things, life still is and will be unpredictable. Sometimes those variations are minor, but sometimes the results are unrecognizable from each other.

CHOOSE TO ATTACK THE PROBLEM, NOT THE PERSON

How does this relate to your coworkers? Hopefully, you have a lot of coworkers who you enjoy. You share the rosy glow of compatible values and shared experiences. And yet . . .

Unintentionally, we define our self-image and our self-identity through watching another's reactions. We tentatively state something, and if someone agrees, we feel a sense of acceptance.[9] "You hate it when he mansplains at a meeting? I do too!" we delight with identity-enforcing joy.

Quick science lesson to explain what's happening here: After making a statement, three parts of our brain are activated to gauge people's reactions to our statement.

1. The temporal lobes analyze the expression that we see on someone's face and interpret it (wide eyes indicate fear or surprise, upturned lips indicate joy, etc.).
2. The frontal lobes are constantly adjusting what we think, feel, and do depending on our surroundings, and anticipating how someone might react to those adjustments.
3. The insula takes this external information and internalizes it. This tells our body how to make adjustments in our communication to get the desired reaction.[10]

In the workplace setting, these processes in our brain are typically working together to get us a desired reaction of acceptance, respect, stability, affirmation, and connection. If we have read the social cues correctly and responded appropriately (for instance, we say something funny and our coworker laughs), we feel a sense of affirmation and connection in the workplace. We read the cues correctly and we did the right thing—yay! Such workplace relationships and communication are important for helping us feel safe and in normalizing our behavior. They allow us to let down our guard and feel like others accept us, that we are okay, we have made good decisions in life, we are likeable.

Similarities make us feel a sense of connection. But this is also why conflict can be scary—we are afraid that if we run into differences, we will lose that connection. This is confusing when our brain can no longer interpret the signals and understand how to reestablish that connection. Our brain responds by deciding either that we have done something wrong (feminized response) or that the other person has done something wrong (masculinized response) to break that connection. "There is a general consensus that women agonize more and blame themselves more and that men get over their blunders faster and tend to point their fingers at others."[11] It can hurt when you run into a difference of opinion, especially when it involves something meaningful that has percolated up from a deep value.

Let's say you and a coworker are very similar, but you have developed different views of management. One of you feels the importance of treating managers with utmost respect, whereas the other values honesty and tells a manager how they feel even if it is disrespectful. These two approaches of respect and honesty have very similar roots, but these values were measured, blended, and heated differently—so they are expressed differently in the world.

This is where things get tricky. You thought that you and your coworker had similar values, that you had a friend you could confide in, someone who accepted you. But then they go and develop their own belief, their own thoughts, that are different from yours. How dare they! This is a betrayal! An abandonment! A clear affront to your friendship!

Depending on your personality, you have two choices: run or attack.[12] You can avoid the difficult conversation and eventually abandon the relationship, walking away knowing that at least you didn't ruffle any feathers. Or, you can attack them for being so wrong, and thus destroy the relationship, but walk away knowing that at least you stood up for your identity.

Could there possibly be a third option? Yes. *Mediating Dangerously*,[13] *Getting to Yes*,[14] Mary Parker Follett's[15] ideas, and, well, hundreds of other mediation books describe this other way as attacking the problem, not the person. The problem is not the person. The problem is not knowing how to talk to that person. Once we know how to have that conversation, it can proceed remarkably well. Try framing this conversation with ingredients—"See, I am made up of connection eggs, and you have more respect cocoa." No, you don't think that would work? Okay, I have a better suggestion below.

"Attack the Person" Conversation

Imagine if I tried to reconnect with the childhood friend I mentioned earlier, and it went poorly. If I don't know how to have that conversation, it would probably look like this:

- This conversation could easily go off the rails because of a lack of my own self-confidence.
- If I don't feel completely comfortable with myself, then when I am placed around someone tougher than myself, I might need to tear her down to feel better.
- I might feel threatened and go out on the attack.
- I might interpret her normal statements as judgmental, because I am judging myself, so I am hearing her comments through my negative self-filter.
- I feel ashamed, guilty, frozen.[16]

If we were to try to speak at this point, it would be tentative, guarded, and I would likely replay the conversation over in my head all night.

I would feel attacked, or I would come out on the offensive and covertly attack her. By attacking her, we would never make any progress, and I would have lost the opportunity to reconnect with an old friend. She would feel defensive, and she would likely attack me back.

Unfortunately, this is our normal response, isn't it? When things go wrong, we either internalize or externalize the problem instead of looking for a middle ground. We assume that things are wrong because we either a) internalize the problem: "I have done something wrong" or b) project the problem: "there is something wrong with you."[17]

There is a study, "Robust Sex Differences in Jigsaw Puzzle Solving," about how different genders responded to conflict. Interestingly, women were able to put the puzzle together faster as they developed a strategy first that saved them time (put together the outline, organize by color, etc.) whereas men jumped in with a trial-and-error approach.[18] When given an incomplete puzzle, females typically blamed themselves. "I must have messed up. Maybe I dropped a piece, or I put it together wrong." Males typically blamed others. "They gave me a faulty puzzle. They messed up on the assembly." But neither of those responses actually solve the puzzle, do they? Instead of blaming oneself or blaming others, a more effective response might be, what is wrong here, and how can we fix it?

Deborah Tannen,[19] professor of sociolinguistics, explains that the difference is in how culture taught men and women to communicate. She says that women typically engage in rapport-talk, whereas men often engage in report-talk. Rapport emphasizes the emotional connection; report emphasizes the information. Responses to her work have suggested that the most effective conversation would be learning how to have both rapport and report conversations. Which is why we are studying a variety of approaches in this book! The report and rapport style, the intrinsic and extrinsic focus, the feminine/masculine approach are all incomplete and too limiting. Workers today need to have another approach—the ability to focus on both the information and the emotions.

"Attack the Problem" Conversation

If we switch the focus from each other to attacking the problem, workers can identify both the facts of what happened and also the emotional response.

What if my childhood friend and I tried to have the conversation again? What if I didn't blame myself or blame her? What if we just needed to figure out how to discuss our differences?

What if we could both honor each other, our similar values and backgrounds, and see each other with true curiosity about how our paths have changed?

> CURIOSITY: What if we could frame the conversation as, "I can't wait to get to know the new you! How should we do that?"
>
> ACKNOWLEDGMENT: Or, "Things have gotten awkward—we need to work on that!" Notice here, I am acknowledging that things are awkward and we are different.
>
> REMOVE BLAME: "Time has definitely pushed us apart, but I'd like to reconnect." With this statement I am not blaming myself or her. We simply are, and there is an external force on us that is causing the conflict. When the difference is caused by time, or past experience, or

pressures of work or children, then we can have an open discussion about fixing it without feeling judged. The second I feel judged, I will close up and judge you back, and the whole discussion is shot. It turns into an argument about who can be tougher and who is right, and we completely lose sight of the goal.

"Attack the Person" Conversation

The first type of conversation, where both sides attack each other, can feel really good, really righteous, in the short term. You each spit out everything you want to say, your adrenaline is raging, and you feel like you are finally standing up for yourself.

Unfortunately, your long-term self is already cringing, knowing that you are actively sabotaging what could just as easily be a good relationship on its way to getting better.

"Attack the Problem" Conversation

The second type of conversation allows both sides to be heard. Neither had to lose face. This paved the way for reconnecting respectfully and with dignity. This is what paves the way for long and sustainable friendships.

In workplaces we often end up working with people who have similar values but very different personalities. If we establish right from the beginning to be curious and open and interested and honor those differences, then this workplace will be founded on trust and respect.

CHOOSE HOW YOU FIGHT

For some reason, workplaces thought that women shouldn't fight.

That we should sit in the corner and look pretty. (Picture Betty Draper in *Mad Men*.)

So, most of us weren't taught how to fight well. Either we avoided the fight, or we came out swinging without taking stock of the damage.

Instead of feeling confined to these options, though, let's take a different approach. I am going to show you a few different tools—some historically called "feminine" or "masculine." You pick up whatever tools you need, or use these as a start to design your own tool.

Women typically have higher levels of estradiol and progesterone, which is associated with a low level of aggression. Instead, women tend to vent their frustration through indirect, more passive-aggressive options. Men tend to have higher levels of testosterone, which correlates with a high level of immediate and physical or verbal aggression.[20]

A stereotypical masculine fight response involves two guys duking it out, whether physically or verbally. Taking aggressive positions and testing each other's power to determine who wins. And sometimes power and resolve and determination have to be tested. (*I have two boys with masculine conflict instincts, and they are prime examples. Recently, for April Fool's Day, my younger son replaced the vanilla cream in the Oreos with mayonnaise. My older son took a bite, thinking it was regular vanilla cream. He gagged a few times, and then took off, ready for a smackdown. He found my younger son hiding, laughing, in the closet. They wrestled through it and were finally able to laugh it off.*)

A 2018 study points out that when women fight, they often bottle up their true interests. Once they reach the point where the situation has to be dealt with, women usually take one of two approaches: passive-aggressive communication (jabs and silent treatment) or the masculine approach (power posturing). Neither of these allow women to communicate their true interests and be validated. Without knowing how to get a good outcome from a fight, it's no wonder women have typically avoided a fight.[21]

Think for a moment about the typical feminine responses, and how well these lend themselves to effective conversations:

1. Women have a high emotional intelligence (EQ).[22] They are able to quickly pick up on signs of microaggression, emotional connection, and anxiety. (Men were typically higher skilled at recognizing signs of aggression.) Women can discern the other's emotional state and adjust their response to be the most effective.
2. Women are great at multitasking.[23] Technically, they aren't actually better, they can just do more things quickly and shift between tasks faster. They are able to consider their own interests, the other's interests, and their surroundings simultaneously.
3. Women have a high level of nurturing and empathy.[24] This helps women to see where the other side is coming from.

4. Most importantly: Women are typically incredible at expressing their feelings. Even though men were reported to feel emotions stronger, women were better at expressing these emotions verbally.[25] This is the key to a successful fight—being able to articulate what you want in a way that the other person can hear it. Without this ability, the fight never gets resolved.

So, according to my calculations, women make incredible fighters!

If we had been taught that it was okay to fight, what would a stereotypical feminine fight look like? (Yes, very stereotypical, but why stop generalizing now?)

Woman A: I am upset about X.

Woman B: I can see that you are upset. I feel bad that you are upset. I am also upset.

Woman A: I think that Y would fix it.

Woman B: I understand. I also want Z. If we could do a combo of Y and Z, I agree that would fix it.

Woman A: That makes sense. Thank you for listening. Let's do YZ.

Woman B: Sounds good. I feel heard.

FIXING THE FIGHTING IN TWO STEPS: (1) ASSESS; THEN (2) ACT

The first half of this book contains chapters to help you assess different behaviors and situations.

The second half helps you decide what you are going to do about it.

The assessment half of this book helps you to diagnose and understand the workplace conflict you are dealing with. The action half gives you options for resolving this conflict. For instance, some conflicts you need to resolve with a quiet grace and with firm boundaries. Some conflicts you need to take by storm and let your warrior roar! Some companies can grow from what you are learning and improve as a whole. And some companies just don't deserve this amazing you, and it might be better to move on.

(I) Assess

Gather information about your situation and your coworkers. Understanding your coworkers' particular brand of bothersome bananapants behavior and why they do what they do is surprisingly satisfying. Unfortunately, after understanding what is going on, many people stop there. But understanding is only the first step—this understanding has to turn into action! Through volunteering at women's shelters, I have learned that this was one of the biggest hurdles of getting out of conflict: Once someone understood why something was happening, they would empathize, and this empathy prevented them from taking any action to improve their situation. Don't stop at understanding! Assessment is not the final destination—it is the key to help you decide what to do next.

The first part of assessment, which we looked at in the previous chapter, is to figure out where a conflict came from: Was it internal, external, or systemic?

1. *Internal:* Internal conflicts come from two or more employees within the company that are having a disagreement. Almost all the conflicts described in this book are internal. Which makes sense—you spend most of your time around your coworkers and sometimes you just drive each other nuts.
2. *External:* This is when an outside factor causes the conflict. Say your vendor increased their prices. Or it could be learned from childhood. If someone grew up in a racist household, then that racism might be exposed through jabs or outright harassment or discrimination in the office. This is why it is important to assess the roots of the conflict: When you know where a conflict is coming from, you are better prepared to address it. Some of these conflicts should be handled by a kind conversation. Others need to be addressed by HR or a judge. There are some conflicts (physical violence, racism, abuse, etc.) that are so insidious you should get help instead of trying to resolve them yourself. But what this book can do for these abusive conflicts is to help you identify them and be able to articulate your goals, so that you can plan the next step.
3. *Systemic:* A conflict is systemic if it is affecting the entire company. If you are facing this situation, then a kind conversation with one person is likely not sufficient. This is when you will

need to address the conflict at a higher level and likely work with management to begin change. Remember, many companies have systemic issues—they were built on a competitive instead of a collaborative culture.

The next part of assessing these behaviors is to identify which behavior you are dealing with, why that behavior is being used (in other words—Is it a front? Shyness? What is the psychology behind it?), and how you want to respond to it.

As Brené Brown often says, "You have to name it to tame it." This is why we focus first on understanding the conflict, and then figuring out how to tame it.[26]

We are going to name it then tame it in four steps:

- *Understand* your triggers, your situation, and those around you
- *Name* why the conflict is happening, and be able to impress people by describing it with fancy conflict vocabulary and theory
- *Plan* out your own conflict resolution adventure
- *Act* by standing up for your interests without people writing you off as wimpy, whiny, or wild

(2) Act

Channel your inner Action Jackson and use the takeaways, practical steps, solutions explorer, and workbook sections to help you plan your next steps. You will find this work really isn't complicated. Assess, then Act. Two simple steps that change your whole workplace culture.[27]

Part I

BEHAVIORS THAT AREN'T AS AWESOME AS OURS

Bothersome but Benign Behaviors

3

CLUELESS CARLS

I spoke with a manager years ago who told me, "I don't know what the fuss is—I just need a new assistant. It has to be a woman, twenty to twenty-five, athletic, able to work at my home, all night long, and able to take direction."

Um. Excuse me?

I was speaking with the head of a firm. His staff had asked me to talk with him because they felt that he said things that were out of touch and sometimes disrespectful. Uh, yup.

This type of behavior I call the Clueless Carl, a person who says and expects things that are just so far out of left field you wonder if they are even on the same planet with the rest of us. In general, a Clueless Carl (or Carla) is often an introvert who spends much of the time living in their head. When they do try to venture into a conversation, uh-oh. It can feel forced, awkward, uncomfortable.

The great thing about working with a Clueless Carl is that they are usually harmless and mostly well-intentioned.[1]

In the example above, when the manager called me, I assumed the worst. As the manager was speaking, I assumed he wanted a lithe young woman to spend the night with at his house as an assistant. Hard not to imagine the worst. When I questioned him on his rationale, however, I learned a lot. Mainly, I learned that I had jumped to an assumption. Not just jumped—I had leaped, I had catapulted into an assumption. "I identify with borderline Asperger's,"[2] he explained. "These tendencies help me to think practically and rationally about my strengths and weaknesses. I recognize that I have a linear and male-centric approach. I appreciate a female point of view to keep me balanced, and women often pick up on social cues better than I do. I prefer someone young who does not yet have a family so that they are able to work around my chaotic schedule. I walk while I think, so I need someone athletic who is able to keep up with me. I work at my home because I don't enjoy the social interactions of an office. And I can't sleep so I do my best work in the evenings, and want someone who is able to stay awake to help me draft reports."

Oh. Okay. This all made perfect sense and was much more understandable. Although he was still ridiculously clueless about how it sounded.

DON'T

Don't assume a Clueless Carl's intentions.

If I had responded harshly to this manager, he would have completely shut down. Since Clueless Carls are typically well-intentioned behaviors, they assume that you understand their good intentions. It can be a surprise to them that their communication is demeaning. You must be especially careful when providing feedback. As people who are not skilled with social nuances, they can easily become upset or defensive from your comments instead of trying to understand where you are coming from. Do not approach them from a place of judgment or retaliation. Do not let the conversation become too serious, because then they are likely to panic and retreat.

I learned this early on in my mediation career. I was working with a Clueless Carla, who just did not realize how she was coming across.

"I always have an open door for my coworkers," she said. (Which was true—the door was physically open—but listen to what she said next.) "People walk in with such stupid, petty gripes, and I just grit my teeth and listen to them, and then I tell them how it is. They are being stupid and I let them know."

Well, I was knocked off-kilter, and instead of a great mediator response, I judged her. "You know, it doesn't matter how wide your door is open, if people walk through the door to criticism and judgment, right? It doesn't sound like you're being supportive of your coworkers at all."

And what was the result of my foible? Of judging the person sitting across from me? She locked eyes with me, stood up, and backed out the door. She maintained eye contact for about five feet past the door—it was very creepy, to be honest—and then turned and ran down the hall. It took a few weeks before we were able to meet again, where I had to take a completely different approach to connect with her. I apologized, validated her efforts, and together we brainstormed more effective responses with her coworkers. She learned to ask questions with curiosity instead of criticism.

DO

Understand that we can all be a bit like Clueless Carl—with communication habits that are outside of the social norm. This doesn't mean that we are wrong, and it doesn't mean that Clueless Carl is wrong either. It just means that we all have unique behaviors that might be more or less effective in an office setting.

Approach Clueless Carls with a spirit of collegiality. Learn to work alongside them and ask them about their motivations to understand where this behavior is coming from. And only then discuss options, if you feel that the communication still needs to improve. You should feel as if you are giving them a friendly piece of advice, as if you were telling them about a new restaurant that has just opened. The same way you would want someone to approach you. Open the conversation with a simple statement, such as, "This might not be helpful, but I know I have had better luck in those meetings when I phrase things this way . . ." or "Did you know that when you said *x*, it kind of sounded like *y*?" or "Maybe I misunderstood, but it seemed like you were saying *z*?"

Ideally, if you develop enough rapport with your Clueless Carl, you might be able to give them additional insights to aid them in future conversations. The key is to keep it comfortable. One successful technique can be adopting a funny phrase to introduce the topic: "Oh, that was another out-of-left-field remark. What did you mean?" This moves towards identifying their behavior, helping them to accept it, and helping the rest of the office feel secure in asking clarifying questions.

IS THIS YOU?

If you are reading through this and realizing that you are often a Clueless Carl (or Carla), often saying the wrong thing at the wrong time, or not getting the joke, or saying something that was misinterpreted, the best thing you can do is own up to it. Growing up, I was often a Clueless Carla and learned to be honest about it until I began to understand what was going on. Find a humorous response that identifies your behavior. This lets people know that you are aware of it and are comfortable discussing it.

- "Shoot, did I miss the joke again? You all know I don't get sarcasm!"
- "Sorry, thought the conversation was going in a different direction."
- "Phew, thank goodness I got my awkward comment out. I try to get in at least one a day."

Here are some signs that maybe it is you:[3]

- Your coworkers constantly disagree with you
- Your coworkers are short or sarcastic with you
- Your coworkers ignore you or laugh at you
- Your coworkers don't ask you for your help
- You feel as though you often need to brag about your accomplishments
- Coworkers don't seem to get your witty remarks

STAY OR GO?

If this isn't you, and you are dealing with this personality:

Absolutely stay. If at all possible, find light, gentle ways to give the person some more information on their style or coaching to facilitate their communication. Also, experiment with ways to gain clarification on any of their statements that make you uncomfortable so that you can continue to work with your coworker effectively.

TAKEAWAY

A valuable resource from authors Stone, Patton, and Heen is the book *Difficult Conversations*.[4] It advises us to "disentangle intent from impact." In other words, realize that conversations have two parts—what I meant and what you thought I meant.

I have seen many teams fall apart because a Clueless Carl was having a negative impact on the group. The team assumed that Carl meant to be short, or smug, or to speak dismissively. Once the team was able to disentangle intent from impact, they could realize that Carl had no intention of being hurtful. He had no idea he was hurting the team. It took a few courteous but very blunt conversations with Carl to show exactly what things were hurtful and how he could communicate more effectively.

Feminine Response

As I have mentioned, this book is going to include studies that illustrate historical responses to conflict, which were often categorized as feminine or masculine. I recommend reading through both, regardless of gender, to choose which response you want to use for each situation.

Women in the workplace often focus on finding their place. This helps us to know how to relate to others. A woman once described how difficult it was for her to participate in conference calls when she didn't know the others, because she didn't know how to relate to them. She said, "I will accept anyone. Any color, gender, age, mix, trans, bi, a cat or a dog person, weird sock inclinations—but I need to know how best to be around them. Am I the mother hen? Am I the fun friend? Am I the helpful assistant? It is hard for me not to understand the other person because then I don't know who I am."

This has resonated with me, and, to be frank, bothered me for years. Because I have seen this as a stereotypical feminized response: First figure out who the other person is, then decide who you are in response. If you are tough and funny, then I can hang tough too. If you are talking about knitting and baking, then I'll pull out my favorite recipes. And what's worse, if this is a good ole boys club, then I have sometimes found myself playing the meek assistant. As if somehow they can't handle my personality so I need to weaken myself, and that is my fault. Well, when you have something to offer the workplace, don't hide it under a bushel, this little light will shine!

And this is why conflict in the office can become so personal; because women, and men, and employees in general, often sacrifice parts of themselves to make relationships work. And when that sacrifice is not recognized or honored or reciprocated, it feels like the woman herself is not valued.

It is as if women have taken the middle seat in the workplace. There is someone large on the aisle and window seat, with legs spread wide, arm draped across the armrest. And women are sitting in the middle, trying to hunch their shoulders in and keep their legs pressed together tight so as not to take up too much space. Women feel that if they are smaller or take up less space, those around them will be more comfortable. In a study by Barbara and Gene Eakins, they found that while women spoke more than men in a day when at their home or with their friends (75,000 words in a day compared with 25,000 words from men), women spoke significantly less than men when they were in a meeting together. They attributed this to a desire to take up less verbal space in the meeting.[5]

That Sucks

No matter how many times I mediate with a woman who is trying to shrink within herself, I think the same thing, *This sucks. This isn't right. This woman has such priceless gifts to bring to her office, and she is hiding them!* So we often spend time coaching—identifying values and figuring out how to stand up for them.

Figuring out your values helps you to figure out your own role. Not because someone else needs you to play that supporting role, but because you are confident in who you are and you know what skills you bring to the office. Do you bring leadership? Organization? Ruthless honesty? Zany energy? Quiet support? And once you find your role, that role shouldn't change, regardless of who you are around.

It also means that the same way you don't want anyone to place you in a box, you can't place those around you in a box either.

When we are working with Clueless Carls, we often place Carl in a box too quickly, so that we can determine how we want to relate to him. This is known as the Uncertainty Reduction Theory, which states that when we are working with a person who we don't understand, our brains make an effort to reduce that uncertainty by making a snap judgment.[6] The problem with this is that then we might allow ourselves to misjudge and treat Carl or Carla unfairly because we have prematurely labeled them. If Carl is being inappropriate, we decide that he is a jerk and we are mean to him. If Carl is being clumsy and clueless, then we become a mother hen to him.

My recommendation? Be you! Carl can do whatever he wants, be weird and clumsy and awkward, and if he crosses your boundaries, make sure to let him know. But you know what? You can be hard-working and funny and probably a little quirky regardless of how Carl acts. And once you come to peace with that, then you and Carl can find your own terms of relationship where you both feel respected.

4

SNAPPY SALLIES

"Sally, I am waiting for your referrals to the counseling office."

"Well, keep waiting. Those worthless counselors are a waste of our clients' time."

(The entire office cringes, since the counselors were sitting right there listening.)

Snappy Sallies (or Sals) describe people with a behavior that is, well, snappy. Not quite so far as to be cruel, but a little farther than short. They are snappy. They make snide little jabs and snide comments, and they know they sting just a bit.

The difference between Snappy Sallies and Clueless Carls is that Snappy Sallies are definitely not clueless. They are fully aware that their words might be a tad harsh. They see people bristle or cringe when they say them.

Some common reasons for Snappy Sallies' behavior:

- They feel that in this moment they are better than you and use this snapping as a tool to let you know it. It's not right, and it shouldn't be accepted, but they have given themselves permission to have a snappy behavior.[1]
- They are frustrated about something and don't know how to verbalize their feelings. Just picture a toddler unable to vocalize what they need and how they become anxious and impatient.

- They feel that they are a champion of a cause and feel a sense of righteousness in "saying it like it is."[2]
- They are overwhelmed, and their feelings have trickled into their office communication. Their snappings are a line of defense to make it clear that they can't handle any more right now.
- They are depressed. If things are hard at home, it is inevitable that their frustrations will trickle into work life. This might be the only safe space where they can let out feelings.
- They think that it is coming across as funny, and that people like their brazen sense of humor. The technical term for this (although I think the term Snappy Sally is a much better name) is *katagelasticism*, which means someone who enjoys laughing at another's expense.
- They may be trying to deliver another, perhaps vulnerable, message in a veiled manner in hopes that someone will pick up on it. "Oh look, you showed up on time for once" might be a thinly veiled way of saying, "You keep getting here late and I have to pick up your slack."

DON'T

Don't confront Snappy Sallies and ask them to recant their statement in the moment. This gives them the opportunity to state their opinion even louder and stronger. They have already decided that the best way to handle this situation is by being snappy.

Don't excuse their behavior. As with all of the negative behaviors listed in this book, understanding cannot become enabling. Rather, understanding helps you plan your response. Understanding is a tool, not excusing their behavior or resigned acceptance. Once people understand a behavior, they often feel sympathy for the person and then allow the behavior to continue. Please do not fall into that trap. Understanding a bad behavior, whether in yourself or someone else, is only *the first step* to improving that behavior.

Let me say that part again because it is important: Understanding a behavior does not excuse the behavior. *Don't understand to enable—understand to act*.

Understanding is not enabling.
Understanding guides your action.

Don't respond in a way that makes you seem overly sensitive or whiny. Typically, Snappy Sallies are blunt and forthright and don't get too caught up worrying about others' feelings. Instead, talk to them about the direct effect they are having on the office. Give them a clear example of a time when their behavior went too far, the negative effect it had, and what would be preferable.

I have just finished watching the show *Love on the Spectrum*, a reality show about people on the autism spectrum who are entering the dating scene. There is a Love Guru who gives dating advice. "Don't be too direct" is one of her common pieces of advice. In our culture, we expect that anything hard to swallow is going to be wrapped in a pretty package. It is a sign of respect and a common courtesy, meaning that we don't want to hurt the other one's feelings any more than necessary. But for two of the women with autism, they preferred to say what they thought. They wanted to be truthful and say their feelings in the moment, instead of having to wade through the social complexity of delivering bad news nicely. For instance, on the show, Abbey tells David, "I don't know if I like you. I need to think about it and talk it over with my mom." In another scene, Dani tells Adan, "I need to realize that you can't judge a book by its cover. So even if you are not nice to look at, you might be great on the inside." Abbey and Dani both thought these were perfectly logical things to say. They were just being honest. But the Love Guru explained that if you have something unkind to say, you have to say it in a way that the other person can hear it without becoming defensive. If not, the relationship can be damaged beyond repair.

Don't exaggerate the issue. Don't use hyperboles and absolutes, such as, "You are always mean," or "You never listen." Instead, give them a logical example. "You don't hold anything back, do you? There are times I wish I could be more like that. You know, though, in this team we've got a lot of quiet people and I think they might feel overpowered to have such a strong voice in the room. They really need all of us to give them a chance to speak and acknowledge the validity of their points as well."

STRAIGHT, NO CHASER

This style of communication is called Straight, No Chaser. (This style will be explained in more depth during Part V: Preventing Future Conflicts.) Often when we communicate on highly charged matters, we worry that our feelings are silly, not really worth mentioning, so we exaggerate our frustrations to make them seem bigger. The more effective straight, no chaser approach means clearly stating what the problem is, without adding concerns, issues, or people. Instead of saying, "You *always* interrupt people in meetings. You are so inconsiderate. I am not going to any more meetings with you until you learn an ounce of respect, ya jerkface pipsqueak" (using absolutes and escalations), say, "You interrupted me in the meeting today" (straight, no chaser approach). In lieu of being a straight shooter, we chase our real interest with all of this added-on ammo.

If we could succinctly explain our concern, then the listener has a pretty good chance of understanding it and probably making an attempt to change. When we add verbiage and ranting, thinking it makes our point sound better, it actually dilutes our point so much that it gets lost. The listener reacts to all of the intensification and emotion, becomes defensive, attacks back, and never hears your true concern. In his TED Talk, Niro Sivanathan explains that diluting our message weakens it. When it comes to communication, "less is more."[3] Because of the excess, the person cannot change their behavior, and your relationship has worsened rather than improved. Instead, do your best to give it to the person straight, "I don't like being interrupted," then you have only attacked the behavior and not the person. This allows the person to hear you and you have a pretty dang good chance of neutralizing the snap and at improving that relationship. I mean, do I want to get upset and mean and snap back? Absolutely. Is it as effective as a respectful straight, no chaser approach? Nope.

DO

Remind a Snappy Sally that she works on a team that needs to work together effectively. State that her snappy comments are unhelpful as they make it difficult for others to speak freely and work harmoniously since they can make people feel judged or on edge.

Check in with others around the office. Do they also see this person as a Snappy Sally? If not, there could be two reasons: 1) This person is only snapping at you, which lets you know that they clearly have an issue with you that needs to be discussed, or 2) You might be overreacting. The fact is we just don't click with everyone's personalities. There will be some people that you don't understand, or don't understand you, and you simply will not react well to each other. And that is okay. Once you know that, it is much easier to give this person slack.

Explain what's going on in a straight, no chaser approach. Tell them kindly and succinctly how you feel and what you want. Without apology or malice. Deliver a clear message. This is the key to change.

IS THIS YOU?

As you are reading through this, is it hitting too close to home? Can you think of times when you are making snappy jabs? Do you justify it to yourself, saying someone needs to be willing to say the hard truth and tell it like it is? Someone needs to champion the difficult causes and it should be me! I am fighting for justice here, who cares if people get their widdle feewings hurt because I didn't cater to their every need.

Maybe it's time to fight for a cause without causing a fight.

And, you actually can keep fighting for your causes, just do so without destroying relationships in the process, without stinging others. In other words, attack the problem, not the person. You can and should still champion truth and justice, just don't stomp on people to get there.

STAY OR GO?

This isn't you, but how do you deal with this personality?

If you're dealing with a Snappy Sally coworker, staying should be your first option—but not staying quiet!

- Be firm about your boundaries. When something is too painful, speak up and say, "Ouch!" If it is disrespectful, check in: "Did that come out the way you meant? Because that was kind of a junky thing to say."
- If this doesn't work, ask the person to sit down and explain the effect of their harsh words to them. Remember the clear and direct, straight, no chaser approach.
- If you are still not seeing an acceptable level of ownership or change, get HR or management involved. They might suggest a facilitated discussion, a mediation, or individual coaching for that person (you can review these suggested processes at the end of this book).

- If you have tried all of these steps and the situation becomes unbearable, then it might be time to consider other options. Can you transfer to another department? Can you telecommute? Can you let HR know that this person has created a toxic environment and you are on the verge of quitting?
- If you have tried these options, then you have given the other person and your company ample opportunities to change. If that person is still filling your life with vicious jabs, and it's affecting your mental health, and you feel that their snappiness is making you about to snap (see the dad pun I threw in there?), get the heck out of there.

TAKEAWAY

Some people are fighting for a cause and not always trying to cause a fight.

Snappy Sallies are rarely trying to cause a fight, they simply see themselves as the warriors of a cause. And when you are a warrior, you can convince yourself that the ends justify the means.

Sitting down with a Snappy Sally and showing them how the end result of their behavior is actually detrimental and hurting their cause helps them to make the choice on their own to change their behavior. As an example, you can explain that a tense office environment restricts communication, information is withheld, turnover increases, and quality diminishes. However, when people feel free to communicate, they can brainstorm better ideas, suggest improvements, and strategize together to meet goals and improve products.

Feminine Response[4]

After one of my classes, I noticed something that described the feminine response to snapping for me. I had just finished a Zoom call with about 50 students, and at the end everyone used the hand emoji to clap or wave. I was struck by the colors. Every student in my class that was white had left the skin color on the weird default yellow. There was a peachy skin tone to match a Caucasian heritage, but instead the white students had left their hands that bright yellow. Every other, non-white student had changed their skin color to match their own. It seemed that those with white skin just didn't think about the default skin color.

It is so easy to turn a blind eye to something that we think doesn't affect us, isn't it? This made me think about how often we ignore things that don't bother us, and we think that people are making a big deal out of nothing when they complain. The white students in my class had probably never thought about changing the skin color because it is probably not something that they think about a lot. Whereas I wonder if the other students often have to consider their color and are unfortunately all too aware of the potential reactions others might have.

Sometimes women in the workplace have to go through this same process. We have to be aware of nuances that others don't. We know that we are going to have to be a bit tougher, put our game face on, and roll with the punches. If we overreact, we will be seen as aggressive or whiny, but if we don't say anything we will end up being overlooked or disrespected. We have to be tough, while also being very aware of our femininity. We have to hold our shoulders back and our voice firm while also being aware of how we cross our legs, and the buttons on our blouse, and walking alone to the parking lot. We also know that statistically we will be the one called first if our son gets sick, and we call home in the middle of the day to remind our daughter to take her meds. Simply, we are feminized. We are expected to multitask and be a caretaker and to have an amazing inner strength all wrapped up in emotional awareness. But we also have to realize that some of the world just can't handle our awesomeness. They are threatened by us, or dismissive of us, or expect to treat us inappropriately. There are certain considerations that you would never know without being female/having feminine qualities. Just as someone who is white in a predominantly white and privileged community might never understand all of the considerations that minorities in their community have to be aware of. Men in the office will never be able to fully understand the complexities that a female worker is always juggling.

We want to voice our opinion, but won't do it too loudly. We want respect, but we know we can't demand it. We will laugh at a joke, even if inwardly we might be cringing. Until eventually, we snap. And unfortunately, many women haven't been taught any differently. We haven't been taught how to communicate openly about expectations, or boundaries, or saying no. I can tell you about a hundred TV shows that show us how to manipulate passive-aggressively. And another hundred that show us how to fit in in a man's world. What we haven't been taught is how to say kindly in the middle of a meeting, "No, that isn't correct. I'm not okay with it. Let me tell you what I want." Instead, we will smile and nod, then immediately gossip about the pigheaded jerk to our coworkers.

This section is about diagnosis and assessment, but read the second half of the book for skills to break out of this conflict cycle. If you are stuck in this cycle and you don't like it, take action!

So let me suggest this: If you are having trouble with a Snappy Sally, or if you are a Snappy Sally, perhaps this is a sign that you need more skills in dealing with conflict. This requires two simple things:

1. State your interests, and
2. Listen to others' interests.

5

BAD BRADS VS. MEANY MINNIES

This chapter looks at the difference between Bad Brad, who is just bad at communicating (but not intentionally), and Meany Minnie, who is deliberately unkind. They are often confused because Bad Brad and Meany Minnie look a lot alike. They both look mean. But they have very different personalities.

When someone is rude we assume they're mean, when often they are just really bad at communicating.

You know those nanny cams that parents hide in teddy bears? Do you ever want one for your office to record the absurdity around you?

> One woman, a CEO of a design company, told me that a new male vendor came into her office one day. He looked around and said, "Sweetheart, what you really need to make this place welcoming to us good ol' boys is a bowl of candy and some cigars. I'll tell your boss that he should give you a candy allowance." (The vendor was a Bad Brad.)

> An intern described how her job was to print out her boss's emails and read them out loud to him, then write by hand her boss's dictated responses, which she would later have to type up and send out. Once, she even had to pretend to be her boss and text an employee that she was fired. (Her boss was a Bad Brad.)

One woman told me that after her coworker was shunned in a meeting, she caught him in the fridge stealing someone's lunch as payback. (The coworker was a Meany Minnie.)

Unfortunately, not everyone has read this book—yet—so you will be working with a lot of people who still have a lot of communication skills to learn. It is helpful for you to know if they really intend to be so demeaning and disrespectful or if they are just clueless. They might just have bad communication skills. There are so many examples on TV, social media, stories over cocktails of how, "I got back at them!" "I wouldn't take no for an answer." "I told her what I really thought of her and then walked out before she had a chance to respond." All of these stories make for great drama, but they are teaching horrible communication skills!

BAD COMMUNICATION

Bad communication refers to the conversation style of someone who is simply a poor communicator. Poor communicators may express things in a way that seems dismissive. They may state things in a way that feels like a demand. They may give feedback with a dose of shame and disappointment. But, bad communication doesn't originate with an intention to harm; it typically stems from a lack of skill or awareness. Bad communication is usually the awkward attempt of someone who is trying to connect, trying to impart something meaningful, and is unable to do so well. With a skills upgrade, a bad communicator can actually become a great person to work with.

MEAN COMMUNICATION

Mean communication, on the other hand, is when someone deliberately tries to be hurtful. If their messaging leaves you feeling undervalued or criticized, it is because that was their intention. Mean communication can be an indirect way of someone saying they are frustrated with you. With effective conversation, the root cause of mean communication can be uncovered, and with time and new habits, even this relationship can be saved. However, if a mean communicator is simply mean, intending to be unkind and cause pain, it's wiser for you to distance yourself.[1] This makes sense, right? You can try extending the benefit of the doubt, ask them what is going on, let them know the effect they are having, but sometimes you can't change a tiger's stripes. If someone is just toxic, if they glare at you and ask, "Have you ever danced with the devil in the pale moonlight?" don't waste your time on them!

For the majority of communication styles we discuss in this book, the preferred method is to be honest and transparent about your interests. But an unkind person can turn this information into ammunition, so be on guard to avoid being manipulated. So how do you know?

1. Do you see this behavior from them often? Then document it.
2. Do they treat other people this way? If not, it might be that the two of you just need to work through something.
3. Do you feel belittled and on edge after most of your interactions with them? They might be using manipulative techniques that you can't quite put your finger on. Lundy Bancroft says that if you are having a conversation with someone who is genuinely unkind, you might walk away feeling as if your head is in a washing machine—you simply don't feel stable anymore.[2]

BAD VS. MEAN: THE DATA

In 2011, I researched the main cause of conflicts for small- to medium-sized companies in the United States.[3] A manager in every company ranked their most common cause of conflict. Sixty companies reported that their leading cause of conflict was bad communication, and 49 companies said their conflicts were from mean communication (companies were allowed to select more than one cause of conflict). What we learn from this is that more often communication disputes simply came from people who were bad communicators.

REAL-LIFE EXAMPLE

If you say hello to someone on the way to the watercooler, and they don't say hello back, it doesn't feel good. But how do you know if they are a bad communicator or a mean communicator?

- *A bad communicator* might not say hello to you because they are shy or intimidated. They might have been preoccupied with their own thoughts and not have heard or noticed you. They

Theme	Entrance
Bad communication	60 (23%)
Mean communication	49 (19%)
Unclear job description	23 (9%)
Group/personality conflicts	17 (7%)
Entitlement	14 (5%)
Unclear protocols/feedback	14 (5%)
Business decisions	13 (5%)
Unfair treatment	11 (4%)
External customer/contractor	11 (4%)
Physical office	10 (4%)
Lack of appreciation	8 (3%)
Poor work ethic	7 (3%)
Unrealistic deadlines	6 (2%)
Bad attitude	6 (2%)
Family/home issues	4 (2%)
Scheduling	3 (1%)
Discipline	1 (1%)
Cultural differences	1 (0%)
Not enough pay	1 (0%)
Personal use of resources/theft	0 (0%)
Total identified conflict entrances	**261**

Source: Author.

might have assumed that you were talking to someone else and not picked up on the social cues that you were speaking to them.

- *A mean communicator* doesn't say hello to you on purpose. This silent treatment is intentionally sending you a message. The message might be that you did something to them they didn't like, and now they are paying you back. It might be that they think they are better than you—perhaps they have been at the office longer or they wanted your promotion—and they are trying to remind you of their supposed superior status. Perhaps it is a passive-aggressive attempt at expressing frustration. Perhaps they are angry and do not have the skills to discuss their feelings, so instead they want you to also feel pain. Worst-case scenario, they are just an unkind person and don't want to conform to social norms.

> Unfortunately, until you find out why they are being mean, you do not know their motivation. Brené Brown states that most people don't even understand their own motivations—they probably don't know why they are so frustrated and taking it out on others. They probably also don't know the extent of the impact it is having on others. But a meanie knows that they are trying to control, belittle, or establish their power. Even if they don't know why they are being unkind, they are doing it on purpose.[4]

What we can learn from the data in the table above is that the majority of the time we think someone is being unkind to us, it is simply because they are exhibiting suboptimal communication. They are either lacking in social skills in general or they are not picking up on your cues in this instance. Even if it seems like they are being rude, it often may be that they are frustrated about something and do not know how to express it. This frustration turns into the silent treatment and snappy comments while the person is processing what bothered them.

Of course, if someone snaps at me, I am going to want to snap back at them! It's human nature. But in this book, we will be looking at some of the reasons why people are snappy and learn more effective responses than returning a snap in kind. It could be that they are having a bad day and overreacting, or maybe even you are having a bad day and overreacting. It could be that they are a horrible communicator and this has nothing to do with your abilities. In other words, just because someone is having a bad day, don't let them suck you into it!

Instead, therapist Bill Eddy recommends the EAR response when working with difficult behaviors. Treat them with Empathy, Attention, and Respect. Do not attack back, do not let yourself be pulled into a fight. Listen to their concerns, then defend your boundary and step away. Please visit highconflictinstitute.com for deeper information on this topic.[5]

TAKEAWAY

Most of the time when someone is unkind, it is only showing their lack of skill at explaining their frustration.

To determine their intentions, sit down and ask them what is going on with true sincerity. It is hard to hear criticism about ourselves, but try to listen with curiosity. After hearing what that person is frustrated about, then they are often ready to hear some gentle feedback. If they are well-intentioned, they might be able to improve their communication skills. However, if the person is simply full of hatred or bitterness, distance yourself as much as possible. Work separately, or see if they can work in a different group. It only takes one bad apple to spoil the pie, and you don't want all of your hard work at improving your office to be undone by one bad apple.

Remember that Bad Brad and Meany Minnie are twins—they look alike. The difference is that Brad is just clueless about how he is coming across whereas Minnie is trying to hurt you. Be careful about assuming it's Minnie, when the data shows that more often it is just clueless ole Brad.

STAY OR GO?

If you are dealing with a Bad Brad, then this is someone who might have a bad *impact* but they didn't have a bad *intention*. This person is typically receptive to hearing suggestions for improving their behavior.

A Meany Minnie, however, might be able to change one or two bothersome *behaviors*, but they probably can't change their *intentions*. They are just mean. So even if you work with them to alter one negative behavior, another one will eventually creep in. As a boss, you can probably develop a training or coaching plan that will help to mitigate some of the negative effects of being around a Meany Minnie. If you are a coworker, try some of the suggestions in this book (conversation, work together on a project, explain your intentions, etc.). If they still don't change and you have to work closely with them, you might want to explain the situation to your boss and see if one of you could move.

Feminine Response

I have two boys, and their favorite game is to sneak up behind the other one and pants him. Suffice it to say, I don't understand. I've just asked them to stop doing it in church.

My daughter's favorite game with her friends is to write sweet notes on sticky notes and see who can be the most creative about the hiding place or the delivery. (Also, though, this would be oddly inappropriate if they play this game at church and the pastor finds a sweet note hidden in the middle of their notes on the altar.)

Masculine and feminine communication styles are definitely different. Historical culture roles taught men that actions speak louder than words. If you look at common love languages, the highest-ranked love language for both men and women was quality time. After that, men ranked physical touch second highest, and women ranked words of affirmation the second highest.[6] This means that men often place more value on physical communication and action and women place more value on spoken communication. Male communication can look like working on a project together as a way to express mutual respect. One of my dearest friends (identifies as female but typically has a masculine communication response) hates long conversations but loves to do a craft project or play volleyball together.

Words, jokes, banter are a way that women say, "Hey, we're all cool here. I respect you and you respect me." Women are effusive in compliments and invitations, as a way to say, "Hey, I see you, and I think you're doing great. I like you and I hope you like me." Women use more verbal clues to signify closeness, and even quite a few nonword clues (nods, smiling, agreeing sounds, etc.). Men typically use fewer signifiers, and these are more often nonverbal physical connections (fist bump, playing sports, head nod, etc.).[7]

For men, being a Bad Brad or a Meany Minnie can be seen as strength, as respect that they can handle this tough banter, or as a form of acceptance to the inside club. Many men even report feeling pressured to act tougher around other men than they are really feeling, just to uphold a societal stereotype.[8] Some men even said that when they felt their mental health was under attack, they dealt with it by attacking others instead of dealing with their feelings. For women, who place more importance on the spoken word, tough banter can quickly become hurtful. Women typically speak to each other in an effort to build people up, and when the other person doesn't follow the same social norm, it feels like a betrayal.[9] If we are not careful our emotions can become activated and we can overreact to a Bad Brad by turning into a Meany Minnie. Instead, check your response to determine if you are reacting to what they are actually saying, or if you have become triggered. Being able to separate the action from emotion and apply separate vocabulary to each will allow you to discuss Brad or Minnie's actions without becoming defensive.

"Men attribute their success to themselves and women attribute it to other external factors" according to Facebook COO Sheryl Sandberg.[10] Men in the workplace typically have a stronger appearance of self-confidence than women.[11] According to *Forbes* magazine,[12] while both might be equally qualified and have worked quite hard to get there, women attribute much of their success to parents, education, kind managers, and luck. Men attribute much of their success to hard work, strength, smarts, and confidence. This means that men are often more protective of their success, since they need to protect that magic and personal combination. Women are often more open to others in the workplace, since they see others as helpful in getting them to where they are.

The practical application of this is that men see it as more acceptable to be short with a coworker, or to not share as much information or time. This can look like a bad or a mean coworker, when what they are actually doing is protecting themselves.

This is also a good time to discuss the difference between intent and impact. Intent means that someone intended a comment to be unkind. Impact means that I interpreted the comment as unkind. If the person didn't intend for a comment to be unkind, but I took it as unkind, whose fault is it? Does the intent or impact matter? The answer is both matter. Both of our feelings and both of our experiences are valid. We have to enter the conversation with that assumption. I need to validate your intentions, and I also need to validate the impact.

I'm in a mediation right now between student services and faculty services where the student services rep keeps saying, "Student services puts students first." The intention here is to explain the mission of the student services office. But the impact is very different. The rep for faculty services is offended, saying that it sounds like the indirect implication is, "Student services puts students first, and Faculty services doesn't." The only way that we could progress in this conversation was by understanding both the intention and the impact. Both sides needed to realize that the other was not a mean communicator, maybe just a bad communicator. They reacted without considering the other's perspective and they never tried to clarify. Their homework going forward is to continue to ask each other about comments or reactions that are confusing. So the ideal response to a bad communicator is to simply ask why.

6

HORROR VACUI—THE QUIET QUEEN

Horror vacui. The latest Rob Zombie flick? A Tim Burton nightmare movie?

Nope. *Horror vacui* is a Latin phrase meaning nature abhors a vacuum. In Greek the comparable phrase translates to fear of the empty. It means that whenever there is a vacuum, nature hates that emptiness and tries to fill it. For us, this applies to information. Whenever there is a lack of information, our brain tries to fill that empty space. Sometimes it fills it with real information, and sometimes we don't know what the real information is . . . and our brain makes a guess.[1]

Whenever someone is treating me in a way that I don't understand, my brain will try to supply a reason. If someone is mean to me, I will jump to conclusions in an attempt to explain it. Often, we assume the worst. This is known as "catastrophizing."[2] This book is going to try to explain the difficult behaviors and give you some information about them, so that you can have a bit more control over your brain and not let it assume the worst.

WHY DO WE HATE A VACUUM?[3]

Years ago, my husband and I put in an offer to buy some property. We were going to build our home on it and raise our family there. We were so excited and kept dreaming of the front porch and the tree swing. But then—horror! We drove by the property, there was a car parked there, and the For Sale sign was gone!

Now we were thrust into a vacuum. We did not have enough information. My brain did not know how to respond. Was our dream home gone forever? Or had the For Sale sign just fallen down? Was everything still all right? Or had a tragedy occurred that my brain had to deal with? My dear brain wanted to protect me and make sure I was prepared for the worst. The day before, my brain had the assurance of a warm future in a new home. Now, my brain didn't know what to envision. Therefore, of course, my husband and I started imagining the worst. Somebody else had made a better offer. We lost the property and our dream home. We would end up raising our kids in a van down by the river.

My brain hated that moment of not knowing what was going on, so it began filling that information vacuum with worst-case scenarios. This was devastating. I remember we came back to our rental house and sat on the couch, but the weight of this loss was so heavy it pulled us off the couch and we lay on the floor staring at the ceiling. We were so shaken by this news that we couldn't even move. (We eventually got a call from the realtor saying that the sellers had actually accepted our offer—phew!) What stood out to me about this situation was how my brain felt it didn't have enough information and had automatically created a story—one that was absolutely false and powerful enough to have completely knocked me off my feet for a day. My brain told me that we had lost our home. There was no truth to it, yet I accepted it as such.

My brain completely made it up—and I let that lie shatter me for an entire day.

When you begin to feel your brain spiraling with stories about a coworker, it is important to be intentional about your own behavior. Does the other person's behavior really justify what you are thinking or saying about them? Do your assumptions really line up with their past actions? Or could your brain be filling in a confusing vacuum with false information?

If you can't understand someone's intentions at work, your brain will respond in the same way: It is going to make up a reason for you.

YOUR BRAIN AT WORK ABHORS A VACUUM

Imagine having this conversation with a coworker:

"Would you like to go to lunch with me?"

"No, thanks."

. . . ouch . . .

After a lunch invitation, social norms dictate one of two responses, either

1. accept the invitation or
2. decline politely while giving them a reason why you can't accept.

Simply saying "no" is not the social norm. It is not what you expected.

So, you now face a vacuum. And . . . your brain begins filling in all of the possible reasons. "He doesn't like me. He is mad at me. Did I do something wrong? He is such a jerk—how could he just say no!?"

Without knowing if there is any truth to your assumption, your brain settles on an acceptable reason for his odd behavior from the many options it has just created—he is a jerk. You accept this answer as truth and begin making additional conclusions based off of him being a jerk. This bothers you, and so you probably end up discussing this with other people. "Have you noticed what a jerk he has been lately? I wonder what's wrong. It's probably because he didn't get that promotion; he still thinks he is better than all of us and now he is finally letting us know." And people begin believing that he really is a jerk and treating him that way.

And the made-up story, the lie, spreads like wildfire.

When you're at work and faced with a situation that does not make sense, your brain rushes in to fill the vacuum. This "filling in" happens on a small scale optically—our brain fills in the gaps in our peripheral vision or when we blink. This happens on a grander scale in conflict—when our brains don't understand someone's behavior, our brain fills in the gaps.[4]

Imagine if we had the same conversation as above, where we invited a coworker to lunch, but instead of letting our brains impatiently fill the void, we asked a bit more.

"Would you like to go to lunch with me?"

"No, thanks."

"No problem. Is everything going okay?"

"Honestly, no. I didn't get that promotion, and now I have to go home and tell my partner. This is the third time that the job went to someone else, and I think we have to have a tough conversation about moving to another line of work."

Without taking the time to check in with him, you would never even have the chance to know what's going on with him. This poor guy is having a horrible day, and then you went and judged him—and probably even complained about him to another coworker.

And now, not only did he not get the job with the needed raise to pay for his mortgage so he doesn't have to live in the aforementioned van down by the river, but everyone in the office is suddenly treating him coldly and he has no idea why.

Information is power. If someone in your office is being vague about their intentions—ask them why. If someone is withholding information from you—ask them why. It could simply be that they have a shy personality.[5] But it could also be a power play—call them on it! You deserve to be informed, because if you're not, who knows what kind of crazy story your brain could make up.

IS THIS YOU?

I am mediating between two execs right now who are facing this situation. One exec was recently hired, and she wants to appear confident. She doesn't want to be vulnerable. What this means is that she is staying quiet about any of her concerns or misgivings or true motivations. She is trying to appear tough and powerful and decisive. But by doing this she is also pushing people away. The other exec is losing confidence in her because she doesn't trust the new exec's motivation. My advice to both of them is the same that it has been for pretty much every chapter: Talk. The new exec needs to be willing to make mistakes and ask questions and reach out for support. She needs to share what her concerns are and explain her interests behind her decisions. "I am doing this because . . ." "I think we should include that person because . . ." This is the only way that her new staff can get to know her and trust where she is coming from. The existing exec also needs to take a step to make the new exec feel welcomed and supported. Whenever the existing exec feels that information is missing, she can also take initiative to ask why. I have been working with these women for the last two months and they have both made a concerted effort to prevent horror vacui. They have been sharing their interests and being vulnerable with each other. And things are changing. It requires some significant behavioral and attitude changes, but it is powerful.

STAY OR GO?

Stay. If you are working with someone who is a Quiet Queen, ask them why. They might be shy, or introverted. They might not have confidence in their position. Their brain might see things very linearly, and they simply don't understand the benefit of sharing their interests. Let them know that you will respect their comfort level, but also ask them to respect your need to ask questions when you need more information. Following these steps should make huge improvements in the office, and hopefully within a few months you will be glad you stayed.

TAKEAWAY

We learned earlier that what we may interpret as mean communication is often just bad communication. When faced with a confusing social norm, such as bad communication, your brain will often make up a reason (such as the person is mean).

Check in with the person and ask them what is going on before you let your brain fly into fake-conclusion land.

Feminine Response

There is another vacuum in the workplace: the Values Vacuum. Those who choose to respond with a feminized response historically underrate the value that they add to the workplace.[6] Women more often see themselves as replaceable, or doing a job that anyone else could do just as well. They have been trained to act demure and humble, and over time start to believe it. Men typically need to overrate themselves in the workplace, being trained to act trustworthy, strong, and courageous. There is no problem with either one of these—humility and courage are both admirable qualities. The more capable we are of both of these qualities the more we can choose which quality to use in the right situation.

However . . .

In the workplace, jobs are often assigned based on self-stated qualities. This makes sense when you think about it. A manager is going to give a job to the person who says, "I can absolutely handle that," and not to the person who says, "I might be able to do it. I could try." Until the manager has years and years of experience with each person, the manager is not going to be able to determine who actually is more qualified. So, the manager will make a determination based on who seems more confident and who says they have the skills. Men typically display more bravado and charisma in the workplace, meaning that they historically get more tasks and advance faster than women. Tomas Chamorro-Premuzic[7] points out that this confidence is often seen as leadership potential, so men are promoted because they *act like* they can do the job first and then learn, over women who would listen to others and *learn* how to do the job first.

7

CHATTY PATTIES AND CHATTY MATTIES

> Everything is awesome. Everything is cool when you're part of a team.
>
> —Emmet, Lego[1]

Chatty Patties (and Chatty Matties) can be great team workers. They help offices to create strong relationships and are often in charge of office social events. The fact of the matter is that some Chatters do not know when to stop. They talk. And talk. And talk. And they always seem to talk right when you have a deadline fast approaching. Or you need to make a phone call. Or you have a headache and just cannot listen to One. More. Story.

Chatty Patties don't seem to know that periods exist—they speak with only commas. In other words, the pauses are just long enough for them to catch a breath and then begin again with renewed excitement. Once they start a story you better sit down, because you have just made a commitment longer than the entire *Seinfeld* series. The difficulty is that if you cut them off, they seem to take it personally.

"Why do they talk so much?!" Many employees have asked me this about their coworkers. "Don't they see me backing out of the room?"

The answer is—probably not. And even if they do, for most Chatters, your discomfort is less important than connection. Chatters are also known as compulsive talkers. These are characterized as those who are highly verbal in a way that differs from the norm and is not in anyone's best interest. These people speak with greater frequency, dominate conversations, and are less inhibited than others.[2]

Some common reasons why Chatters chat:

- They need to connect.
- They don't realize how long they are talking.
- They are romantics—meaning they are so taken up with a story they lose touch with your not-so-subtle signals that you have to go.
- They need a social outlet, and you might be the only one they have.
- They might be afraid of silence.
- They need to work through an issue, and you are the safest person around.
- They process information verbally; they need to talk through something to figure it out.[3]

REAL-LIFE EXAMPLE

I am a Chatter (you've probably realized this by now), so I can relate to this personality type way too well. I realized I was a Chatter during our doctoral orientation. We had an icebreaker where we went around the circle and stated what we had for dinner the night before.

Person A: Hmm, spaghetti and meatballs, and leftover birthday cake.

Person B: Take-out Chinese.

Person C: Chicken salad.

Person D: Cheese pizza.

Me: Well, I was getting day care figured out for this orientation, so I was running late. I had picked up chicken because I was going to try this new stuffed chicken recipe I saw—it had spinach and pine nuts and feta—yum! And I didn't want to waste the chicken but I was too maxed out to make something new. So, I just fried it, put it in a taco with fixings, and told my kids it was Taco Thursday! It wasn't my original plan, but sometimes being willing to go with the flow is the best thing you can do for your family.

Only then did I look around the room and realize that everyone was just staring at me, their chatty classmate for the next five years. Probably wondering if it was too late to switch programs.

Let's note a few things here:

- I wanted people to know me and accept me.
- I wanted people to think I was funny.
- I am a verbal processor so I couldn't remember what I had for dinner until I started at the beginning of the story and made it to the nugget in the middle.
- If someone had interrupted me and told me to get to the point, I would have lost my train of thought and needed to start over.

DON'T

If you need the information, do not interrupt. Chatters and other verbal processors typically see stories linearly. Meaning a long, long line that has gotten tangled and wound around itself and they only have hold of one end of that line. They need to start at the beginning of the ball of string and they cannot jump to the end. You interrupt them, and you just popped them right back to the beginning of that ball of string.[4]

Do not ask them to hurry. This often causes frustration and increased heart rate, which for many verbal processors causes confusion. The story takes twice as long.

DO

Be calm, kind, and receptive. If the story appears not to end, kindly state that you have two minutes until some important meeting or phone call.

Acknowledge it, jokingly and warmly. This will give you some social credit in your workplace bank account. You can make a withdrawal later when you need to get out of a conversation. For instance, "You always have the funniest stories!" Then later, "I wish I could hear the end of this story, but I'm going to be in major trouble if I don't get back to my station."

IS THIS YOU?

If you are a Chatter, it is important to be honest with yourself. Chatters have certain strengths and weaknesses. Be aware of these so that you can contribute your strengths to your office and find workarounds for your weaknesses.

Chatter assumptions:

- That you are interested in what they have to say
- That what they are saying is interesting
- That you are also a Chatter and enjoying this conversation
- That the two of you are forming a connection

Chatter strengths:

- Can create a warm office environment with their high sociability
- Can bind a team together with their inclination to connect
- Can deflate tense situations with their humor and quick wit
- Can be the go-to candidate for making speeches and greeting customers and potential clients with their warm style and storytelling flair

Chatter weaknesses:

- Can take time away from discussing important issues
- Can appear as flighty or wishy-washy
- Can be oblivious to verbal and nonverbal cues indicating people need to end the conversation
- Can veer to superficial connection without the back-and-forth of two-way conversation

STAY OR GO?

Stay. You should be able to stay in an office with a Chatter; just make sure to set up some good boundaries. Develop a few conversation exit strategies that are kind but firm.

TAKEAWAY

If you are working with a Chatter, point out their chatty tendency in a kind manner. This lets them know that you accept them and are not judging them, but that you also must protect your time in the office.

Feminine Response

This is an area where women excel. We are great conversationalists! Although the averages vary, recent studies say that women speak about 20,000 words in a day, compared to men's 7,000. In a social setting, this can be 75,000 for women and 25,000 for men.[5] We are great at sharing ideas, having funny personal anecdotes, asking people about their day, and sensing if something is wrong. The area where most of us need work is saying no when it is time for a conversation to stop.

Traditionally, our conversation skills have been minimized and downplayed as a distraction. However, human resource, management, and leadership studies are recognizing the importance of these skills. If you are a Chatty Patty, learn the social cues to determine when the conversation needs to end, and then advertise this as your strength!

Confidently place on your resume that you excel in:

- Nonverbal validation
- Emotion control
- Stress management
- Empathy
- Clarifying tasks
- Reinforcing office culture/setting a friendly office tone
- Open to feedback
- Concern/issue identification
- Strong team player

Remember—these are your strengths, not your weaknesses! This is what your workplace needs! So, work on your instinctual communication strengths and get out there and fight like a girl!

8

THE DUDE AND THE DUDETTE

The Dude abides. He doesn't excel, he doesn't fall behind. He just *abides*.

This is a reference to *The Big Lebowski*'s character, The Dude. If you haven't seen the movie, picture the chill guy who got Cs in high school—good enough to pass, not bad enough to fail. This is the person who manages to do just enough to get by. The Dude is never early, but never late enough to draw attention. The Dude is typically funny and laid-back, and usually a great pal to have around.

When you work with The Dude, or let's say a Dudette, you probably need to come to terms with something: she is content the way she is. We think there is something wrong with her, that she should follow social norms and be more driven in her career. But The Dudette is content just being herself. You might be able to motivate her for a short period of time, but this typically won't be a lasting change. It is important to realize this and plan accordingly. She is difficult to include in a group, as other people will often feel that she is not carrying her weight.[1] This is not intended to be judgmental; it is simply acknowledging the way she is.

WORKING WITH THE DUDE

Working with The Dude can be equally relaxing and frustrating. When things are tense and The Dude shows up with the equivalent of office margaritas, it can be relaxing. Deciding that things have been too tense and taking the time to unwind with your coworkers is a valuable lesson that we all need once in a while.

Once in a while. Not daily.

The problem with The Dude is that most of the time at work you have to . . . well . . . work. And when you have a huge report due for your client coming in the morning that could make or break your company, and The Dude comes in with a pitcher full of margaritas, it can be incredibly frustrating.

What you have to realize is that The Dude is enjoying his time. His primary concern is creating enjoyable experiences in the present moment. And if those experiences can be tied into improving office culture or creating interesting projects, then The Dude can be a benefit to the company. But if The Dude's interests continually undermine the company's interests, it might be time for The Dude to go.[2]

About 20 years ago, I worked with a Dudette. We are still friends, and we both have grown a lot since then. Also, in all fairness, she was planning her wedding and her heart was not in the office. But she was definitely a Dudette. Our office was approaching our major annual deadline. We had one day to get all of our marketing materials finalized: perfectly edited, consistent messaging, clear brand, bold colors, and we were scrambling. She was in charge of the paper, and when she missed our first meeting we gave her space, assuming she was making an important copy paper versus cardstock decision. At lunchtime, I walked by her desk to see that she had spent the meeting time ordering llamas for her rehearsal dinner. When I asked her why, she said that she didn't like the vibe of the meeting and just didn't need that in her life right now.

There was no changing her personality. She was enjoying her morning, and eventually ordered the paper, but she just wasn't going to be rushed into it. After a few months, we parted ways, but I still sometimes missed the "vibe" that she brought to the office.

DON'T

Do not take ownership of The Dude's work ethic. Make sure he knows that he alone is responsible for his behavior. *Forbes* author Erika Andersen points out these personalities often blame others when they fall short, or they tell their bosses that if that one thing could just be fixed, then they would be able to operate fully.[3] When he gives you an excuse, simply point out that something always seems to come up for him, and that next time you can work together to develop a realistic plan.

Do not get sucked into his behavior. His lackadaisical work ethic can seem tempting, but it likely won't help you reach your goals.

Do not go. You might be the best hope this company has for success!

DO

Protect yourself so that your coworker's lack of motivation does not hurt you. In other words, if you are dependent on him, or if you are working on a team together, make it clear to him from the beginning what you expect. Then also make it clear to others what your work responsibility is, so that it is isolated from The Dude's responsibility.

Set clear expectations and consequences. Lay out the expectations in separated columns. Make lists with timelines attached to each of your deliverables. Create a clear process of confirming tasks, accountability, clear standards, and consequences if those tasks are not completed.

Make sure that you are still accomplishing your work.

Maintain a positive attitude. You will get the credit you deserve for your hard work eventually, and The Dude's work habits will eventually be exposed. Keep your head high in the meantime, even if things do not feel fair.

IS THIS YOU?

Communicate with your coworkers. If you are not operating at your full capacity, let your coworkers know. You do not need to share personal details, but let them know that you have other things going on. This is necessary to work well with others, but also to protect your mental health while you are working through something.[4]

If you have realized that you are a chronically low-performing worker, are you able to change? Can you change your habits to meet deadlines? Can you remove distractions? Would you be a better worker in a different job or different environment? If there is something around you making you ineffective, speak to your HR department about making changes.

If you have simply reached your limit in your office, then be honest with your coworkers. For instance, if you are expected to type a summary of a meeting in the next half hour and you know you are not that fast of a typist, it is much better to let your team know up front that this will take you an hour. Creating deadlines that you will be able to meet, and then meeting those deadlines, will make you a more trustworthy employee.

STAY OR GO?

If this isn't you, and you are dealing with this personality:

Stay, but develop clear expectations and consequences. Suggest projects for The Dude where his low-stress approach will thrive. If you are in management, you might have to consider if it is time for The Dude to go. A Dude-ish, low-energy, do-the-bare-minimum mindset can infect an entire office. Keep an eye out for diminishing productivity, and work with The Dude to prevent a spread of his apathy.

TAKEAWAY

There are lots of reasons why workers underperform, and it is important to understand why. Are they having home troubles or personal stressors? Are they not getting along with their coworkers? Are they confused about their tasks? Are they in the wrong job and not feeling challenged, or too challenged?

A manager should work with an employee to find out how to help him or her flourish.[5] However, some employees simply enjoy being low-key, and no amount of motivating will change that. In some cases, consider a flex schedule, a shared shift, or a job description that more accurately reflects The Dude's fun, but oftentimes frustrating, personality.

Feminine Response

Women have a unique response to being around The Dude. They want to fix The Dude. Women often adopt The Dude and think, "If I can just find the right way to motivate him, he will be a more productive member of the office." And then women beat themselves up when The Dude doesn't change, and they have created tension with a person who never asked to be fixed.

Oxfam International notes that the majority of those in poverty are women, and one of the main reasons is that women tend to be caretakers. In the office, this means that women often step in to help other coworkers who need support, so women are picking up the slack for other workers, but not being paid for it. Oxfam anticipates that women are doing 10 times as much unpaid work caring for other employees than men do. They value this work as $10.8 trillion annually.[6]

Your relationship to The Dude should be the same as I have described in previous chapters: Set your boundaries and be firm about them. It is okay to step in and help, but don't tie your identity or responsibilities up with The Dude/ette. It is okay to offer advice, but there is no need to mother hen someone who is not your child.

Of course, sometimes women take on the role of The Dudette. Many career-oriented women strive to be people pleasers and being responsible at work is a great way to please people and advance in the office. However, let's face it—we have all had times in our lives where we just didn't care that much about our job. Typically, it is when we were young and working a throwaway job, or our home responsibilities were taking most of our attention.

Masculine Response

I recently interviewed a man dealing with this situation. He said, "If we were working together on a project, I guess I would be annoyed. But if it didn't directly affect my everyday job, why would I care?"

Interestingly, director Judd Apatow talks about how the slacker-striver romance has become one of the most socially acceptable norms for the movie plot. There is a driven female, typically a high-powered executive, striving to advance her career. She eventually falls for the slacker male, who is the typical Dude personality. He does just the bare minimum to keep his job. Apatow points out that this role is the new culturally acceptable male, which allows a man to fit into his workplace, without appearing threatening and allowing his female coworkers to find their place. Men uniquely seem to understand the confusion in the masculine role in the workplace, and they therefore seem to be more supportive of The Dude personality.[7]

The masculine response to working with The Dude is often a laissez-faire, live-and-let-live approach. Instead of taking responsibility to fix everyone, men are able to work alongside someone without needing to fix them. A manager I consulted with at an office noticed that there were some problem employees and shuffled them around in order to avoid the conflict, but she never spoke to them directly about the conflict (this was a cisgender female, with a masculinized managerial style). Instead, she moved them from department to department, without really explaining why or expecting growth. I watched them move into another department with a female manager who had more traditionally female responses. She took these employees and set up performance improvement plans with HR and brought in a coach to talk to them about staying engaged in the office. Incidentally, one employee responded well to the attention and became a much more motivated employee. The other quit, saying, "Stay out of my business."

Simply, when working with The Dude or The Dudette, you can either respond by accepting them or trying to change them. If you try to change them, however, don't allow them to affect your work ethic and don't become personally invested, as The Dude will change only if and when he decides to.

9

THE PEOPLE PLEASER

If you are the type of person who typically downplays situations, tries to take on more, and continuously pleases, then you might be putting up with more than you should. This is typical People Pleaser behavior. You probably justify this behavior by saying, "If I am able to handle it, why shouldn't I? I can figure this out on my own, so why take time out of work or make things awkward just to cause a big stink about something?"

The upside of this personality type is that you are probably very easy to work with. I mean, you are a People Pleaser, so you are probably pleasant. It is rare that you rock the boat.

The downside of this personality type is that, well, it is rare you rock the boat. And sometimes, the boat needs to be rocked. Things need to be improved. People need to know where your limits are in order to respect your limits. Coworkers often report that they are not sure where they stand with People Pleasers, not sure if they really know them. They actually want to know sometimes where the limits are in order to understand you as a person. People Pleasers can also be seen as wishy-washy if they are too nervous to stand up for their beliefs. It seems as if The People Pleaser can say whatever another person wants to hear, which makes it hard to know if The People Pleaser is actually telling the truth.

If you are a People Pleaser, chances are it is hard for someone to bring up a difficult topic. A difficult conversation plays into your deepest fear: that someone doesn't like you. So, you feel attacked and you need to defend yourself. And when you feel attacked, you can't hear the deeper issue—you are distracted, worrying that someone doesn't like you. After such a conversation, People Pleasers routinely feel drained. They often feel guilty if they spoke too firmly, or they feel resentful if they weren't able to say what they wanted. They will typically blame the other person for not letting them speak. Instead, they will either hold their resentment inside or voice their resentment to whomever is around who will listen. Many women, according to the Medium website, say that they are People Pleasers because it is normative, it is socially assumed. They say that people pleasing is their superpower—it allows them to know how to read a situation and adjust accordingly. They can identify a person's need and be what that person needs—funny, compassionate, patient, hardworking, quiet, and so on. Which is a wonderful superpower! But it doesn't allow a lot of room to bring up a difficult conversation or to stand up for one's own interest.[1]

You are a people, please you!

For most People Pleasers, the thought of standing up to someone is terrifying. If this is you, it is important for you to be honest about your abilities and your restricted comfort zone. You are a people, please you! (Please ignore the 75 grammar atrocities in that last sentence and appreciate the sentiment: You are a person, and you deserve to do what it takes to impress yourself as well!) If you are taking on too much work and finding yourself stressed, you are not operating as effectively as you should be for your company. If you are putting up with difficult personality types, you are likely ending up distracted and not communicating effectively. Standing up for yourself here is not a sign of weakness, saying that you couldn't handle it. It is actually the opposite. It is saying that you are going to do what it takes to be the best employee and coworker that you can be. It is saying to yourself and to those around you that you will take on what work you can, but also be honest about when it is enough.

People pleasing on its own can be a completely innocent and even effective behavior. One of the problems with people pleasing is if the person is being fake, or disingenuous, which can destroy relationships once discovered. One of the other problems with people pleasing is the motivation. Often people pleasing comes out of a fear of not being needed and that fear motivates people to continue pleasing others. The problem here is that there is no trust or growth in the relationship.

FEMININE RESPONSE

What is the feminine response to people pleasing?

Many women place a high value on relationships. They can understand when someone takes action to improve a relationship. So they can empathize with a woman who is fawning to get in someone's good graces, or to strengthen a friendship. Or if a woman is people pleasing at work, and then conspiratorially draws you in to explain that she is putting in extra hours today so she can leave early tomorrow, this feels like she is strengthening your relationship. However, if a woman finds out that someone was just people pleasing to get something from her, it feels like the ultimate betrayal. Finding out that someone was being fake or manipulative means that the relationship was not that important. It feels like the person was willing to sacrifice the relationship for their own selfish desires. And this stings.

So, the typical feminine response to a People Pleaser is to understand and encourage the behavior, unless it endangers the relationship.

MASCULINE RESPONSE

There are some times when employees use people pleasing as a strategy to advance their career. And it is a great strategy. But I have worked with many employees who felt burned because they thought a People Pleaser was their friend and didn't realize that they were a rung on a ladder.

So, let me encourage you to take a masculinized response with People Pleasers and act a bit competitively. Take back control of the relationship and choose how you respond to a People Pleaser. For your sake, if an employee is befriending you, I truly hope it is because you are friends. But be aware of these signs that a People Pleaser is only using you to move up the ladder:

- They compliment you, then ask you for a favor.
- They vary in their friendliness—one day they seem to want you involved, and then suddenly lose interest.

- They do not give you credit in front of others, especially those in authority.[2]

TAKEAWAY

Most People Pleasers justify their behavior in the office by thinking that by handling more they are making it easier on everyone. And let's be honest, for a short period of time, that is true.

But long term, The People Pleaser cannot maintain that pace. They need to take care of themselves. They need to know that their coworkers support them as well. Their coworkers also need to be able to do their job, instead of The People Pleaser always handling it. Remember—put your own mask on first, then take care of others. So figure out what you need to feel supported in the office. This might be setting clear boundaries, delegating tasks, working with a team on difficult projects, setting more realistic timelines, and maybe even saying no. If you are managing a People Pleaser, have a talk with them about what they need to be validated and supported in the office. You might also want to clarify your standards, such as, "I approve of the work that you are doing, and I commit to letting you know right away if I ever have a concern."

Additional nonconfrontational options coming soon to chapters near you (Freelance Problem-Solving, Delegating Disputes, and Rising Tides Raise All Boats).

Potentially Painful Personalities

10

INAPPROPRIATE INGRIDS AND IVANS

"So, two guys walk into a bar," begins Inappropriate Ivan. The whole office groans, knowing that with this worker, there is going to be an inappropriate joke following soon.

What makes a joke inappropriate? Inappropriate is anything that is detrimental to your office or office culture. Every office defines its own level of what is appropriate behavior. But it usually makes one group feel marginalized or unsafe.

Common complaints center around inappropriate jokes or language. Some jokes are appropriate for an office—they build relationships, they reinforce the culture, they place people in the same circle, they release tension. Jokes are inappropriate for an office if they breed mistrust or make an employee feel uncomfortable.

Conflicts arise when one person's definition of inappropriate crashes smash-bang into the rest of the office culture.

SITUATIONS WHERE I HAVE WORKED WITH INAPPROPRIATE IVANS AND INGRIDS

Tomasz worked in a call center. It was a high-stress job where employees had to deal with many negative calls. During breaks, the employees would unwind by trying to top each other with the worst client call. They would make fun of their clients and often their jokes would turn personal. "I am not kidding you—it took forever to get this lady on the phone. Then once she started talking—she wouldn't shut up! She must have yacked on for hours. Just like my marriage—took five minutes to get into it and a lifetime to get out."

Tomasz smiles at the jokes but is feeling more and more uncomfortable. He doesn't like how rude everyone is being about their clients and their families. He is withdrawing from the group. He also wonders if they are that rude about each other—what do they say about him behind his back? He used to enjoy working here, but it has become such a negative environment. He has started to fake being sick on days where he just feels like he can't take it anymore.

Let's look at another example to put this in perspective.

Misaki has worked as a server for three years at a busy restaurant. It is run by a family patriarch, whose son is the chef. A couple of times they gave her advances on her check when she had unexpected bills. They've been great about letting her come in late when she has to pick her son up from school. She was glad at first that it seemed like she was getting closer to her coworkers, but she doesn't like where it's heading. She walked into work once and the manager said to his son, "Hey, get over here. Misaki is wearing her sex kitten skirt!" Misaki laughed and teased them back, but she was shaking inside. A few weeks later, the son saw a food critic was at her table, so he half-jokingly asked Misaki to hike her skirt higher so that they would get better reviews.

Misaki went home and looked up the definition of harassment (which will be discussed later in the book). She didn't think this was harassment or verbal abuse—they weren't doing it to be mean. They really thought they were complimenting her. Yet, she is feeling herself withdraw. She is wearing more modest clothing. She is withdrawing from conversations. She is feeling emotionally abused; she is feeling her mental health taking a hit. She even realized that she is making sure she is not alone in a room with either of them.

Let's look at the effects of inappropriate behavior to help her decide if she should stay or go.

Inappropriate behavior can take a variety of forms. People might tell crude or dirty jokes, use profanity, make direct or indirect sexual comments, or make fun of their coworkers or clients. Most people who are inappropriate simply feel comfortable around their coworkers and they are using language or telling stories that they are comfortable with personally. Telling a dirty joke in a hushed tone is saying, "Hey, I know we're close enough friends that you can handle this." Making fun of your clients says, "Hey we're on the same team. We've got each other's back against those crazy clients on the phone." However, inappropriate communication is simply communication that does not belong in the office. It might belong in a bar, around a dining room table, or on a shrink's couch.

These are the effects of inappropriate behavior, according to the Human Resources Director website:[1]

- makes you feel small
- diminishes trust in your office
- sparks worry about them saying something inappropriate around your manager, clients, or family
- establishes a tension between communication you are comfortable with and wanting to be a team player
- instills a fear that if you complain, they will think you are uptight
- creates a negative environment

Simply put—inappropriate behavior is not helpful and not worth it.

DON'T

If you work with someone who engages in inappropriate behavior, it is typically not helpful to challenge them. Confronting someone who is inappropriate often puts them on the defensive. Once someone is on the defensive it is difficult to have an effective conversation with them. "Feedback is the breakfast of champions," says Ken Blanchard, but unfortunately most workers become too defensive to be able to hear feedback.[2]

DO

Be clear with yourself about what you need to be able to work effectively. If the jokes are distracting, if the behavior is making you withdraw from the group, if the tough attitudes are making you call in sick to avoid going to the office, then this inappropriate behavior is affecting your ability to work. This means that you need to define boundaries for yourself: What behaviors are simply unacceptable for you? If someone exhibits one of those behaviors around you, let them know that you actually don't find it funny.

- Gentle approach: In many offices, people only have to be told once, gently, that their behavior is unacceptable and they will change. ("Hey, I have a hard time with those kinds of jokes. Can you not say those in the workplace?" or "I don't really think that's funny and it's making me uncomfortable. Can you try to avoid the _________ (sexist, racist, ableist, etc.) jokes? Thank you.")
- Humor approach: With some people, humor works better. ("Hey, if you guys keep talking about the assistant behind her back, then I'm going to have to keep listening to make sure I'm up on the latest gossip, and then I won't get my work done, and then I'll get fired, and then my kid won't get his bike. So could you keep it down so that Billy gets his bike?")
- Firm approach: You might find that you have tried the gentle approach and the humor approach and you just have to go straight to the direct, kind-but-firm approach. ("Enough already. The only one who gets to make jokes about my body and what I'm wearing is me—got it? Keep the rest of your comments and your wandering eyes to yourself. I'm trying to get work done here and I don't like all the comments I hear as I walk by.")
- Short and sweet approach: "Cut it out." You don't owe them any more of an explanation than that.
- HR approach: If you have tried all of these approaches, then their behavior might fall into a behavior disorder, be mean, or be abusive. If so, it is time to go speak to your manager or your HR department. They will have a variety of processes for resolving this dispute. These options will be discussed in later chapters.

IS THIS YOU?

Many of us can relate to some of these behaviors—gossiping about the boss a bit too much, telling too long and detailed of a story about our weekend, speaking a bit too loudly when someone is on the phone. However, if you find that these behaviors are becoming the norm for you instead of the exception, then think about the effect your behavior is having on those around you.

THUNDER TURTLE SYNDROME

Everyone wants to be liked by their coworkers. For most of us, we try to be liked by telling funny stories, cracking jokes, or paying attention to our coworkers. Sometimes, however, we take this too far. We tell a joke that is a bit off-color and it upsets a coworker. The typical response is that the coworker withdraws a bit. This response is *turtling*—they withdraw into their shell while they watch and see if this was just a one-time bad joke or if this is indicative of more bad behavior. They will stay in their shell until they feel it is safe to come out. Now if you are the one who told the crass joke or made a comment that someone felt was inappropriate, you can feel that the response is that the person withdrew a bit. They might not be approaching you to talk about their weekend or may be acting a little cold in a meeting. Your response might be to try to reconnect with them and find out what happened. So, you shower them with attention. John Gottman,[3] renowned relationship expert, describes these as bids for affection. Too much attention, however, begins to feel like *thunder*. The more you thunder, the more your coworker turtles. In other words, the louder and funnier and chattier you try to be with your coworker, the more they will see you as being unsafe and obnoxious and they will continue to withdraw.

You can't force a turtle out of its shell.

My first suggested course of action is always to try to talk to the other person. And that works more often than you would expect! But people can have a variety of reactions. When a coworker withdraws, try not to be frustrated with them. Instead, be grateful that you picked up on this clue about how your behavior is being received. If you find that you are pushing a conversation on someone and they are withdrawing, back up and try a different tactic. For instance, focus on defining goals and creating a timeline for reaching those goals.[4] Make an effort to be friendly and courteous and give your coworker a chance to realize that you are a safe and kind person. After repeatedly seeing your kind behavior, most people will begin to approach you again and you will reestablish your normal friendly relationship. If not, you might need to approach them (kindly and respectfully) and ask them what is wrong. If they are willing to tell you, say thank you and that you will work on it (or think about it). Do not defend yourself at this time. You might think that your behavior is completely acceptable, but if it is bothering another person then you should probably think about making some modifications. Hey, better you figure out some new jokes on your own before your boss tells you to! The other coworker might also just be quiet. They might enjoy the quietness of work where they can just focus on their projects and don't enjoy other people asking them about personal details. And that response also deserves to be respected.

STAY OR GO?

If this isn't you, but you are dealing with an inappropriate person, you will have to decide how much you are willing to invest in changing the situation, and how much you are willing to put up with if they don't change.

If you enjoy the rest of the job and the inappropriate person is open to change, then stay. But consider going to HR with your concerns. Make sure to document the inappropriate comments so that you have specific examples to demonstrate these concerns. If the rest of your job isn't worth it, or if the person is not open to changing, then it is time to go.

DISRESPECTFUL CULTURE

Tomasz and Misaki (the call center rep and waitress in the earlier examples) both have an added challenge because they are not dealing with a single inappropriate person, but an entire culture.

Tomasz works at an office where the culture is gossipy and disrespectful. This is clearly more complex than dealing with a single inappropriate person. Interestingly, disrespectful cultures often begin with a single person whose inappropriate behavior was never challenged.

When I began working with Tomasz, we discussed that he might not be able to change the entire culture, but he can change how people treat him. Picture a weed beginning to take root in the ground. The roots will move to the least resistant spots in the ground. Firmer ground will prohibit the weed from spreading there.

What Tomasz did in this situation was to be that firmer ground. As people tried to gossip to him and tell jokes that made him uncomfortable, he resisted and changed the subject. He tried to rebuff the gossip with something positive. People eventually realized that Tomasz will not gossip. They began to approach him with a more appropriate conversation. And this happened quickly—after two conversations where he drew the line, people got the hint. Hopefully, Tomasz's example will have an effect on the overall office culture. Just like a weed whose fertile ground has dried up, the gossip weed should eventually wither.

Tomasz is able to be firm with his coworkers about his decision not to gossip. He also is interested in a long-term career at this company and is willing to wait for change. Tomasz stayed in his office and is glad that he did. He experienced some initial blowback about being the "office joke police," but over time the office noticed a) they all felt a bit safer around each other and b) Tomasz was a more comfortable, productive worker.

Misaki also worked at a place where she had to deal with a larger culture of disrespect instead of just a single person. The difference between her story and Tomasz's is that Misaki was being treated inappropriately, not just hearing inappropriate behavior. She needed to make it clear how she should be treated and not back down. I arranged a meeting with her and management where she discussed how she expected to be treated. How the management responded determined whether she would stay. And they didn't respond well. Even though I continually validated Misaki's concerns in front of management, it was clear that they weren't taking her seriously. Misaki was not interested in a long-term career with this company. Since they were not acknowledging how they were treating her, they will likely never change. She left the company. But she walked away with her head held high. She knew that she had tried to make the situation work, that she had defended her boundaries, and that hopefully she planted a seed for them to reevaluate how people should be treated.

If you are an employee, you can take control over your own circle and change that culture. If you are a manager, take an aggressive zero-tolerance response to a disrespectful culture.

TAKEAWAY

Office gossip is like a doughnut. It looks tempting and delicious, especially if everyone else is having one. And then you have one and it is enjoyable. But then you start to feel the sugar crash, sick to your stomach, and the regret. Gossip is just like this. It might feel nice for the first few minutes, until you regret it and realize that it takes too long to fix the damage.

Feminine Response

Remember that these descriptions of a feminized response are based on historical studies on females. I strongly recommend reading both the feminine and masculine responses so that you can walk away from this chapter informed and ready to choose your response.

Dealing with inappropriate coworkers is a great opportunity for women to rely on their inherent social and communication skills. Reach out to another woman or someone who is using feminine conflict resolution skills in the office for feedback. This can be a mentor or someone you trust. Tell them your goals for your career and that you would appreciate their help. Ask them if you can rehearse a confrontation conversation with them. And then practice how you would confront an Inappropriate Ingrid. Sound weird? What is weirder is considering that masculine coworkers have spent a lifetime practicing—through trash talk, posturing, and badgering. Guys have been doing this since they could talk. Confrontation and criticism don't come as naturally in female relationships, and so this is simply something that you might need to practice to make sure this conversation plays out the way you want it to. This mentor might also be able to give you feedback about times that you are being inappropriate.

Some workplaces have picked up the African proverb "Each one, teach one," meaning that every woman in the workplace takes responsibility for mentoring a new hire. As you become more skilled at standing up for your boundaries and what you deserve in the workplace, teach other women in the workplace these skills. Our society and media are drastically lacking in examples of women who are skilled in respectful but firm communication. It is time for all of us to become our own example.

I also suggest working with a mentor to plan out your steps after this difficult conversation. The *Harvard Gazette*[5] shows that while men might be more comfortable bringing up a difficult conversation, they are also more likely to forgive and reconnect after the conversation. Women are resistant to bring up a conversation, and then are resistant to forgive afterwards. Being able to speak with a coworker or mentor about this can help to give you some context. Simply, "I feel like I have every right to be mad at Pablo for correcting me, so I'm not going to speak with him today. Does that sound like a good response?" And a good mentor can say, "Uh, sure, that's a great response, if you're in kindergarten!" They might also suggest, "If you want a relationship with your coworker, state what you want and then put time into developing that. Let's come up with a plan."

Masculine Response

Inappropriate behaviors are often tolerated by men for a few reasons. (1) Men often try to outdo each other in how inappropriate they can be—almost a show of strength to see who can tolerate it. It's like a verbal game of chicken, and you don't want to be the first one to back down. (2) Banter and teasing are a common conversational tactic for men to feel connected, which means that they give less validity to jokes that cross the line. There is an assumption that the person wasn't being serious.

Since workplace culture has historically said that men will put up with more in the workplace, this is why it can be incredibly powerful to go against the norm. When a man stands up and says, "Whoa, whoa, too far, buddy. That one is crossing the line," it takes on a tone of power. This means that it can be a powerful tool to change a culture of inappropriate behaviors.

If you choose this response, it means that you are willing to put up with a few inappropriate jokes and that you appreciate the banter. But it also means that it will send a powerful message to your coworkers if you decide to put your foot down.

11

MICROMANAGERS

Replies to the question *"How would you explain 'micromanagement' to a nine-year-old?"* on LinkedIn:

"Do you remember when we were driving to see grandmother and you constantly asked 'Are we there yet?'"

—*Olli-Pekka Manninen*

"It's like cooking with my mum. When every few minutes she checks actions I have taken and suggests what to do next. Without being asked."

—*Kasia Więckowska*

These descriptions of micromanaging for a nine-year-old are surprisingly accurate. Micromanaging behavior is checking up on you constantly, with an assumption that you may be doing something wrong. Managing details does not mean it is a micromanaging behavior. Managers can continually manage details, but they can do it in a way that makes you feel supported. This chapter provides tips for those managers who assume that their worker is constantly making mistakes.

There are two common reasons why people micromanage.[1]

1. **They want to** (It is their personality).

Some people are by nature more controlling, or have a keen attention to detail coupled with a dash of paranoia, or they might even have borderline obsessive-compulsive disorder (OCD). These people can be the miracle workers at organizing their summer office picnic, are fantastic editors, and are great at tracking vacation requests and ordering office supplies. They are curious and interested in everything. They are often very capable and thus very confident. This has led them to think that they know they can do a good job on most things, and so over time they have simply taken on more and more things to do. And they get frustrated when everyone isn't as perfect as they are.

2. **They have to** (It is their job).
   People with micromanagement tendencies might feel that they are the only ones who can do the job correctly. This might be a rational concern if they are concerned about the lack of quality from their employees. However, their desire to control can lead to an irrational fear. For instance, they might have found a single typo in a report and decided that from then on, they need to type every report.

Common responses to being micromanaged:

- Become resentful. Every time you hear them speak, you start picturing in your head how you really want to respond. If you have been envisioning the smashing scene from *Office Space*, you are probably resentful.
- Give up. If my work will never be good enough for my boss, then why try?[2]
- Rise to the challenge. If the manager is also encouraging, or if you have a strong fight reflex, then being micromanaged might inspire you to try harder and meet their goals next time.
- Take it personally. If you know that you are trying and the manager is still critical, then the logical conclusion is that the problem is not your work. A masculinized response is that the problem is with the micromanager—"They are too critical and a jerk." A feminized response is that the problem is with herself—"I must have done something wrong to make them not like me." (This will be discussed in more detail later in this chapter.)

If someone is micromanaging you:

- Ask them why—maybe you did something that required them to micromanage you?
- Maybe they are simply nervous about their business or project and need to review every detail to make sure it goes well.
- Maybe you have also reinforced this behavior by handing them more and more to oversee.
- Maybe you have reinforced this behavior by knowing that they would review the details, and so you have let some of your own quality control slack.

DON'T

Do not try to wrench control from someone who is micromanaging; secure your own control in another way. They feel the need to control the current situation. If they sense you're trying to take some of that control away from them, they will only try to tinker and manage further.

Don't relax on your quality and force someone to micromanage you.

Don't label someone a micromanager just because they are editing your work.[3] It isn't helpful to label someone at all, as this makes it harder to see them as a person. When you label someone, you are just seeing their behavior and not who they actually are.

DO

Discuss procedural safeguards. With micromanager behaviors it works well to counterattack with a plan. For instance, "I will complete steps A through F. That will give me a chance to brainstorm freely, and I will refine my thoughts on my own sloppy copy. Once the report is refined and edited, at step G, I will email it to you and ask for your review. Does that sound like a good plan?" This makes it clear that you appreciate their input, but that you also need freedom to work. Design a plan that gives you space from them looking over your shoulder and also a definite time for them to step in.

IS THIS YOU?

If you tend to micromanage, then you should be aware of the effects of your behavior. Have you been told that you are a micromanager? Do you feel that you spend the majority of your time checking in on employees? Have you given them what they need to succeed on their own? Micromanaging can be done successfully and lead to a positive overall effect. For instance, if you are able to bring up concerns to your employees in a way that makes them still feel respected, you might be able to improve the overall work product and keep employees involved.

The problem with micromanaging behavior is that providing feedback or concerns often comes across as condescending. Employees feel disrespected, as if the rest of their work was worthless or not appreciated. Micromanagement often diminishes their sense of ownership, which then leads to an overall decrease in motivation, quality, and attention to deadlines. Employees afraid of being micromanaged tend to be less forthcoming with their work (often subconsciously and without realizing they are being evasive or withholding). They will hide reports until the last minute so that there is less opportunity to be micromanaged.

A good strategy is to communicate candidly with your employees.

- *Be first*. You must be the one to broach the subject first so that your employees know it is safe to discuss openly. Come prepared with a few suggestions. Discuss definitive points where you would appreciate reviewing the work.
- *Be honest and humorous* about your tendencies in your next meeting. "Okay, people, so you might have noticed I can be a bit controlling"—pause for nervous laughter—"so let's go ahead and discuss ways I can still feel in control and be involved but you are able to freely do your job."
- *Discuss timelines*. When do you need the work delivered to you? How much time do you need to review? Is feedback more constructive delivered via email or in person? A piece at a time or all at once? Make sure that you validate all of the suggestions, even if you do not agree with each one.

STAY OR GO?

If this isn't you, but you feel that you are being micromanaged, it would be good to remember that micromanaging can be an incredible asset to the company—and to you. However, you must establish a relationship where you both feel respected. When you are trying to have a relationship with a micromanager it is easy to slip into habits that leave both of you feeling that your efforts are not being valued. You feel that they are not appreciating the quality of your work because they may have found one typo. They might feel that you are not appreciating how perceptive they are to have combed through so much detail to find that single error. Without intervention, this relationship can quickly deteriorate into bitterness and outright animosity.

TAKEAWAY

> The best executive is one who has sense enough to pick good men to do what he wants done, and self-restraint enough to keep from meddling with them while they do it.
>
> —Theodore Roosevelt

Micromanaging can quickly cause deteriorating morale in a company. Simply put, if people are being micromanaged, then there is an assumption that they are not good enough. This assumption can cause employees to become frustrated, resentful, and despondent.[4] It is important to deal with micromanagement behaviors quickly before they spread dissension. It is also important to analyze your reaction to being micromanaged: Is someone being critical because (A) you need to improve your work, (B) there is just a personality difference, or (C) the person really is a micromanager and is overmanaging you?

Feminine Response

Stereotypical feminized behavior is people pleasing (please read the earlier chapter on people pleasing and understand the strengths and possible downsides). Women strive to keep their home perfect, their kids fed, homework helped, schedules organized, and family healthy. (At least I have heard that is what other women manage to do. I may need to give up trying and hire a cleaning company.) When we work with someone who is micromanaging, who is never satisfied with our work, then it can throw us into a cycle of hopelessness and frustration. Women often have a deeper value of wanting to be accepted and to take care of those around them. They will try to be flexible to meet their manager's expectations, and it is disheartening when that is a moving or unachievable target.

Women often internalize criticism. They will work excessively hard to try to meet their manager's expectations. If the micromanaging lessens up, this will reinforce the woman's belief that the problem was entirely hers, and she will continue to self-evaluate. If the micromanaging does not lighten up, she will typically become frustrated, resulting in fight or flight, which in this situation looks like passive-aggressive behaviors or burnout.

This has a disastrous effect on our mental health. The requirements for our mental health are clarity, pride, and hope. In other words—we figured out how to solve a problem, we are proud of ourselves for solving it, and we have hope that we can get through any other problems. The opposite factors attack our mental health. If we are confused about how to solve a problem, and we do not have a sense of accomplishment from fixing it, then we begin to lose hope and slip into despair. The point is: Working with a micromanager can have long-term negative effects on our mental health. This situation must be dealt with before it gets worse.[5]

When an employee tries the feminine response of conversation and it doesn't work, they will often switch tactics and try a masculine response, or vice versa.

Masculine Response

The typical masculine response to this situation is that there is something wrong with the manager or the company. The male worker will complain about the manager to coworkers, who will of course reinforce his belief that the manager is a raging jerk who needs to be brought down a peg. Eventually, the worker will also have a fight-or-flight response. The masculine version of this is typically confronting the manager ("I need to stand up for my rights and those around me!"), confronting the company ("I don't deserve to be treated like this. I am going to show this company how to respect people!"), or quitting ("I won't be treated like this. I'm going somewhere that can respect my skills."). In other words, women respond by trying to understand what they did wrong and why, and men focus on the bottom line of the problem and their reaction to it.

Male managers report that when they are supervising female employees, they micromanage them more than male employees. The reason is often that they are not as comfortable communicating with women, so they keep the conversations focused on ways to improve, and they keep the conversation closed-ended instead of engaging in a collaborative dialogue. Male managers also report that when men are being micromanaged, they focus on the bottom line: What have they done wrong? They seem to spend less time asking why, what it means, and how they are going to fix the problem.[6]

When the Feminine and Masculine Response Are Not Enough

When a worker, regardless of gender, adopts a feminine or masculine response, that response is typically well, y'know, in response to something. This usually means that it takes a behavior and then a response to that behavior to form a complete picture. For instance, if I were to yell at my kids about doing the dishes and they took an aggressive stance back with me, then that conversation would not be complete without looking at both of us. However, the workplace is starting to see a new personality that is complete on its own. This personality has a sense of completeness and confidence on its own. It can navigate the workplace with a consistency, regardless of who it comes into contact with. There isn't enough data yet to discuss this personality, nor have I seen it being named, but I've been looking for suggestions. YinYang Personality? Fusion Response? Self-Sustaining Ecosystem Worker Profile? Hmm, I guess I can see why none of these names have really taken off.

The problem with both the feminine and the masculine response is that they are not enough. For many of these personalities, the feminine response is to internalize the problem: "What did *I* do wrong?" The masculine response is to externalize the problem: "What did *you* do wrong?" But these questions only get at half of the answer. An extreme micromanagement situation is usually caused by a) a manager with extreme attention to detail and control tendencies and b) an employee who needs a bit more attention to detail. For this situation to be truly fixed, both the employee and the manager need to make some improvements. They both need to acknowledge their contribution to the situation. The employee needs to consider if there are ways to improve the quality of the work, and the manager needs to find a more effective way to communicate feedback and instill trust in employees. The manager needs to work on their feminine social skills, and the worker needs to work on their masculine rise-to-the-challenge competitiveness.

In other words, for the best outcome to dealing with difficult personalities, both the feminine and the masculine response are needed. It will be difficult to take ownership and change the situation without the complete picture from both of these viewpoints.

Destructive Dorky Behaviors

12

THE HULK

Side note: When we are talking about The Hulk, picture the old one—the green monster who couldn't contain his anger, with the shredded clothes and veins popping out in rage and unable to calm himself down.

THEY-ARE-THE-REASON-I-WANNA-QUIT COWORKERS

Settle in. There's a lot to say about angry, they-are-the-reason-I-wanna-quit coworkers.

Sigh. Why do so many people fall into this category?

Some people, as we discussed earlier, just have bad social skills (Bad Brads). Some people we just don't connect with (The Dude). We are prepared for these personalities; we take it as part of life that you won't connect perfectly with every single person.

But The Hulk? These people are harder to figure out. These are the people who don't say good morning. They fly off the handle when you make a simple request. They take credit for your ideas. They wait until the night before to tell you about a report, then complain to the boss that you didn't get it to them on time. They don't support your ideas. They are cranky every morning. They eat your sandwich from the fridge.

In other words, these are the people who have gone from bad communication to mean communication to mean behavior. They are intending to be unkind and don't seem to have control over their anger. This goes beyond angry vibes, and instead adds to the fear and tension in the workplace.

CHARMING ANGRY PEOPLE

Surprisingly, many angry people have learned how to be charming as a social skill coping mechanism. This is known as the "awestruck effect," according to Cambridge scholar Jochen Menges. This is when someone uses charisma to cover up their anger or motivations. They are charismatic and full of life. They feel confident and have little problem communicating. They know that they can succeed and carry a sense of optimism around with them. And they use these skills to push things in their direction.[1]

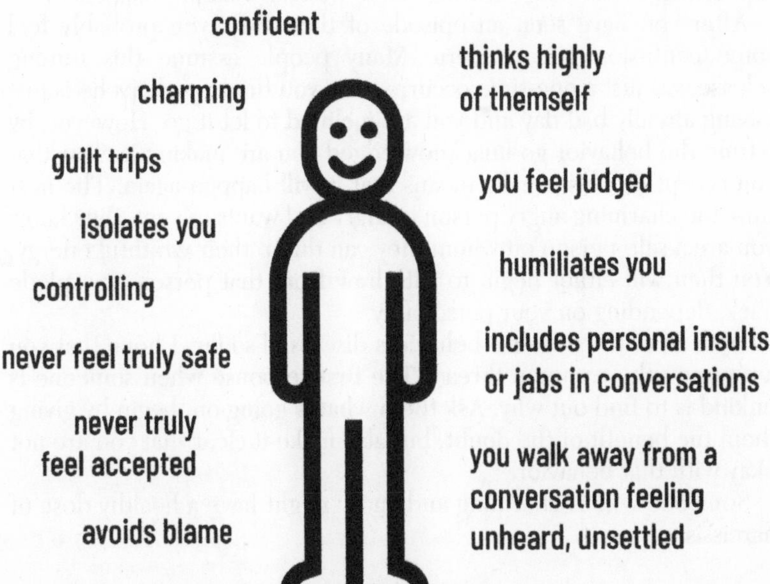

Charming and Angry Personalities. Source: Author

Charisma is their strength, but also their dark side. The confidence they have to say something kind is the same confidence that allows them to say something unkind. They are skilled communicators who know how to say just the perfect funny joke in a staff meeting, and also just the perfect jab to deflate you for the rest of the day.

Charming angry people can be difficult to detect. Most of the time they are on good behavior—and everyone thinks they are wonderful. "Carlos, he's such a nice guy. He always asks about my kids." "Prashma? She's so funny. I can't picture her ever saying the things you are mentioning. You must have misunderstood her." If you haven't seen a charming angry person switch from Jekyll to Hyde, then it may be hard to imagine. And what adds to the problem is that your coworkers might not believe your concerns.

Such a transition can be quick. Charming angry people often have their emotions right at the surface, meaning their feelings are often expressed. This typically comes out in sincere displays of kindness or perfectly timed humor. But when offended or challenged, their anger can seem to explode forcefully out of nowhere—often catching you off guard and speechless. After they have exhausted their outrage, they can promptly slip back into charming—leaving you to wonder what just happened.[2]

After you have seen an episode of their fury, you probably feel some confusion and concern. Many people assume this fuming release was just a one-time occurrence—you think, perhaps he is just having a really bad day and you are inclined to let it go. However, by letting the behavior go unacknowledged you are making it clear that you accept it. This usually means that it will happen again. The next time the charming angry person is angry and wants to vent, they know you are a safe person on whom they can dump their wrathful energy. You then will either begin to withdraw from that person or explode back, depending on your personality.

With all of the negative behaviors discussed so far, I hope that you are seeing the common thread. The first response when someone is unkind is to find out why. Ask them what is going on, begin by giving them the benefit of the doubt, but also make it clear that you are not okay with that behavior.

Someone who is charming and angry might have a healthy dose of narcissism.[3]

- They know that they have great skills and they quickly get annoyed with anyone who doesn't have their same skills.

- Intelligent, funny, and witty personalities have also given them a Texas-sized dose of self-esteem.
- They have a lack of empathy for others.
- They are typically cold unless they are using their charisma to get something.
- They have the confidence to put you in your place when they decide that you deserve it.

They also have a tendency to make confrontations personal. They are feeling frustrated with you, giving off the vibe that you are wasting their time by being so stupid. So, they turn their attack into criticism. This goes beyond just pointing out behavioral improvements. It can turn into personal humiliation. They will not be satisfied until you, and maybe everyone around you, has realized just how wrong you are.

The preferred management motto is "Criticize Privately; Praise Publicly." The rationale is to build a person up in front of their coworkers and to have a private conversation about improvements where people can listen and not need to defend themselves. But charming angry people often do the opposite, almost as if they think they are helping you by pointing out loudly where you need to improve.[4]

SULLEN ANGRY PEOPLE

There is also the person who shows you that they are sullen and angry. This person has a deep brooding concern about life. They might be angsty; they might think that the world has wronged them; they might just be a quiet person who tends to be critical. This person also keeps their emotions at the surface, making it easy for them to explode out of the blue. But they have a negative undertone, a pessimism that things won't work out. This pessimism helps them to feel justified in exploding.

Characteristics of a sullen angry employee (defined as "Desk Rage" by the Society for Human Resource Management):[5]

- Quiet, but a well-spoken communicator when needed
- Unpredictable; their explosions are unexpected
- Unskilled at calming themselves down without venting
- Prone to switching moods easily
- Entitled, feeling justified in their right to explode

- Righteous; simple put-downs seem to take on more meaning than merited, and small misunderstandings can lead to extreme indignation

We have a golden retriever. My son named him Dirtbike. Yes, Dirtbike. When Dirtbike was a few months old we bought him a stuffed penguin from the Wildlife Foundation. He loved his penguin. He slept with it and kept it by him while he ate. When he ran around the yard, he would hold his penguin tenderly between his teeth.

One day there was a different sparkle in Dirtbike's eye. He was bored and hungry—easy prey for a bad idea. Our dog knew what was going to happen—we all knew it. He suddenly looked at his penguin differently. Without warning, he began shredding the penguin. Like a shark with his first scent of blood, there was no stopping his insatiable hunger for penguin stuffing. Chewing and loving it and high off of that delicious microfiber filling exploding into the breeze.

And then? He had an empty penguin. There was nothing left of his much-adored penguin. He hung his head, and we all saw the remorse dripping from his big, brown eyes. He was sad and the only thing that could have cheered him up would have been his beloved penguin. He wishes he hadn't destroyed it, but he has also tasted his first penguin microfiber flesh. He now knows with a certainty that the next time he feels the urge he will again destroy it. Oh, poor Dirtbike!

Every time I see an employee explode out of the blue, I see the same voracious indulgence that we saw in Dirtbike. Where they have given themselves permission to attack. It's a mix of hunger and remorse and power all mixed into one. At the same moment they are regretting their actions they are getting a high off of it. It is that feeling of power they get that reinforces their action—and that means they will probably do it again. Even though they are sad that they have destroyed the trust and the relationship they enjoyed earlier.[6]

We will go into more depth later about the psychology of conflict, but let's make a quick observation here.

When someone's anger is controlling them, they are doing what feels good to them in the short term: attack! These short-term decisions come from our amygdala, which is responsible for protecting and directing us in the moment when we are under duress. The problem with our amygdala, however, is that it is not prioritizing long-term thinking in our brain—it is not envisioning the long-term consequences that an action might have. Which explains why in the moment someone might think it's a good idea to lose their temper and tell you how they really feel but later on regret their actions and the damage it caused to your relationship. This is known as the amygdala hijack.[7] You were going along trying to make great life choices, and that dang amygdala jumped in and took control and made a bad decision. Shows like *Jerry Springer* and *Cops* should have a credit screen that says, "This show is sponsored by the Amygdala Hijack."

ANGRY ESCALATIONS

Most initial interactions, even with an angry person, are fairly benign. The problem with conflicts is when they escalate.

Let's say you ask the new intern to grab more creamer for the office kitchen. He comes in the next day with almond milk creamer, and you wanted half-and-half. Not a big deal, right? You let him know, and the next day he grabs half-and-half. Now you have what you need to make your coffee taste like not-coffee.

But then, he does it again. He comes in with almond milk creamer!

Now, clearly, the intern has disregarded your request on purpose. What an insolent, entitled little snot. You extended him mercy the first time, but this time? Let your wrath rain down!

This could be a simple little conflict, right? Ask him why, and maybe he tells you that the rest of the staff appreciated the almond milk creamer. Maybe he actually bought both types. Or maybe he is just really dim and forgot. This *could be* a simple conflict resolved with a simple conversation.

But it escalated. You felt like your wishes were ignored. The common respect that you show to those around you was not returned and this betrayed a deep sense of how all humans should be treated. Your amygdala kicked in. You started thinking about your short-term desire for vengeance instead of your long-term desire for mutual respect. Without consciously realizing it, your inner warrior needed to be validated and defended, standing up, as it was, for Truth, Justice, and Delicious Creamers!

What does this mean? By escalating it, you might have overreacted. A simple issue of buying the wrong creamer escalated into blatant disrespect, and so your behaviors escalated right alongside it. Instead of asking him why, you assumed that he did not respect your request and bought the wrong creamer on purpose (see the chapter "Horror

Vacui"—when we don't know someone's intentions, we often make up negative intentions for them). This begins the escalation path:[8]

- assumptions
- labeling
- passive aggression
- silent treatment
- guilt trips and shaming
- verbal insults
- threats
- violence

Note that we do not immediately resort to violence, and in fact few people become violent. Most of us try to get conflicts resolved through talking, but when we are worked up, we are not using our highest-level talking and reasoning skills. Rather, we throw out a guilt trip or a passive-aggressive maneuver. The other responds in anger. Thus, our negative assumptions about that person are validated, and we feel justified in escalating the conflict further. (The psychology of conflict says that when we are escalated, we ignore the other's attempts at de-escalation and are hyperaware for any aggressive behaviors.) This process is similar to the cycle of abuse that many psychologists discuss: Building tension, Attack, Reconciliation, Calm.[9] The cycle continues until we have exhausted all of our verbal escalation weapons and we resort to nonverbal techniques, or physical reactions. This might start small: crossing arms, walking away, or slamming a door. But if the conflict still isn't resolved, and the value betrayed feels so great, then this physical escalation can continue. In my research, I found that approximately 10 percent of workplace conflicts escalated to some form of violence.[10]

As conflicts escalate, people lose their perspective. An ancient, instinctual warrior takes over, and their original motivation is forgotten. Instead, the warrior cries out for justice at all costs. The conflict escalates to a battle of winning, instead of the original desire for basic respect.

As conflicts escalate, our goals change. What was originally simple ("I want half-and-half for my creamer") becomes wrapped in our values and our needs and our identity. As you look at the different stages below that our goals take, can you identify with any of them? Can you see where you might occasionally turn into a green monster? Can you identify this path in your coworkers and see how their goals change?

Here is how our goals change:

- Understanding—"I want someone to understand my goal."
- Being heard—"I want someone to understand why this matters to me."
- Being right—"I need them to know that I am right."
- Winning—"I need them to know that I am right and they are wrong."
- Including other people in our fight—"Other people feel this way."
- Including other issues in our fight—"Other examples of your behavior prove that you are not a nice person."
- Revenge—"You have hurt me; let me hurt you back to show you how much that hurts."[11]

One of the other reasons why conflicts escalate is because we unfortunately are not taught how to respectfully explain our interests and respectfully listen to others. Instead, we are taught that there are two options: be nice or be tough. How many times have I heard my own family say, "Stand up for yourself, son," and "Play nice, sweetie." As if those are the only two responses: attack or give in, fight or flight, soft or hard negotiating. Alternatives to these two social norms are not popular—or modeled—in movies, in social media, or in most families. Most families place a priority on strength or kindness, as if a person could not be both strong and kind.

In movies, we typically have a few tough characters who argue, and then a few meek characters who support them. I would love to see a scene where characters could be both strong and supportive. Imagine this movie:

Thor: "Hello Hulk, I would appreciate it if you would let me finish punching first before you began punching."

Hulk: "Thank you for telling me, Thor. I appreciate and understand your point of view. I will gladly let you finish punching. I would also like it if sometimes I could punch first."

Thor: "That is an excellent idea, Hulk. We should take turns. I have heard your interest and am glad that you also listened to my interest."

Maybe it is just me, but I haven't seen that movie yet.

Most movies/social media threads/families encourage two options: stand up or shut up. But there is a third option: speak and listen. Kindly state what you want and then listen to what the other person wants.[12]

So, we get swept up in conflict and it begins to escalate, and most of us have not been given the tools to de-escalate a conflict and explain what we really want. The combination of these two—escalation and the lack of verbal tools—leads to conflicts growing into a violent, undesirable ending.

But wait! Don't give up hope—we are going to look at tools for resolving these conflicts soon!

WORKING WITH ANGRY COWORKERS

Most people respond to conflict in one of three ways:[13]

1. *Fight*: Stand up to and attack the other person
2. *Flight*: Leave the conversation and avoid the person
3. *Freeze*: Inability to decide what to do, not sure if you want to flight or fight, sometimes resulting in shame or depression, a general sense of lethargy where you are afraid to do anything

If you work with someone who has a tendency to get angry easily, she is probably programmed to be a fighter. This means that when faced with an unfair situation, her response is to defend herself and make sure that she is not hurt in the process. Conflicts escalate to a mythical degree. What might have been a simple misunderstanding over creamer has now become a crusade to defend honor, tribe, and the horse you rode in on. Douglas Noll and Thomas Jordan,[14] two researchers on escalation theory, state that the more a conflict escalates, the more we regress to childish habits. We are no longer communicating like mature adults, but moving into an accelerated, back-and-forth type of an argument, without pausing to consider the impact of our words. "He started it." "Did not." "Did too." "Oh yeah, well, you're a jerky jerkface." You know, those kinds of arguments, just with adult words.

The problem is that when conflicts take on mythical proportions it becomes so easy to see yourself as the mythical warrior slaying a dragon, instead of realizing you're just a coworker steaming mad that you have almond milk creamer. And once you start seeing yourself as a mythical warrior with a noble cause, then suddenly you are justifying actions that you probably wouldn't normally consider.[15] You are allowing yourself to intensify the problem because "this is about respect," instead of realizing, no, it's seriously only about creamer.

And, let's spell it out: Once you see yourself as a mythical warrior slaying a dragon, then you are seeing your coworker as, well, a dragon. And everyone knows that you can't be nice to a dragon.[16] They'll take advantage of you and turn you into a BBQ special. You do indeed have to stand up to a dragon and slay them at all costs. It is important to teach them a lesson so that they don't repeat the action or take advantage of other coworkers. What a righteous undertaking! Protecting the innocent villagers of ABC Corp from the terror of subpar creamers!

Except your coworker isn't a dragon. They might mess up sometimes, but that doesn't mean that you get to treat them like a ferocious beast. No matter how just your cause might feel in the moment, there isn't a rationale for treating people with less respect than you are requesting.[17]

DON'T

When you have a Hulk coworker, don't retaliate, don't assume that you have all of the information, and don't run away. I think that's the same advice for dealing with an angry brown bear.

Don't challenge an angry person with a verbal sparring, because once their feelings register a righteous cause in the air, they'll have no restraint with this conversation. When you have seen that someone is being controlled by anger, then you have to be careful how you respond. Gently protect your boundaries, but if you appear challenging it is throwing gasoline on a potential forest fire.[18] You don't know how much or for how long it will burn, but you know the destruction will take quite some time to remedy.

How angry can they get? As angry as you let them.

DO

Be careful not to get sucked into the interaction and let it spiral downwards. Instead, if you notice a conflict escalating, take a break. This is for your mental health as well as your safety.

When you have an angry coworker, try to understand their concerns—and explain your concerns—with the same amount of care. *Care about their needs* and *care about your needs*. This can work whether that person is your supervisor, you are their supervisor, or you are equals. The conversation might need to be framed differently depending on your positions, but everyone likes to be heard and most people are pretty good at extending the same kindness back to you.

Author Bill Eddy has spent decades working with high-conflict behaviors, including angry outbursts. His work is full of practical advice. He recommends that when having a conversation with someone who is displaying anger, use the BIFF method:[19]

- *Brief*. Explain your interests briefly, so that it does not feel like a lecture.
- *Informative*. Don't try to persuade them, just provide them with information. ("This is what I need," or "This approach might be more effective because . . .")
- *Friendly*. Try to avoid being either condescending or meek, but be warm. Let them know that you are having this conversation to try to establish a relationship.
- *Firm*. Relationships are like a scale—if one side is pushed down the other is pushed up and vice versa. As mentioned above, avoid being condescending—this can make you seem like the dragon and will make them feel like a victim. Avoid being meek—this can make you seem like the victim and will make them feel like a dragon.[20] Instead, be firm. Be confident in what you are requesting. Give respect and expect respect.

When someone is having an angry outburst, let them know somehow that such behavior is not okay with you. Most angry people act like they can't control their outbursts, and yet . . . they seem to conveniently explode only around people who are safe. People say they can't control their behavior, yet rarely explode to their boss. Or, they explode differently in a public setting versus a private one. So as much as they tell themselves that they can't control their outbursts when they see red, clearly they have learned how to manage their behavior. It is important to remember that they are able to control their behavior. Do not allow them to explode on you.

Setting up a firm boundary is key. It could just be, "I am not going to have this conversation with these circumstances." Which might mean that you don't want to speak to the person when they are angry, or maybe you are busy, or maybe you are feeling triggered and you know that you need a break. But you are making a clear statement that angry behaviors are not effective with you.

Angry people are actually just people who have learned angry behaviors and can control their outbursts!

IS THIS YOU?

Are you constantly surrounded by stupid people? Are you amazed by the idiotic mistakes that everyone makes?

Hmm, ever thought, maybe everyone else in the world is not the problem?

If you find yourself constantly becoming angry, it is likely because you are assuming everyone should be like you. How can this person be so thick and just keep talking in the meetings? Well, maybe it is because this person is a verbal processor, or they have a need to be liked and appreciated. How can they make so many mistakes in their report? Well, maybe they have a brain for big ideas and not details. It's time to realize that everyone you work with has their own set of strengths and weaknesses. Including you.

And whatever knuckleheaded thing they might do is probably nothing compared to how daft you might appear while losing your temper in the office. I remember years ago working in an office with a Hulkette. She was constantly irritated by people in the office and had no problem losing her temper. I think that she assumed she was helping people to speed things along or do a better job by pointing out their errors. I think she also assumed that we all agreed with her that she was better at the job and that everyone else needed her to point out errors. But she was wrong. We didn't agree with her; we were just afraid of her. And instead of respecting her, we all talked about how we didn't trust her in high-pressure situations because we didn't think she was stable enough to handle the stress. Of course, I never said that to her face. I was young, okay? I didn't know how to handle complex confrontations yet.

If you find yourself losing your temper in the office:

What price are you paying to be right? How long are you willing to keep sacrificing relationships for that, er, privilege of standing up for yourself?

STAY OR GO?

If this isn't you, but you work with someone who is continually angry, I wouldn't plan on seeing a transformation anytime soon. However, over time, as you respond to their behavior differently, they might slowly change, but you cannot count on this. The only thing that you can do is define and reinforce your boundaries. *If they respect those boundaries and treat you in a way that you can accept, then you have gained a respectful coworker.*

"Hey, Tim, you can't keep dumping all your work on me when you've got too much—I've already got too much on my plate. We gotta figure something else out."

"Hey, Marika, it's been a blast working with you on this project—but it's not working when you blow up on the team like that."

"You know, I get that you're trying to be funny, but it's getting really old when you call me a pipsqueak in the morning meeting."

If, however, you stand up for yourself and your coworker continues to be angry and belittling, then this might not be a healthy environment for you. Hopefully you can de-escalate this conflict before it becomes physically violent. We have later chapters on keeping yourself safe—if this is a potential concern, please read these. Even if the conflict doesn't become physically violent, please don't discount the other harmful effects of working with angry behaviors. The mental and emotional assaults take a huge toll on people. Angry environments change your temperament and comfort level. Your anxiety level rises. You dread coming into work, you are reluctant to voice your opinion, you begin second-guessing your value, you are more worried about self-preservation than doing your job and forming relationships. Without realizing it, bitterness for the angry behavior begins to grow inside of you. Long term, this has disastrous effects on your well-being. Short term, your company is likely not getting their money's worth out of you if you are retreating, unwilling to voice your opinion, or unable to fully show up. This kind of stress can't be vented at the workplace, and therefore is likely spilling out into your personal life, onto your family and friends. So, if you have tried to work through things with a person who is angry and it is getting worse, then blow that popsicle stand.[21]

If you manage a Hulk, be very clear about what behavior is/is not acceptable. Outline clear expectations of what is a supportive behavior, what is not helpful, and what the consequences will be. Chances are that your expectations will be tested, so make sure to be firm on any infringements. This is letting everyone in the office know how important it is to you to create and defend a supportive and safe culture.

TAKEAWAY

Hulks can only improve if they want to, and there might not be anything that you can do to motivate them. So, if you are working with an angry, unchanging Hulk, get out of that office and move on to greener pastures. (Get it? Cuz the Hulk is green.)

Feminine Response

Many women hate working with The Hulk because it strikes a sense of fear in them: They simply do not feel safe around that person. Women can't control that sense of intimidation. Fear is such a driving, overwhelming instinct, that logic is overridden. I had one woman flat-out refuse to be alone in a room with another woman for more than a year. There was even an HR report, where it was detailed that the angry woman had intimidated the other woman so much that she was not able to think straight around her. Women typically shrink from being around angry behavior.

Until they explode like a caged animal.

Without being taught that it is okay to stand up for themselves, women try to stuff those feelings of intimidation into a bucket. But eventually their subconscious says the bucket is full. Something in our subconscious begins to realize that our sense of self and self-respect and our boundaries are being eroded. And then our subconscious says *enough is enough*. And we snap because we can't take it anymore.

Unfortunately, by snapping at the angry person, we are not going to get the response we want. This is known as reactive abuse, where someone reacts in an abusive way after being abused. There is some evidence that shows that an abuser might push their coworker until their coworker explodes. In other words, they want the coworker to lose credibility and so they continue to antagonize them until the point where the coworker can't take any more. But reacting is ineffective with someone who is abusive by nature, instead of having a behavior that occasionally seems abusive.[22] First off, they are probably much more skilled at arguing than you are. Second, now you look like the person who is emotionally unstable.

Which is why we have to be able to articulate our interests and our boundaries early on, before our inner Hulk takes over.

Masculine Response

Around The Hulk, men often respond by showing that they are not affected or scared by this person.[23] They don't want to show that they are afraid. They play it off by saying, "Oh, that's just Tim being Tim." They know that a woman can cry or be afraid and it is socially acceptable. But they have to pretend that they are not affected. Culturally, men are supposed to be able to handle it and take it—which is one reason why there is such a lower number of cases of abuse reported by men than women. When it becomes too much, however, men will explode because they still have emotions, they just haven't been able to vent them or discuss them along the way.

There is a joke that the masculine response is mad, sad, glad, or hungry. The complex masculine response to anger, however, shows that men have just as many emotions as women. It just might not be socially acceptable to display them. Around women, many men note that they curb their responses. This seems to be either because they don't want to appear intimidating or because they don't want to be seen as weak. Many men say that they are increasingly curbing their responses around their male coworkers as well. "I find it hard to express my feelings. It makes me sound weak." And "I am frustrated that as a male I am blamed for so many of society's ills. It makes me feel like I can never bring up a frustration, because there is an assumption that I am so privileged I don't have the right to complain." And "Men are always bringing each other down. Women raise each other up."

With all of these responses, The Hulk is slowly being reinforced. Men are feeling like they cannot complain about difficult situations and that their complaint would not be taken in the right way. Instead, many men respond by either hiding their frustration or aggressively defending their position.[24] A more effective response would be to let The Hulk know as soon as they are being inappropriate. "Hey, not cool, don't talk to me/her/them that way." This allows the target of The Hulk a chance to take some of their power back. This allows The Hulk's target to stand up for himself, or to vent her emotions, and changes the habit of The Hulk.

Resolve Response

Either a feminized response or a masculinized response might be the right choice for most situations. But are there times where anger might be the right response?

What should you do when you see someone being mistreated? Perhaps an appropriate dose of anger is acceptable? It sends a loud message that the behavior is unacceptable. If you are able to respond with anger, without demeaning the other person, then anger can also be a powerful tool. The problem with anger is that it can be a fire—once it starts it is hard to put out. But if you know that you can control the fire, then applying a bit of heat to a situation might be enough to change it.

If someone is being a Hulk to you, and you have tried ignoring them, and stating your boundaries, and being funny, it might be time to add some heat to your voice and say, "Stop it! Enough is enough!"

13

HIGH-CONFLICT BEHAVIORS

High-conflict behaviors seem to have a righteous anger fueled by, well, it could be fueled by just about anything. When they are upset, they get upset big and fast and loud. As author Ken Kesey says, they just seem to take up more air than others. They are more than comfortable with conflict—they might even enjoy it. High-conflict people are quick to find a wrong done to them, and to use that wrong to justify high-conflict behavior. If you are hunting cougars, this is the person you want on your team. If you are in a criminal defense case, this is the person you want for your lawyer. If you are trying to work effectively with them every day in your office, however, this person can make it difficult to relax and focus on your work. They will also make it difficult to engage in everyday conversations, since you are never sure what is going to push them over the edge.

High-conflict behaviors are different from angry behaviors. Angry behaviors are just triggered easily, are often offended, and you can tell that their feathers are ruffled. They feel a high need to defend themselves. High-conflict behaviors are not triggered—they are accepting righteous causes. They need to argue positions that seem unfair or policies that are unjust. They need to point out ways that you are not performing well or are taking advantage of the team. They combat outdated company policies. They have a high need to defend every cause. Anger is typified by an internal slight; a high-conflict behavior is typified by an external cause. To apply our psychological understanding—an angry person is operating from a short-term amygdala response. In other words, the angry person is being controlled by their emotions. A high-conflict person is operating from a long-term prefrontal cortex response, where they are making a calculated response.[1]

While they might have a different motivation, dealing with angry and high-conflict behavior is pretty similar.

Let me provide you two ideas to help you with your immediate decisions.

1. BIFF. I have discussed this concept in the previous chapter, but let's review it here. Whenever you must interact with someone with high-conflict behaviors, Bill Eddy[2] recommends using his BIFF method. You may or may not be able to change that person. You can, however, change how you speak to them, which can result in more effective conversations and resultant actions. Regardless of how they are speaking, keep your communication Brief, Informative, Friendly, and Firm.
2. You can teach an old dog new tricks, but it's still the same old dog. Mr. Eddy's studies have found that there are effective methods for changing the habits and behaviors of someone with high-conflict behaviors, but it's harder to change their personality or basic beliefs. For instance, through effective communication, time, consequences, and reinforcement, a worker can learn to stop their abusive behaviors. But if they are choosing to be mean, then their basic belief set, the impatience, entitlement, and anger often remain firmly in place.

If you are dealing with high-conflict behaviors:

- Are you safe? Review the chapter on abusive personalities for additional information, but if you have any doubts about your safety, immediately take steps to protect yourself in the office, to and from the office, and at home. Discuss the situation with your manager or HR department. You might even need to request a leave from work. If you request a leave, also decide on the explanation you will supply to your coworkers.
- Are you willing to stay and change your communication patterns while this person takes the steps to change their behavior? Remember, this can easily take a year. There is a myth that it

takes only 21 days, but this is assuming that you are continuously and intentionally changing the behavior and having positive reinforcement for the change. The reality is that it will probably take 2 to 12 months to make a deep, lasting habitual change.[3]
- Will you be able to work effectively with this person if their belief set does not change? If their destructive, high-conflict behavior changes, will you be able to stay now that you understand this person's view of the world? If they just don't like you or respect you, can you still work with them?

DON'T

- Don't expect them to change.
- Don't lecture them about their behavior.
- Don't waver on what you need.
- Don't let them get away with treating you poorly.

DO

- Be Brief, Informative, Friendly, and Firm (BIFF).
- Be brave enough to speak up when you are being mistreated.
- Recruit the allies you need for support, both at and away from work.
- Realize that most high-conflict behaviors prefer things in black and white and have no patience for anything in between.[4]

IS THIS YOU?

Do you have high-conflict behaviors? If so, please realize the effect that you are having on other people. Take responsibility to develop some self-calming and listening techniques. Most people with these high-conflict behaviors are also quite confident. Use this confidence to build up your coworkers and improve your office instead of tearing them down.

STAY OR GO?

If this doesn't describe you, but you are dealing with this personality:

This one is tough. Unfortunately, high-conflict behaviors are hard to work on. Because this behavior allows people to get what they want, it is more difficult to change. According to *Psychology Today*,[5] these are four of the most common high-conflict behaviors:

- They need to make it clear when others have done something wrong.
- They think in terms of absolutes: always or never, good or bad, they like you or they don't.
- They give themselves permission to behave intensely, often beyond social norms.
- They act with extremes, pushing an issue forward beyond the typical boundaries.

This means that high-conflict behaviors can be a tornado of turbulence. Your first response, as with all of these behaviors, is to discuss it with the person. You might have mislabeled them or they might not know the effect of their behavior. However, if they are unwilling to change and the behavior is continuing or escalating, you could easily get sucked into the perpetual maelstrom. If you have the option to find another job or move to another department, you might want to get away from this behavior while they are working on it. Another option, however, is to talk to your manager about this behavior. Chances are good that your manager has already noticed that everywhere she goes this person causes tornadoes. She takes the office peace, the ruby slippers, and the little dog too. Your manager might be willing to put this person through a performance improvement plan or move them to a different department with less potential for chaos. But if your office isn't taking this situation seriously, it is probably time to leave.

TAKEAWAY

The high-conflict person is usually a warrior. If they are fighting for your office, this is great. However, you need to be prepared for this person to attack you whenever they feel like you are in the way of their righteous warpath.

Feminine Response

Females often have two reactions to high-conflict behaviors. One is they take up the righteous cause. This is part of their mother hen personality, or desire to make things right. This is where the original

"Karen" meme has come from—where if something isn't right, I will call your manager. But the other reaction is often complete avoidance. Unsure of how the high-conflict person will react, it becomes easier to just avoid them.

Once again, these responses are the typical fight-or-flight response. A more useful tool is engaging in the middle by validating the other's interests while protecting your interests as well. This method does not mean that the other person's cause is any less important. And it doesn't mean that your interests don't deserve attention. Rather, this is a method of empowering all involved. The high-conflict person will feel heard, and you will feel respected.

A high-conflict person typically doesn't respond well to a fight-or-flight approach anyway.[6] A fight response causes the high-conflict person to escalate and fight back. A flight response shows the high-conflict person that they can get their way around you. Instead, approach them with a firm conversation. Ask them about their interests, and then confidently state your own. This takes work on your part, and it requires you to be the first to offer forgiveness and hope. But you might find that the high-conflict person is actually a great coworker who just needed to work on their high-conflict behaviors.

14

BUSIER-THAN-THOU

Every person I have ever met—including myself—thinks they do the most in the office. Every. Single. One.

Have you ever met that person who really seems to be the most important person in the world? No, seriously, the amount of work that they have to do and the small amount of time that they have to do it is so unprocessable by your puny brain that they just don't have time to explain it all without getting frustrated.

So, they won't explain all of their work. But they will complain about it. And huff. And be frustrated when you knock on their door. And just make you feel like it really is your fault for daring to breathe.

How can you identify these people? They are usually late—and it is always someone else's fault (probably yours). They slam their fingers against the keyboard. (After all—how dare you ask them to send an email?! The nerve!) They huff when you ask them for anything. The book *Difficult Conversations*[1] identifies this behavior as having a negative contribution to conflict. Specifically that by putting up an armor of saying, "I'm too busy," the person is really saying, "I'm unapproachable. Don't bring anything difficult to me. Don't talk to me about anything. Don't bring up a conflict."

REAL-LIFE EXAMPLE

I mediated a case with just this issue—one coworker made it clear how overworked he always was, making himself completely unapproachable to the other employees. There were two men in this case; one was new to the office and was always flustered. He routinely told everyone how many projects he had and was predictably annoyed if anyone tried to small-talk about their weekend. His coworker, on the other hand, had worked at the office for years and was pleasant to work with. He could be counted on to have a kind word for coworkers and always had a minute for stories (more than a minute and he would politely excuse himself). Their boss told me that the seasoned employee had about twice the workload of the new guy. The quality of his work was also much higher. The flustered, busy worker turned in rushed, sloppy work. Unaware of how to prioritize, delegate, or work with supervisors to determine which deadline was the most pressing, this worker tried to do it all. He had frustrated himself. His heart was in the right place—he wanted to please everyone. But the truth was that his stress level made him almost unapproachable. His coworkers complained that they were unable to ask him for updates on projects.

It took a few weeks of retraining his habits and coming to terms with the effect he was having on people before he was able to change. He began to prioritize his projects, ask for help when he needed it, and be patient enough to treat his coworkers with respect.

Many, many people think that they are too busy to handle additional projects. Or to communicate effectively. Or to even take a moment's breath to tell you when something is due. Or to let you know that something else might be late. Or to explain what they need to do their job and when they need it by. They think the problem is that they have so much to do. And in today's overworked environment that *is* definitely part of the problem! But for people who are constantly acting frazzled and overworked, the large part of the problem is that they have not figured out how to communicate about timelines, expectations, needs in advance, and any delays. They have not figured out how to have conversations about what is on their plate.

When someone is constantly too busy, time pressure is rarely the issue. The issue is their inability to communicate well.

WORKING WITH BUSY PEOPLE

You may or may not be able to help busy people. What you can do is give them the opportunity to succeed. Give them assignments early, be clear about deadlines, and then approach them with the confidence that their stress is not your fault. Ask them about deadlines when you need to. If met with resistance, call them on it: "Did I do something wrong? What's going on? Anything I can help with? Would you like me to get you this project sooner?"

These conversations can be a bit intimidating to have face-to-face. And the person might be so flustered that they might not hear what you have to say in person anyway. An email might be better. A sticky note on the desk—*Could you email me an update on this project?*—is unobtrusive. Or, blame it on the boss—*I need an update because our micromanager boss is breathing down my neck*. But be prepared for resistance. There is still that unspoken belief on their part that, *what I am doing is super important and who are you to check in on me?* From a boss's perspective, this may indicate that the employee is taking their work seriously (a great quality). However, it can be a nightmare to deal with day after day.

DON'T

Don't let "busy" people control the workflow. It is important to listen to their concerns, but that does not mean that you should be afraid to hand them work. That would essentially be rewarding their declarations.

At the same time, don't ignore their complaints either. If someone is protesting about their workload, ask them *when* will they have enough time to get to your project. Or, if they have too much on their plate, ask them what they can give up. For many people it is easier to gripe about a problem than to fix it. Force the ever-busy to realize that they are either

a) truly overworked and it is affecting the rest of the office or
b) grumbling too much and they need to do something about it.

It could also be part of the office culture. Busy culture is typically rewarded. It seems like people are working hard and contributing to the success of the company. This creates a culture of producing instead of impacting. Of working hard instead of working smart. And there are usually one or two key people who lead this culture. If you can find that person and help them to change then it can trickle down to the rest of the office. This might mean that you need to ask the busy person to set boundaries and protect those boundaries for the rest of the office—such as saying no to projects that are not an absolute requirement, being approachable, and making it okay for people to take a business day to respond to email.[2]

They might need to reprioritize. Perhaps they need to be more realistic about the time it takes to complete a project. Could be they need to talk to their manager about letting go of some tasks. Or they may possibly need to examine if they are organized and using their time wisely enough.

I am cringing as I write this chapter, because I know it is often me. It is easy for me to slip into the Busier-than-Thou mindset. I become frustrated when people interrupt. But it's okay—I'm going to read the next section on what to do. Then I'll know how to handle my frustration before it turns into a conflict.

DO

There are two approaches for dealing with the Busier-than-Thou: validate or challenge.

- *Validate*: Some people are *sooo* busy because they want to feel acknowledged and important. The more you challenge them on how busy they are, the more desperately busy they will act so that you will hopefully validate all that they do. What this person needs to hear is that you can see they add a lot to the company and that you appreciate their work.[3]
- *Challenge*: If you have already tried validating The Busy and they are not easing up on the grousing, then it might be time to let them know that everyone on the team is working hard. They can't remain unapproachable or continue to imply that others have less work or don't work as hard. Instead, work with them to develop a protocol. When they are completely overwhelmed, perhaps they're allowed 20 minutes of Do Not Disturb time. But the trade-off is that the rest of the day, they need to be kind and respectful when people make requests of them.

IS THIS YOU?

Practice listening with patience when someone is asking you for something. It is also acceptable to kindly say, thank you, now I really do need to get back to work, and excusing yourself after a moment. Write down a schedule—3 minutes on this email, 10 minutes on this file, and even schedule in 2 minutes for making coffee, walking around the office, catching up on weekend chatter. And then realize that everyone else might be just as busy, but handling it better. If you are still feeling out of control and constantly behind, have a conversation with your manager about next steps for your workload. Make sure to bring in your documentation about steps taken to improve your time management and increase your efficiency.

Through hundreds of mediations and private conversations, I have realized that when someone acts really busy, their coworkers often don't think that person is really busy. They just think that person complains a lot and can't handle their workload very well. Whether or not that is true for you, you might want to ask someone you trust how you are really perceived by the rest of the office. There might be a few miniscule changes that you could work on—like listening when someone asks for help.

Or it could be that you just are feeling stressed and overwhelmed with your current tasks—can you ask for help? Can you switch to a different project that better suits you? Maybe let your office know that this month is going to be really tight and you are going to need to protect your time, but after that you can be a team player again?

STAY OR GO?

If this doesn't describe you, but you are dealing with this personality:

This type of personality might be frustrating, but it is not abusive nor should it have a long-term effect on your self-esteem. It is recommended you stay but force the person to ask the question: What are you going to do about it? Every time they complain ask them the same question: What are you going to do about that? Eventually they might take responsibility and do something about it. Even if they don't take responsibility,[4] at least they will realize that you are no longer receptive to their complaints.

TAKEAWAY

When people are incredibly busy, they often do not realize that they are contributing to the busy culture of the office. When they are stressed, they stress out others. When they are late, the delay trickles down. A good approach for working with busy people is asking them what their contribution has been to the things that are frustrating them.

Feminine Response

I have yet to meet a parent who doesn't feel like they are managing 37,000 things. And chances are—they are managing 37,000 things. Yup, I'm looking at you, lady, and applauding everything you do for your family and your job. But here's the catch: It's not an excuse to be short with other people. The more that women can come to terms with what actually has to get done, then they can manage to let a few things go. Or get to them later. Or trust someone else to do them. Or realize that they don't have to do them perfectly.

This is a hard one for me, and I think for many people who manage work and a home, because so many things have historically fallen on our plate. And by moving into the workplace we added more things to our plate, without taking very much off. And if I'm being honest, I'm incredibly proud of everything I can handle! It is part of my identity, and when I feel like I can't handle it all, my Superwoman identity is challenged. And if I'm being vulnerable, just because I think I can handle it all, doesn't always mean I should. What pride is there in checking 37,000 things off of my list if I'm not doing them well, if I'm not a nice person in the process? If I'm constantly snapping at my coworkers, or taking it out on my friends or my family, then I need to shuffle some things right off my plate. And I might do only 36,000 things. Which means I might not be seen as Superwoman. But I will be seen as approachable, a team player, someone who can get things done but is also honest about what they can't get done. I will be able to work with people. And wouldn't you rather work with SuperTeamPlayer than Superwoman anyway?

Resolve Response

In 2004, about half of US workers said they felt overworked.[5] US employee workload has increased during COVID, and with the staff shortage, the end result is that many workers are taking on more than ever before.

Increased workload can have many negative side effects—such as anxiety and mistakes. It can also lead to increased conflicts. Before the workload begins to cause conflicts, set your boundaries. Talk to a manager or HR and discuss a plan. Tally up how much time different tasks take you and ask if you can brainstorm a solution. This might mean cutting out a redundant task, bringing on help, or setting up more realistic expectations.

15

HONEY BADGERS

A honey badger is a funny little African animal that loves sweet honey. A honey badger gets its name from its particular method of acquiring food. The honey badger depends on a bird, the honeyguide. The honeyguide is a small bird that eats bee larvae—and of course also enjoys honey. It is believed that the honey badger waits hungrily in the background, watching the honeyguide. As soon as the honeyguide is on the scent of bees, the honey badger stalks behind. Just as the little bird gets there, the opportunistic honey badger swoops chunks of honey with its big paws and its sharp claws into its open jaws.[1] The honey badger often destroys the beehive. Hopefully that honeyguide is still able to get some of that sweet nectar that it worked so hard for.

This biological backstory illustrates a few characteristics of the Honey Badger:

- They let someone else do the hard work.
- They do not appear to be a threat in the beginning.
- They do not feel remorse for taking something from someone else; rather they feel pride at their cleverness.
- Charm is one of their tools, so coworkers and managers often like them.
- They often win.

Another name for the Honey Badger is the Golden Child, the favored one, he who can do no wrong. This is the employee who lets you do all of the work on the project, then swoops in and presents it to the boss, reveling in all of the praise. All of the praise that should have been yours.

WHY DO THEY DO THIS?

But let's take a moment and be really honest. Like, I'm going to be so blunt you might start writing me hate mail—but just keep reading for a moment. There are lots of reasons to hate the Honey Badger. They take your glory, you thought they were your friend and they betrayed you, they are not giving you the credit you deserve, your boss likes them more, and all of it is just not fair. But let me shoot out a very unpopular suggestion. There is one more significant reason that you might hate the Honey Badger.

Perhaps . . . people think the Honey Badger is better than you because . . . they are better than you.

Don't throw this book across the room yet! Let me explain.

The Honey Badger has important skills in the office and you might be upset with him because those are skills you need to work on. Perhaps your hatred of the Honey Badger is actually a form of jealousy. Perhaps even frustration with yourself.

THE HONEY BADGER GOT THE PROJECT DONE, WITHOUT REGRETS

Often, we overanalyze our work. Then, when we finally turn it in, we are almost apologetic. "Sorry it took so long." "I know I should probably still pump up the numbers section." "This is just a first draft." "I can change the wording here, just let me know."

No! No regrets! Take pride in your work. Be your own Honey Badger! Get the honey and be proud of how you got it. If anything needs to be changed, you'll hear about it. Exude confidence; people will notice and start demonstrating more respect for your work.

THE HONEY BADGER IS CHARMING

One of the things that is so annoying about a Honey Badger is that everyone likes them, while you want to scream from the rooftops,

"There goes an annoying little peacock! Why are you playing to his ego?"

But as the saying goes, if you can't beat 'em, join 'em. In other words, if there is a Honey Badger in your office charming their way to the top, maybe it is bugging you so much because you want to be a bit more like that. Maybe you want to be at the top. You want the managers to notice you and your hard work. So, make them! Dress like a Honey Badger. (Okay, true, honey badgers don't wear clothes. And it might be weird to go to the office naked. But, you know, dress for success and all that.) When you present your ideas in meetings, overprepare with numbers and timelines so that you can speak with confidence. Develop ideas for the company. If the Honey Badger is bothering you, it is probably because you want some of what they have. So, learn those skills! Develop your own confidence and swagger. Listen to your manager's concerns and create suggestions that address them. Then *you* can be the office Honey Badger. But the really cool, nice one.

THE HONEY BADGER WINS

The Honey Badger will continue to steal your glory as long as you let them. Just stop letting them. If you have put work and time into something, make sure that you win your part of the recognition.

DON'T

Don't trust the Honey Badger until they have earned your trust. If someone has already proven that they value their career over their relationship with you, that is not likely to change any time soon.

Don't let it pass. Promote yourself in meetings. Kindly but firmly contradict someone who passes off your idea as their own.[2]

DO

Do let the Honey Badger motivate you! Stand up for yourself! Be proud of your work. If the Honey Badger has a skill you envy, develop that in yourself.

Make sure to keep records of specific instances where the Honey Badger has stolen your ideas. These might be important during a performance review, or if you present your concerns to HR. You might also want to discuss these concerns with your boss. Even if you don't want them to take any actions, you might want to make them aware of the situation and get their advice.[3]

IS THIS YOU?

If this is you, please decide what is most important to you. Is it success in your job? Recognition from your supervisors? Now ask, what are you willing to do to achieve that? Do you want to destroy your office relationships, the people that you have to see 40 hours a week? Do you want to become someone you are not proud of? There is nothing wrong with being a golden achiever, but the best achievers also give credit to those around them.

STAY OR GO?

If this doesn't describe you, but you are dealing with this personality type:

Don't you dare leave this office! Don't let someone Honey Badger you out! Show people what you are made of. Show them the quality of your work. And show them that you can be successful and be kind.

TAKEAWAY

Honey Badgers will take as much glory as you allow them. Don't let them!

It is important to realize that you need to be your own champion. If anyone else were being overlooked or unfairly treated in the office, I am sure you would come to their aid. Don't you deserve that too? So come to your own aid!

Feminine Response

The book began by acknowledging all of the amazing characteristics that women bring to the office. Use these amazing emotional awareness, multitasking skills—and be your own Honey Badger. Look at everything you can do. Why are you letting someone else stand in your way? Decide what honey you want—and go get it!

16

THE PASSIVE-AGGRESSIVE

A passive-aggressive person is described as someone who is upset but holds it in. Instead of confronting someone when they are upset, they stuff it down and wait for a time where they can get revenge but avoid the conflict. They indirectly and covertly express their frustration instead of addressing the other person.[1]

Let me give you an example:

It was a normal staff meeting. Half the people looked like they were taking notes, which were probably grocery lists. The other half were trying to talk over each other. They reached Item 3, which prompted Susie for an update on the new phone installation. Susie reviewed the completion date, how it would affect everyone in the office, and then gave an updated price.

Pablo piped up, saying, "Sorry, Susie. Forgot to tell you, that piece has been cut from the budget. So, we will have to go with a less advanced system. Can you get me an updated price by this afternoon?"

"No problem," Susie responded with a smile.

Later that afternoon, Pablo was in another meeting and furtively pulled up Facebook (or Instagram or Snapchat or TikTok or whatever they are using). He was stunned to see the following post from Susie: *Can't stand coworkers who pull funding from you on a major project, don't tell you about it until you have done all of the work, and don't have the decency to tell you privately—but blurt it out in front of the entire office. #norespect.*

Now what does Pablo do? Susie has made it clear that she is upset, but also that she doesn't want to talk to Pablo about it. Other coworkers have begun to comment on her post, however, so Pablo thinks he should step in and do something.

FLIGHT RESPONSE/SOFT NEGOTIATION

Pablo briefly considers doing nothing. In this instance, the world would keep spinning. Susie was able to vent and indirectly save face in front of her coworkers. Their relationship might be tense at work for a few days but should be fine in the long run. But what about the precedent this has set for the rest of the office? Pablo is convinced this would turn into a nasty habit, which could quickly destroy office morale.

FIGHT RESPONSE/HARD NEGOTIATION

Pablo thinks about replying to her Facebook comment. He even types out a few potential ideas (still looking like he's working hard, of course). "Susie, if you are upset, please come talk to me." "Posting negative things about your coworker on Facebook. #norespect." "The inability to speak to someone face-to-face. #chicken." As his comments become increasingly aggressive, he takes a deep breath and closes Facebook. There has to be a better option.

Pablo sees Susie working in her cubicle and thinks about walking over and loudly saying, "Susie, please get back to work and stop wasting time on Facebook." He daydreams about this scenario for a while—the satisfaction of seeing her embarrassed, knowing that she was caught. Then, he quickly realizes she might realize he was on Facebook as well. He needed a new plan. He begins typing up a staff memo, along the lines of "If you are frustrated with company changes, please refrain from blasting this company on social media sites." As he's writing this, however, he knows that he would be just as guilty of passive-aggressive behavior. He would continue to act pleasant in front of her but would be indirectly aggressive.

EFFECTIVE RESPONSE/FIRM NEGOTIATION

Pablo realizes there is no way to avoid a difficult conversation. With some conflicts you realize that you can't go over it, can't go under it. You just have to go through it. There is no way to get past them by a flight-or-fight response, but to take a deep breath and walk right through the middle.

Pablo picks up his phone and calls Susie, asking her to come into his office when she has a moment. Before she comes in, he preps himself for the conversation. He wants to be frustrated, exclaim so that everyone can hear how *posting her frustrations on Facebook is unacceptable behavior! It is inappropriate, childish, and if it happens again she will receive a write-up in her file!* But our lovely, dear Pablo has already read this book (Be smart. Be like Pablo.) and he knows that in the long run this will not reinforce the type of behavior he wants. He knows that Susie would become defensive and wouldn't hear anything he said. So, Pablo questions if there was anything he could have done to prevent the situation. Then he identifies how to shift from blame to building positive habits for the future.

Susie walks in, half sheepish, half furious. Pablo can tell that by this point her friends have added fuel to the fire.

"Susie, please, take a seat. Help yourself to coffee. Suze, excuse me, I mean, Susie, I saw your post on Facebook. Which made me realize that probably neither of us should be on Facebook while at work, but let's save that for a different discussion," Pablo says with a tense laugh, hoping to break the ice. Susie offers a tight laugh back but remains wound tight. Pablo continues, "Well, I was surprised at what you wrote, but it did make me think. As soon as I knew the budget was changing, I should have let you know. To be honest, I forgot about it until you mentioned it in that meeting. I realize now that was probably frustrating."

"It was," Susie says quietly, some of the wind leaving her sails. "It was frustrating that I have spent a lot of time researching a system at a certain price point, and now you are telling me that time was wasted. I just, I guess you're right. I was frustrated."

"Thank you for letting me know," Pablo responds. Then, he doesn't say anything. He is trying out these conflict resolution ideas for the first time, wondering if they will work. So, he lets the silence hang . . . and hang . . .

Uncomfortable with the silence (this is a very effective technique, by the way),[2] Susie blurts out, "I guess I could have talked to you about it too. I don't think the staff meeting was the right place for you to say something! And I didn't want to embarrass you back in front of everyone like you had done to me!"

"I get that, Susie. But what you did was still embarrassing, and it made it difficult to talk to you about it face-to-face. I want you to come talk to me if you are concerned. More than that, I want the rest of the office to know that we need to talk to each other if we are frustrated. I want people in this office to trust each other, so if we say everything is fine, that needs to mean something. If things are not fine, speak up. Find the right time, and then talk to the person. That's the only way things can improve."

"I understand that, and I really am sorry, I just wish I hadn't been cut out of the loop. It seems like this has happened before, where I am working on a project, but I don't have enough information to do an effective job," Susie vented.

"Susie, that is true, but I also have other matters that sometimes take my attention so I can't get you the information in a timely manner. I need you to understand that. But—you know what might help? Why don't you just come to the monthly budget meetings? Then you have the information you need at your fingertips, and I won't risk forgetting what pieces to pass on to you. Deal?"

"Definitely a deal." Susie smiles for the first time and begins to stand up, then pauses. "Hey, Pablo? I guess, well, I shouldn't have . . . I'm glad we talked. I'm feeling much better about this whole thing. Thank you."

Pablo maintains his cool and says, "You're welcome" with a smile, while he's mentally giving himself a high five.

CHARACTERISTICS OF PASSIVE-AGGRESSIVE BEHAVIOR

There can be a variety of reasons for passive-aggressive behavior. Passive-aggressives are typically afraid of direct confrontation, but sometimes they just don't know how to bring up the difficult conversation or they try to ignore it.

Regardless of the motivations, there are some common characteristics.[3]

- People who are passive-aggressive are concerned with keeping the peace in the office.
- Passive-aggressives strive to maintain the appearance of peace and maturity.
- Passive-aggressives begin to resent their self-sacrificing decisions.
- This resentment begins to override their passive behavior and seep out into aggressive behavior.
- These actions are indirectly aimed at hurting the other person.
- Passive-aggressive employees often complain that they are not being respected or understood.
- Passive-aggressive behavior might be posts on social media, anonymous complaints, "forgetting" to pass on messages, and bypassing someone for a promotion. They are posts that are aggressive and hinting around the conflict without directly addressing it.

CONFRONTING THIS BEHAVIOR

The Passive-Aggressive often has a righteous anger, meaning that they know the other person did something wrong first, making their passive-aggressive actions justified in their mind. Unfortunately, until the initial wrong is discussed, The Passive-Aggressive will probably not be able to recognize the wrong in their own actions. When a coworker approaches a Passive-Aggressive to discuss what they did wrong, you will need a delicate touch. The Passive-Aggressive often behaves like a turtle in a thunderstorm. The louder you try to get your point across, the further they retreat into their shell.

- In order to get The Passive-Aggressive to acknowledge and ultimately change their behavior, you will need to identify the initial wrong. This does not necessarily mean apologizing, but pointing out that something happened that was less than ideal and probably frustrating.[4]
- The Passive-Aggressive is typically not skilled in handling confrontation, so a direct conversation is less effective than other routes. Instead, you can ask the person how things could have gone better. Ask them for suggestions for the future. Tell them that you are mostly concerned with maintaining office morale, or trust, or strong working relationships. Speak to them in a way

that does not directly embarrass them but allows them to engage in the conversation.[5]

- Judge the sin, not the sinner. Attack the problem, not the person. It is still important to let The Passive-Aggressive know what specific action is unacceptable. "In this office, our policy is not to do *x*" is easier for the listener to accept than, "I thought I could trust you, but now you have done *x*. Why did you do *x*? What were you thinking? What's wrong with you?" Pointing out the wrong action helps the person to focus on what they did that was inappropriate, instead of becoming defensive and unable to participate in the rest of the conversation. A passive-aggressive person is just someone who has a couple of passive-aggressive behaviors that they need to work on—don't confuse the behavior with their identity. People can do dumb things and still be great. Just like when Ryan Reynolds made *The Green Lantern*.
- Ask The Passive-Aggressive to consider actions that will promote more effective communication and a stronger office. Such as being assertive about hurts and interests.[6]

DON'T

If someone is behaving passive-aggressively, don't directly confront them. People who are passive-aggressive are usually very conflict averse and will have a tendency to fight or flight instead of being able to have a direct conversation with you.

DO

Do have a gentle conversation about passive-aggressive behavior. Ask what would be more effective and what would improve office morale. Ask if there is something you could do to be more approachable.

IS THIS YOU?

This is a pretty common tactic for people who are frustrated but are unable to or feel unsafe expressing their frustration. There are times when we all behave passive-aggressively. But how can you tell if this has become your primary response to office conflict? When you are frustrated:

- Do you hide cocktail shrimp behind your coworker's computer? You might be passive-aggressive.
- Do you smile sweetly to a colleague's face and curse at them like a sailor in your head? You might be passive-aggressive.
- Do you tell your boss that you don't mind taking an extra shift, then go home and scream about it to your spouse while eating a plate of injustice nachos? You might be passive-aggressive.

The Passive-Aggressive often has healthy self-esteem; they simply haven't found the right way to express it.

STAY OR GO?

Sounds like this isn't you, but you are dealing with this?

Stay in the office, and show your coworkers that you really want to hear their concerns. That you can handle difficult news. Maybe even preface it with, "I'm working on office communication. What do you think we could improve on?" Have a weekly garbage can meeting, where you meet up and point out any potential problematic behaviors before they worsen. Get the junk out of the office before it builds up. So, stay, but develop techniques for improving the passive-aggressive behavior.

TAKEAWAY

So, your homework is to figure out how to kindly have a conversation with someone while delivering bad news. Practice telling your coworker that you cannot pick up another shift. Practice telling your boss that she needs to treat with you more respect (instead of smiling to her face while picturing putting Lactaid in her coffee). It might not be as satisfying, but it is more effective to talk to people about your concerns.

Feminine Response

Passive-aggressive behavior is a common response by a lot of the women I have worked with. They are frustrated and want to act out! But they don't want to directly confront the person. They might be afraid of the anger or backlash, or they might have learned growing up that they weren't supposed to confront others.[7] So, the frustration just squishes out the edges. Sharp words. Not including someone on an important email. Taking the stress home.

We know that avoiding the problem isn't working. And blowing up on the other person isn't going to work either. We need a third option. We need to figure out how to bring up the behavior. And for some of this—it takes practice. You need to role-play the scenario with a friend, or write down what you want to say.

Go ahead, write out a couple of sentences you could use in the type of difficult conversations you tend to avoid at work. Don't be meek. Don't be condescending. Don't attack the person. Be firm and attack the problem! Here are some examples to get you started:

- "It is frustrating to me when . . ."
- "I am noticing that . . ."
- "This behavior is having a negative effect on the office."
- "What can we do about that?"

17

RUDE COWORKERS

You're not going to get along with everyone. You can't. There will be some people you work with who just rub you the wrong way.

Some of these people might have bad communication skills—not necessarily mean, but somewhere in the vicinity of really, truly annoying, they-are-the-reason-I-drink coworkers.

RUDE COMMUNICATION

A fellow workplace mediator told me about a case that stunned her. It was about an office that was having a hard time with their new HR director. She never smiled at them. She barely said "hi." She provided the bare minimum of information to the employees. Instead of firing her, the forward-thinking boss asked a facilitator to come in and investigate.

The HR director hardly made eye contact but expressed a strong need to keep the job. The facilitator gently told the HR director some of the concerns the employees had—"she was too rude to work with," and "she acted like a snob who didn't have the time of day for anyone around her." The HR director looked down and thought about this for a long time. She finally looked up at the facilitator and smiled, revealing some pretty horrible teeth. She explained that she had been in an accident the previous year and didn't have dental benefits at the time. She needed this job to have her teeth fixed but was too embarrassed to have extended conversations with anyone. She was simply avoiding people and avoiding smiling because she was self-conscious. She knew that she was coming across as rude but thought as long as she did her job, she would be fine. The facilitator explained that she might need to share this information and be more aware of the impression she was giving if she wanted to keep her job. It took time for the employees and the HR director to be able to trust one another, but they were finally able to build an office with open communication.

I like this story as an example of rude communication because it shows that people can have a legitimate reason for being rude, and they often don't realize the disastrous effects of their communication habits. The impact was rude, but it certainly wasn't her intention. When people are hurt by the impact, they often invent the intent. The HR director felt like she didn't have the skills to explain her situation and had not looked beyond her inner experience to realize that she was hurting others. She knew she was being distant but was too embarrassed to care. People are often locked in their own world, due to being secluded, overworked, busy, stressed, or preoccupied and not tuned in to what's going on around them.[1] In such cases, we encounter a poor communicator, someone who is not trying to be unkind but does not have the skills, in general or in the moment, to communicate well.

ANNOYING COMMUNICATION

Some coworkers' behaviors have moved beyond simply being introverted, as in the last example; they're outright bothersome.

A past client told me the following story:

> I began working in a law office surrounded by many traditional male lawyers. I remember, not fondly, one elderly lawyer who couldn't understand that I was anything other than his assistant. (She was a junior partner in the firm.) "Dear, when I come into your office, I expect you to stop what you are doing and talk to me, even if you are talking to someone else." "This cup must have a hole in it and now my shirt is stained. Go buy me a new one and take this to the dry cleaners."
>
> After realizing that I had no investment in this office, that I would never be able to advance, and that my coworkers were unwilling to

change—I decided to go. (And now I have my own fancy shirts that I can pick up myself from the dry cleaners, thank you very much.)

This is an example of plain rude communication—he was being hurtful. Likely he was reinforcing the power imbalance in the office. He was making it clear that he had the most power in the office and that she needed to play by the rules.

PLAIN OLE ANNOYING

We all have a few quirks that annoy other people. Whenever we are talking about annoying coworkers, we're talking about things that go a bit further than just your odd habits. These are habits that disrupt the workplace. Consider . . .

- the person who continually plays music too loudly and disturbs the other cubicles,
- the person who swears inappropriately,
- the person who is the Golden Child and gets credit for everything,
- the person who is an Eeyore and is negative about everything,
- the person who one-ups every story,
- the person who is unsanitary (sneezes without covering, eats without washing their hands, double dips),
- the person who is always late, and
- the person who won't stop talking. And talking. And talking.

Sure, for small idiosyncrasies, we can probably suck it up and deal with it (and hope others extend us the same courtesy). There are harmless eccentricities that don't bother the office and are not rude, and we need to extend grace. Consider the guy who laughs a bit too loudly, or the woman who talks a bit too much about her fiancé. Nothing actually harmful. Putting up with these small frustrations are the price we pay for having our job and an investment in relationships.[2]

But the truth is that some of these eccentricities are not so harmless. It is one thing for your coworkers to deal with someone who tells inappropriate jokes. It is a very different matter for this person to tell an inappropriate joke to a customer or a client you are trying to impress. Because of such broader ramifications, it is important to address these inappropriate behaviors before they grow and to discuss better options.

WHY DO PEOPLE ACT THIS WAY?

Most people are not annoying on purpose. It is simply a habit that they picked up. Chances are, no one has ever discussed their maddening habit with them, or its effect on others.

One common reason why people display an irritating behavior is because they are trying to get some sort of attention but do not know a better way. If someone is always one-upping your story, for instance (meaning that you tell a story and they always have to follow it up with something better), they probably want some form of attention. They might be trying to establish their place in the office. Maybe the office culture is highly competitive instead of collaborative, and the person doesn't know how else to succeed in the office.[3] Maybe they feel threatened by you. Maybe they have a strong desire to be liked. If this is the case, then the best way to help them stop their dysfunctional comportment is to satisfy their desire. Reaffirm their story. Compliment them. Make sure they feel like they are part of the group. And then point it out to them.

Another common reason for these irksome tendencies is simply because those habits were acceptable in their family. Things like loud music or crass jokes are learned behaviors that were likely encouraged. Nevertheless, these behaviors are clearly not helpful to the office. The tricky thing is to figure out how to bring up the matter without making the other person defensive. Suggest some options or guidelines: "When it's just us, bring on the dirty jokes! When clients are here, though, let's try to act a little more reserved, prudish even. Channel your inner *Little House on the Prairie*. Thanks."

WHAT TYPE OF COMMUNICATION IS IT?

In these last few chapters, we have looked at a lot of communication styles. Let's go through a checklist to help you decide what type you have the misfortune of dealing with.

Look at examples from your office and ask yourself a few questions:

- Is this bad communication (the person doesn't realize the effect of her detrimental habits)?
- Is this mean communication (the person realizes the effect of her callous habits and she is trying to have a negative effect)?

- Does this annoying behavior bother anyone else? If not, it might just be something frustrating that I have to deal with.
- Could this behavior bring down morale or make the company look bad? Then we have moved into rude and it is time to confront it.
- Have I actually seen my coworker change in other situations? If you are dealing with someone who cannot change, they might simply be a mean person, as opposed to a nice person with a few mean behaviors. "You may not know which end of the spectrum you're dealing with until you actually address the behavior. If it's a bully, it can be difficult—if not impossible—to get the person to change," says Gary Namie, founder of the Workplace Bullying Institute.[4]

To shift the focus to yourself and your reactions, ask yourself these additional questions:

- Why does this particular behavior bother me so much?
- Have I expressed specific ways that I would like those habits to change?
- Have I tried to find out their intentions (to determine if this is mean communication or just bad communication)?
- Do I see any patterns—do they bother other people in the office?
- Do I always have a hard time with this type of personality—if so, why?
- Do they seem to behave poorly only around certain kinds of people or in certain situations?

Now that your mind is spinning with immense, introspective questions, in part III, "There Are Solutions," I will provide you with some suggestions for your one big question:

WHAT ARE YOU GOING TO DO ABOUT IT?

But you're not at part III yet, and I don't want you to skip all the good, juicy stuff to come, so let's take a minute and work through this while it is fresh in your head. Respond to the questions below and think about conflicts that you are dealing with.

THE "WHAT ARE YOU GOING TO DO ABOUT IT?" WORKSHEET

- What is the annoying behavior?
- Is this bad or mean behavior? (You might have to ask them to find out their intentions.)
- If it is mean (intentionally unkind), write down examples of this behavior, with dates, for your records.
- Write out how you are going to clearly, concisely, and consistently explain to the other person that this isn't acceptable.
- If it is simply bad behavior, why do you think they are behaving this way?
- Write out how you can gently bring up this behavior in a straight, no chaser: gentle, but clear format (e.g., "It bothers me when you interrupt me.").

DON'T

When someone attacks you or says something unkind, your instincts of self-protection kick in. This means that you (and me, and all of us) respond with fight, flight, or freeze. Our brain registers that we are in an unsafe situation so we need to confront the problem, run from it, or stand real still and hope it doesn't see us. This is an instinctual response that is difficult to change. It is written into our brain's code as the best way to protect us in that situation.[5] Our brain is trying to help us, and if we were facing a cougar then this protection might save our lives. *When dealing with a rude coworker, however, this "protection" might cost us a fine, harmonious working relationship*. When we respond to a jab by attacking back or becoming defensive, we are assuming that the person intended to be hurtful and that we are justified in our response. We treat them as "rude," we respond rudely, they see us being rude, they attack back. Next thing you know you are flinging chairs at each other on *Jerry Springer*.

DO

When someone is being rude to you, the best thing you can do is take a breath before you respond. The simple act of taking a deep breath or counting to 10 tells your brain that you have control over this situation, that you have a plan. It allows your brain to move from anxiety to curiosity. *This means that the conflict is not controlling you; but you are in control of the conflict.*[6] When you respond from a place of fight or flight, you are often not dealing with full information. Give yourself enough time to get the broader perspective to be able to come back with an optimal, or at least more suitable, reply. If you want to avoid a firefight, the best thing you can do is . . .

STOP, DROP, AND ROLL

Stop

Before you blurt out a nasty response, pause. Take a deep breath. Go for a walk. Close your eyes. Do what you need to give yourself the space you need. When you stop reacting, you are allowing the reptilian part of your brain to relax. You are telling your brain that it is not in danger. It does not have to hide or attack. This will give you room to get more information and formulate a more accurate response.

Drop

If you feel yourself escalating a conflict, it is likely because you feel attacked and you are starting to spiral out of control. You are spiraling up and away from the person and the facts of the situation and exaggerating them to fit your story. Negative emotions or experiences cause our brains to create false assumptions and even false memories. Unbelievable, right? The National Library of Medicine published a study of recalled memories that showed people most often created false memories when remembering a painful or infuriating experience.[7] In other words, one rude remark turns into "He is *always* rude." Hyperbolic comments (he *always*, or she *never*) are red flags that indicate you are spiraling into exaggerations. Another red flag is when you begin attacking the person instead of the behavior (not "his comment was rude," but "*he* is so rude"). When you notice these red flags, drop back down to reality. Reality allows you to remember who this person really is and see their comment in context (such as, "normally he is very kind, but I remember he is going through a divorce and maybe that is why he snapped at me today").[8]

Roll

After you have *stopped* your knee-jerk response and *dropped* back down to reality, then you need to *roll* with the situation. Roll alongside a person instead of against them.

An attack response: "Why are you being such a jerk?"

A rolling response: "Whoa, ouch, is everything okay? What's going on today?"

A rolling response acknowledges that there is a difficult situation but you are willing to roll through it with them. Some mediators refer to this as conflict aikido or dispute Tai Chi, which is a fun image.[9]

Even if the person has a legitimate beef with you, you can still roll through that conversation with them. "I didn't realize I was coming across that way, thanks for letting me know. Maybe just tell me next time instead of barking it. Dealio?"

This is why mediators refer to this concept as conflict aikido. The idea here is that you take their energy, roll it to the side of you, and come alongside of them to find out what is going on. This takes an amazing amount of emotional maturity, but it is also incredibly effective.

Stop your defensive response.
Drop back down to the facts.
Roll alongside them.

IS THIS YOU?

Are you reading this section and thinking, *Oh, fudge, that sounds like me*? Let's face it, at some point we all have said something harsh and come across in a way we didn't mean to, or let off steam on an innocent coworker. So, what do you do about it? 'Fess up as fast as possible. This doesn't have to be a gushing exposé, it can just be a gentle, "Shoot, sorry for the snark this morning, I was hangry and took it out on you." The key is to clear the air as fast as possible before ideas have cemented in other people's minds. In the short term, there is likely some confusion about why you acted that way. After snapping at someone, a sweet spot remains for a few hours where the other person's brain is sifting through reasons and trying to understand your behavior. The ground is still soft and malleable and open to new ideas. At this point you can still plant a seed in that ground that says, "Oh! I'm actually a nice guy! I am just in a really bad mood today, sorry."

But eventually their brain will harden. This typically happens within a few more times of thinking about you—so this might happen within minutes or hours. Eventually their brain will decide that you snapped at them because you are in fact a world-class jerk, and once that realization has been reached it will be very hard for them to forget it. This is based on the Uncertainty Reduction Theory, which says that brains hate the unknown. To avoid the unknown, our brains make snap judgments to reduce any uncertainty with another person. We will often use a social interaction ("Hey, how's it going?") as a tool to determine if someone is a friend or foe. And if that person doesn't respond back kindly, our brain alerts us that they are a foe.[10]

What this means for us is that as soon as you realize you have breached basic decency, own it. By bringing it up you are making it clear that you are willing to have a conversation about your foibles and missteps and that others can call you on it if you do it again. And that you're an awesome human being and not a world-class jerk.

STAY OR GO?

Sounds like this isn't you, but is this a personality type that you work with?

Do you work with someone rude? Probably—there is one in just about every office. Whether you stay or go depends on if you can establish and stand by your own boundaries. If you have let someone get away with being rude to you for years, it will be harder to change that dynamic. If they have been ill-mannered and disrespectful without you saying anything, you have been letting them know that you accept that behavior. If you are unwilling or unable to communicate that times are a-changin', then you might need to go. For some people, that is easier than shifting an imbalanced relationship.

If you are able to establish a new boundary, however, then you should definitely stay. This will be an uncomfortable change process for both of you. It will take time. Research[11] says that forming a new habit takes approximately three weeks of intentional work, but it can easily take a year if it is a deeply entrenched habit and you are not truly focused on change. Realize this is not an overnight fix. But deciding where your boundaries are allows you to determine what behavior you are comfortable with. It will also force the other person to grow and become a better person, even if they don't want to. You can stay if you feel that you are ready to take on this challenge, but many people are sick of dealing with it, which means go if you don't want to continue to stand up to this person.

TAKEAWAY

Sometimes people are just mean, and it is understandable that you want to be mean back. But that will destroy your relationship and your peace and the office environment. You deserve better. So instead of responding to an attack with another attack, find a tool that gets you the response you want. Stop, Drop, and Roll alongside them to find out what's going on.

Feminine Response

Unfortunately, I have seen many mediations where women called each other rude or power hungry, simply out of envy. Perhaps a woman asked for what she wanted—and got it. The other one didn't. This show of confidence is not as common (yet!) in women, so when a woman does come into the office with confidence and bravado, she is often labeled as stuck-up or a gold-digger. The book *Women Don't Ask* discusses a study in 2003 where 57 percent of male graduates negotiated their starting salary, but only 7 percent of women. The point is that the men asked to be paid more, and so many of them were. The women did not ask because it was socially not expected, and so many of them were paid less. And that should upset you. Ask for what you deserve.

The takeaway here is check yourself—is someone actually being rude? If so, talk to them and tell them what your communication boundaries are. But are they just being confident and asking for what they want? And are you jealous because you never gave yourself the freedom to ask for what you wanted? If so, on behalf of all womenkind, I not only grant you that freedom, but admonish you to go out and ask for what you deserve.

Warning! Warrior Personalities

18

FAMILY BUSINESSES

Families have their own special kind of nuttiness. (If you have ever sat through a Thanksgiving dinner with obscure distant relatives and in-laws, I'm sure you can agree.) This is head-scratching, no discernible excuse, "would they just stop being so weird" behavior. And family businesses take their weird ways and try to systematize and monetize them.

WHAT THE HECK ARE FAMILY BUSINESSES?

For this book, a family business is limited to a small- or medium-sized company (between 2 and 50 full-time employees), where the owner is related to the original founders or many of the employees. This number falls nicely within the Census Bureau's definition, which means we can use census and Small Business Administration data. Family businesses often protect their family vibe and familial network and draw prideful attention to them. Just picture the joy of working with the Kardashians—doesn't that sound like a calm and friendly atmosphere?

STRENGTHS OF FAMILY BUSINESSES

Families bring into their business the same ties that keep them together as a family. The strength and effectiveness of these ties clearly depends on the type of family, but there are certain characteristics common in all family businesses.

- *Commitment*: The success of a family business looks different than a typical business. Success means:
  - Their children will have a stable income.
  - Their grandchildren will not have to struggle in the same way that the founder did.
  - They have low turnover.
  - They will be able to work together.
  - They sacrifice individual goals for the collective business.

  This vision of success is a much more personal motivating factor than simply looking at shareholder profit and loss statements. It represents a value, a vision, a belief that by making the business succeed the family is taking care of each other.

  For instance, picture a deli opened decades ago by a mom and a pop. They have three sons who currently work at the deli, who mom and pop hope will take over ownership and management someday. What happens if the neighborhood changes and it's no longer the best place for that deli? An investor would make a decision based on practical profit and loss margins, close the deli, and possibly move to a different neighborhood. The mom and pop, however, will make a decision based on their values. They have made a commitment to provide an income for their children, so they will fight to see the deli survive in the same neighborhood their children live in. This commitment to the business might not make business sense, but it represents the values of the family.
- *Lifespan*: Families often discuss the lifespan of a business in terms of generations, rather than fiscal years. This means that families are more likely to make long-term decisions that might not make sense in the moment. They are working to create an enduring, sustainable future for their business. Families also often make decisions based on past actions. For instance, a vendor who was kind to the family in the past will often receive preference over other vendors.

- *Communication*: Family communication has high context, meaning that you can share more information in fewer words, in a shorter amount of time. This can make the business operate efficiently and with a high degree of quality, since there is likely an understanding of expectations. With a business that has been around for generations, they likely have the benefit of building on successful business strategies. They are able to communicate ideas quickly and think about what has worked in the past. It also means that those who are not part of the family might not understand the context of certain communications.[1]

WEAKNESSES OF FAMILY BUSINESSES

The same traits that can strengthen a family business are often the same traits that can weaken it.

- *Commitment*: A common characteristic of family businesses is the amount of commitment the founding members have put into it. Almost as common is the lack of commitment from additional members of the family. The newer members of the family business often do not feel the same level of ownership, investment, and commitment to the enterprise. They might see it as a temporary employment while they are looking for something else, or they might develop bitterness at being pushed into a position that they do not want. This commitment imbalance places tension not just on the family members involved, but can permeate the whole company.
- *Lifespan*: Many family businesses do not make it past the third generation. Only 12 percent of family businesses make it to a third generation, and only 3 percent make it to a fourth. The primary reasons these businesses fade out are the lack of commitment mentioned above and that the owners are making decisions based on personal values instead of business sense.
- *Communication*: Family businesses can be fun and enjoyable places to work because communication in them is typically less formal. This same informal communication, however, can also result in an unprofessional and possibly disrespectful environment. This can be hard on the family members, but also hard on the employees who are not related and would like to be treated with more respect and more typical standards of professionalism.

WORKING FOR A FAMILY BUSINESS WHEN YOU'RE NOT PART OF THE FAMILY

Family is first.

The needs of the family often come first, favors go to the family first, the boss will side with the family first, and time will be carved out for family things first. For instance, if you are working at a hat shop and you need a new fabric supplier, and one of the potential vendors is a little more expensive but is also the owner's cousin—who do you think will get the contract? If two employees are trying to get the same time off, and one is going to a family reunion and the other is going on a personal vacation—who do you think will get the time off?

This is often one of the biggest surprises that employees run into when working in a family business: There are a lot of perks and special exceptions given to family members!

The second surprise is that most managers do not realize the inequity. Most managers I have worked with have full intentions of being fair. They try to make sure they are not giving extra leeway or preference to family members. They are often startled when confronted with a clear example of family preference, simply because over time they begin to develop a blind spot to the preferential treatment. I remember one conversation where a manager had so rationalized her preferential behavior that she could not see anything wrong with it:

> Me: Svetlana, some of the nonfamily employees are stating that you are treating them with less respect than the family employees.
>
> Svetlana: I make all of my decisions based on what is best for the company. I don't have time to listen to all of these newbies squabble if I don't curtsy every time I walk by.
>
> Me: That sounds like you are spending more time listening to your family than to new members of the company. How do you think treating them with less respect is best for the company?
>
> Svetlana: Simple. I know my family, and they function best when they are treated well. If I treat them like they are the best employees and their opinion is the most important, then I don't have to spend all day and night listening to them complain. This improves their morale, and it also means I don't have to waste my time listening to their petty complaints. That seems to me like it is best for the company, right?

Unfortunately, Svetlana feels completely justified in her response. She is giving privileged treatment to her family and is convinced that it is the right thing to do. She is not trying to be unkind or unfair in any way. However, she does not realize that she is making short-term decisions to appease her family, but in the long term these decisions will hurt her company. She does not recognize the environment that she is creating for the nonfamily employees.

Storytime: We had an office-wide meeting. One nonfamily employee tried to speak and Svetlana told him to stop interrupting. Then a family member got mad and *pulled a gun* on Svetlana, telling her to shut up so he could finish talking. Not even kidding. Only time that has happened in one of my meetings. He pulled a for-real, black pistol out of a holster I hadn't previously noticed on his hip. She just rolled her eyes at him and kept talking. The upside? This made for a very good example to use in this book of how family members got preferential treatment. "Svetlana, would you let a nonfamily member pull a gun on you?"

Obviously, in this situation, we had to quickly identify office safety policies. Which included, y'know, no guns. The office voted and created policies that everyone had to abide by—even the family.

FACTIONS

Unless you are careful, the company can divide into two factions: family and nonfamily. Offices with different factions often find decreased communication between factions, and eventually bitterness and resentment can spring up. (And it is even more exciting when the family itself divides into factions! Makes for great drama, though. Have you ever watched *Sons of Anarchy*?)

A great suggestion is to propose a strategy for balance. For instance, for every family member who moves into management, elect a nonfamily member to balance them out. Create fair processes, such as anonymous voting, to ensure that processes include everyone's opinion.[2]

DON'T

Don't try to be part of the family. You are not. Blood is always thicker than, well, you. Let them be their own crazy family. Your job is to enjoy the relationship and the fun family dynamic you observe, and then getting to leave at the end of the day and thank your lucky stars you are not related to them.

DO

When working in a family business:

- Realize it is different.
- Realize it is not going to change.
- Decide what you can accept.
- Enjoy the quirks of the particular family you work for. Every family is based on its own set of values, and those values will work their way through every element of the business.[3] Are they casual? Conversational? Combative or collaborative? Serious or party-time? The Duggars or the Kardashians?

IS THIS YOU?

If you are a family member working for your family business, then you already know your situation comes with additional complications. If you are trying to decide to stay or go, ask yourself these questions:

- Is my family able to leave family issues at home, so that we can operate a business successfully?
- Am I treated with respect based on how well I perform as an employee?
- Will I be able to advance based on my work performance, or will I always be treated as a subordinate family member?
- Do I enjoy the family culture enough to continue putting time into this business?
- If I were to leave, am I willing to accept the strain that it would put on my relationships with my family?
- If I were still working here in 20 years, would I feel satisfied with my career?
- Am I able to make decisions based on business values, or am I forced to make decisions based on family values?

STAY OR GO?

So you are working for a family business, now what?

If you are able to deal with the characters and oddities of such a business, you might want to stay—for a time. However, if you are planning on advancing your career and moving up the ladder, a family business is a difficult place to advance. It is difficult to compete against the boss's son for a vice president position. If your long-term plan is to move into management, then you will likely need to move into another company. Another option is to become close with the family. If you are seen as a cog in the family machinery, and not as a threat, then you might have a chance at taking on a position of leadership. But keep in mind that it will be more complex than advancing in another company. In order to be seen as important to the company, you will need to excel not just in the business but also in strengthening your relationship with many family members. This might mean attending after-hours functions that would not be expected in another position. Many employees find it is worth it to put in the time to become accepted with the family, feeling their career becomes more stable than it would be at a nonfamily-owned business.

TAKEAWAY

Family businesses can be a blast to work with, but you have to know what you are signing up for.

Feminine Response

This is where Mama Bear comes out. When it is a family business, you have to realize that no matter how great of a manager someone is, a parent will always protect their children.

If you are working in someone else's business, you are going to have to define your role. You are not the Mama Bear or the Mother Hen, or even the Queen Bee. But you are not a meek little daisy either. That business pulled you into their inner ranks because of something unique that you offer them. So, hold your ground in that office. And enjoy the show.

19

DISMISSIVE BOSSES

A dismissive boss is one who gets their power based on their role, not their skill as a leader. They do not see the value in empowering their employees.

A boss, supervisor, or manager has to be treated differently than a coworker. There is a power imbalance. You simply do not have as much leeway in your conversations as you might with a peer, where there's a presumed balance of power.

If you have a dismissive boss, develop some appropriate tactics in advance. A boss will dismiss you only as long as you let them. Find reasons and ways for them to stop it. Hang the meat low enough so the dog can bite. Speak to them in their language. Give them a reason to care about your concern, focusing on:

- *Overlap*: Find a similar interest in movies, food, Fantasy Football. How can you aid in a project that they are working on? Do a bit of homework and discover the places of overlap.
- *Entrance*: Once you have located the overlaps in interests or work responsibilities, use those as an entrance. Building on any overlap is usually a much more effective entry point than coming in guns-a-blazin', demanding, expecting, hoping that someone is nice, responsive. So, use material related to that overlap as your on-ramp in building the desired conversation.

- *Utility*: Have a prepared plan for once you begin the conversation. What service or information do you have that is useful and significant? "I was noticing that inventory was low. Perhaps I should plan on taking over inventory duty the beginning of every month?"
- *Growth*: Once you have become useful in your area, do not let that area be diminished. Grow the importance of it. Grow in the quality with which you do your job. Grow in giving detailed presentations. Grow your areas of responsibilities.
- *Defense*: Defend your zones of responsibility. Perhaps you are in a meeting and people are rushed, and you can tell that your presentation is about to be cut short. Employ a preemptive strike, "I can tell that we are running out of time, but there are some numbers coming up that I think you all will need for your own jobs. How about I end the presentation now and we finish this up at the first five minutes of our next meeting?" or "This information is imperative before we make a decision. I will go through it quickly to make sure you have time to hear it all."
- *Reminders*: All of us get locked away in our own worlds and often do not notice what is going on around us. It is important to remind people of your areas of responsibility so that they are not dismissed. "Ma'am, I just want to say that I have enjoyed taking over the inventory responsibility and I have also begun researching lower-priced vendors. Perhaps we could have a conversation at some point about streamlining delivery."

Think through, talk through, and make lists about your options. Here are some to consider:

- Do nothing, and everything stays the same.
- Quit.
- Talk to your boss.
- Talk to your coworkers.
- Deal with it differently.
- Buy expensive gifts and charge them to your boss's card. (Okay, fine, it's illegal. But it is fun to daydream about.)

Think about the short-term awkwardness of your desired conversation and allow yourself to live in that awkwardness for a moment and be okay with it. Then push through that feeling and envision the long-term benefits to you, your job, and your family. It is similar to saying going on a run in the morning will be uncomfortable, but the long-term effects are well worth it.

If you want your boss's behavior to change, there are two ways to have that conversation, and one will blow up in your face.

1. *Position conversation (wrong approach, this attacks the person)*: State your position and demand that she listens. Tell your boss to change. Positions are a statement of what you want, without any insight into your motivation or reasons.[1] "You need to include me in morning meetings. You have to listen to my ideas in meetings. You've gotta stop being a flop doodle and give us more realistic timelines." Your boss's response? "No." If you try to have a position-based conversation there is only one outcome: The person with the power wins. This is like you and your older brother arm-wrestling when you were a kid: The person with the most power wins.
2. *Interest conversation (right approach, this attacks the problem)*: Find out what your boss is interested in and explain what you are interested in. This explains your motivations behind your stated position. This is why I want something.[2] Not like "I'm interested in good mochas and long walks on the beach," but "I'm interested in sharing some ideas I've had that I think will improve our turnaround time in receiving." Find out what your boss is interested in, such as company efficiency, meeting payroll, fewer squabbles, fewer people quitting, not having to listen to Sally from HR complain about communication policies, or whatever. Then find a way to merge your boss's interests and your interests in a discussion. "If we improved turnaround time in receiving then we wouldn't have so many people quitting." This drastically changes the conversation. This is no longer about who has the most power. It is no longer an arm-wrestling competition but a handshake. A handshake that your boss might not have been prepared for, but by asking for her interests you are asking her for a bit of trust—to extend her hand, so to speak. And by explaining your interests you also extended your trust. Instead of a metaphorical arm-wrestling, your hand just grabbed her hand and they started a-shakin'.

DON'T

Don't try to strong-arm or trick your boss to get what you want. Many of them think that they are doing a great job and won't believe you if you point out their flaws directly. Bad bosses are usually those who did a great job in their previous position, and so they were promoted. But they were never trained how to be a manager. As a result, they likely don't know how to be a good boss, and instead they just dismiss any idea that didn't work for them when they were in the employee's shoes.[3]

DO

Do find out about your boss's concerns for the company, and see if your interests can help alleviate any of those concerns.

IS THIS YOU?

Are you a dismissive boss? Can you name your employees? Do you know what is going on in their lives? Do you know why they work at the company or what they are good at? If not, do a quick reset. Take your employees out to lunch. Go on a walk with them. Employees are often the ones with the best ideas for improving the company. Do you seriously think they are going to bring you the million-dollar, save-the-company-at-the-eleventh-hour-when-all-hope-is-lost-right-before-the-commercial-break ideas if you keep putting them down?

STAY OR GO?

You may not be a dismissive boss, but if you work with one:

Try to stay. And to make your stay enjoyable, speak with your boss, expressing your interest, explaining your long-term plans for the company.

Sometimes you can help to change the office environment. You can model better communication habits, create new systems, change policies, or have a discussion with the team at large about more effective conversations.

But sometimes you cannot be a part of that change.

Let's assume that you have made change efforts in your office, both personally and systemically, and that your office was not receptive to the change. Then it is likely time to go.

TAKEAWAY

When a boss is dismissive of you it is because they see you as a zero sum—that there is zero reason for them to take time to give you attention. You can be upset with them for it, or you can change their mind. Make sure you are doing something of value for the company, then make them notice, then make sure they treat you like the asset you are!

Feminine Response

As I've mentioned, when faced with adversity women look for the answer within themselves, and men look for it outside. This means that if your boss is being dismissive towards you, your first response might be to look at yourself to see what you are doing wrong.

Don't you dare.

If your boss is showing repeated signs of being dismissive, toward multiple people in the office, then don't you dare let that boss silence you. Don't you dare think less of yourself. That you haven't worked your butt off to earn that job. And here's the clincher: Right now, as you are reading this, a typical feminine response is to think of a time where you weren't perfect. Where you were late or had a typo, and you can justify your boss's response to you. Like, "Oh, but I completely flubbed that one slide, so it's okay for my boss to dismiss all of my ideas."

Don't you dare.

Don't you think every single worker around you has made a mistake? If you are self-aware and continually working on improving, then chances are you have made way fewer mistakes than they have. So don't you dare hide behind your couple of mistakes as if that was an acceptable reason for you to be dismissed.

It is time for you to be honest with yourself. About your worth. How lucky that office is to have you. Realize that you can loudly and proudly state your ideas in a meeting, stick up for your interests in the office, be firm on your boundaries. Dare to be treated how you deserve. Dare to kindly and firmly let people know when they've crossed a boundary. Dare to be proud of the skills you bring to the office.

Do it—I dare you.

20

THE BOXER

The Boxer has likely had more positive experiences with conflict than other personalities, such as The People Pleaser. This means The Boxer is likely more comfortable having difficult conversations than other people in the office. The Boxer might even have learned that conflict can be a great way for things to improve.

The upside of working with a Boxer is that you always know where you stand. People often report close relationships with a Boxer, if you can get past the sparring. The Boxer isn't afraid to fight, because she knows that fighting is the way you win. This might be winning the prime contract, winning over a new boss, winning a better position, or even winning a friend. If The Boxer sees an opportunity for improvement, The Boxer isn't afraid to speak her mind. Who cares if a little disagreement occurs, if it means that things end up better in the long run? The Boxer is comfortable fighting to win something, but is also comfortable fighting to defend. The Boxer will defend her ideas, will defend the values of the company, and will defend her friends.

The downside of working with a Boxer is, well, the boxing. Having a disagreement with a Boxer can be exhausting. Boxers typically experience a norepinephrine and an adrenaline rush while arguing. In other words, they feel good and they want more. Some even develop an addiction to these chemicals. They want the rush, as well as the connection you experience with another when you are boxing.[1] They are thinking, "Finally, we are getting somewhere. Things are changing. Let's get over with the pleasantries, and get to the heart of the matter. Let's do what we have to to move this thing forward or make it better or make it right." Boxers are able to think clearly and quickly during an argument and enjoy knowing that they are being heard. Boxers become focused—either on the principle of the matter, or on defending what is right, or pointing out something that is wrong—to the point where they can forget about the person they are talking to. This can cause attacks to become personal, when instead The Boxer is actually focused on the issue. The Boxer speaks her mind loudly, clearly, and completely—then walks away from the conversation energized and satisfied.

REAL-LIFE EXAMPLE

I mediated a dispute between a Boxer and a People Pleaser. The Boxer loved digging into disagreements and difficult conversations. The People Pleaser constantly felt on edge. I was called in when The People Pleaser said she was being, "Targeted by a sociopath."

"What do you mean by a sociopath?" I asked.

"Well after he fights with me, he whistles!" she said. "Clearly he enjoys picking on me and is doing this on purpose." And it was true. He was becoming addicted to the rush of the energy, the intensity of the conversation, the oxytocin hit he would get with the arguments.

We had to teach her some techniques for standing up to The Boxer and teach The Boxer the negative effect he was having on the office. We brought HR into the situation so that there would be some protections and an improvement plan in place. And we banned the whistling.

TAKEAWAY

If you are working with a Boxer, don't take their attacks personally. It really is them, not you. They are enjoying the thrill of the attack, the rush of the conversation. But that doesn't mean you have to put up with it. Bring awareness to what is going on. Set up a meeting with The Boxer and your manager or HR. Explain the situation, and that you need some safeguards for when you are feeling Boxed-in in your office.

Identify your boundaries and defend them. And you will probably have to defend them repeatedly to change the relationship. But if a month goes by and you are still not seeing any change, ask yourself if it's worth it. You can brainstorm with a supervisor or the ombuds office. But if the behavior isn't changing, it is likely time to lodge a more formal complaint. It is time to speak to the HR office and put your company on notice of the aggressive behavior.

21

ABUSE

The Bad, the Worse, and the Ugly—and What Protections You Have

We have been talking about behaviors in the workplace and how you can best work with them. But there are certain behaviors that you shouldn't try to work with. Run far, far away.

ABUSIVE WORKPLACES

Abuse is defined as repetitive and intentionally mean.[1]

According to Reach MA,[2] there are six different types of abuse. The first two (physical and sexual abuse) are more common in relational/romantic disputes, but the remaining four types of abuse can easily be seen in the workplace. There are multiple types of abuse to watch out for:

- Verbal/emotional abuse: Using words as weapons. The injuries are harder to spot and take longer to heal than physical abuse.
- Mental/psychological abuse: When one person slowly wears away at the other's sanity, making them doubt their own understanding or worth.
- Financial/economic abuse: When one person holds money over an employee's head as a sense of power.
- Cultural/identity abuse: Using someone's culture as a way to control or manipulate them. For instance, if a coworker comes out

as a member of the LGBTQ+ community, and another coworker holds it over their head before they are ready for that identity in the workplace.

You might notice any of these six types of abuse in your workplace. Many support sites discuss workplace bullying, but HR offices are starting to realize that there are actually many more types of workplace abuse than just bullying. They are now starting to offer support for all six types. According to the Workplace Bullying Institute, in 2021 19 percent of Americans reported being bullied at work, and many more indicated they experienced other forms of abuse.[3] What do you do if you suspect abuse?

1. Document it. This will prepare you for the resolution options in part II.
2. Determine the scope. If there is one person being abusive, then you can likely report them to your manager or HR and allow them to deal with the situation properly. If there is a culture of abuse, get out.

CRIMINAL WORKPLACES

If you discover that someone in your company is doing something criminal you have protections available.

If you have to take whistleblower steps against your company, prepare for this process:[4]

- Describe the incident.
- Note who was involved—are they friendly, what was their involvement, and are they still employed?
- List supervisors who were manipulated, aware, or complicit.
- Make a list of any rules or laws that you believe the company has violated.

The Whistleblower Protection Act is designed to protect you. In 1989, Congress passed a version of the Whistleblower Act that says employees who report evidence that a reasonable person would deem evidence of a criminal activity need to be protected. Specifically, employees are protected from demotions, pay cuts, or being fired.[5]

Make sure that your allegations are founded on truth, however, or you could be guilty of libel or slander.

Libel is when you have written something false that defamed a person or a person's business dealings. In other words, you wrote, drew, printed, published, or created a written record of someone that was injurious and untrue.

Slander is a false spoken word, when you have said something negative about another person that has injured them or their ability to work.

UNSUPPORTIVE WORKPLACES

Over the past half-century, our workplaces have made gigantic leaps in worker protections. Most of these have become integrated into our expectations of the workplace, but there are a few that are less well known.

Civil Rights Act of 1964: This prohibits discrimination on the basis of sex, race, color, or religion.

ADA: The Americans with Disability Act of 1990 (modified in 2010) prohibits discrimination based on disability.

FMLA: The Family and Medical Leave Act of 1993 allows employees to take unpaid, but job-protected leave for family and medical reasons.

EEOC: The Equal Employment Opportunity Commission was established in 1964 to enforce civil rights concerns of workplace discrimination. They set the standards for determining reasonable accommodations for neurodiversity, age, and religion.

FLSA: The Fair Labor Standards Act determines the age when employees can begin working (between 14 and 16) and in what conditions (e.g., you have to be 18 or older to work in a hazardous environment).

Concerns about fair pay, reasonable accommodations and protections, or minimum wage? Look into the US Department of Labor for their current standards.

These protections mean that your employer must make a reasonable accommodation to support you. For instance, if you are easily startled by loud noises, then your employer should make reasonable efforts to help you work in a quieter part of the office or provide you with noise-canceling headphones. If not, the EEOC is there to help you.

BFOQ

BFOQ, or Bona Fide Occupational Qualification, means that there are times when a certain demographic is part of the job requirement. Demographics are usually forbidden from being part of the job application process. At an interview, an employer cannot ask you about your age, gender, religion, sexuality, pregnancy, or ethnicity.

There are times where your employer might be exempt from discrimination laws. For instance, flight attendants and firefighters have specific physical requirements that are required to complete their job. This BFOQ allows employers to ask questions about their employee's height, weight, and physical fitness. This is how Hooters can hire only females to be their waitstaff. Another example: a temple might ask a rabbi about their religious affiliation to ensure that they have similar beliefs. This allows employers to claim exemptions for hiring on the basis of demographic considerations.

AT-WILL VERSUS JUST-CAUSE

At-Will Employment: This is the most common type of employment in the United States. It means that your employer can fire you at any time for any reason, except an illegal one (one of the protected statuses above). Similarly, an employee is free to leave their employment at any time for any reason. It is wise to review your employer handbook to understand the company policies before making any decision. For instance, your company might require a 14-day resignation letter.

Fired for Just-Cause: This means that your company has fired you for a reason, such as misconduct. However, they have to prove their cause—that it was justifiable to let you go, that it was not an At-Will termination, and that they are not firing you for a protected reason (such as race, pregnancy, etc.). The employer must be able to prove that they abided by the seven Just Cause principles:[6]

1. Notice. Was the employee warned of his/her conduct?

2. Reasonable. The rule or order cannot be arbitrary and must be related to safety or performance.
3. Investigation. Did management conduct an investigation?
4. Fair. Can management prove that their investigation was fair?
5. Proof. Did the investigation prove guilt?
6. Equal. Did the same treatment/rules apply to others in the office?
7. Appropriate. Was the penalty proportionate to the offense?

NEXT STEPS

I am part of a kickboxing self-defense class. The majority of the participants are 70 to 90 years old, female, and in amazing shape. These women have worked hard and are confident and tough. Seriously—don't cross these ninja retirees. They have skills.

When we first began kickboxing, we were all pretty flimsy. Bouncing around as if it were a normal aerobics class. But our amazing teacher, Livia, a New Yorker with bright red hair, taught us something. She helped us go through the mental preparation as well as the physical. Self-defense is about much more than learning the steps—it is a mindset. We learned about the mental transformation that victims of abuse must go through to change the abuse.

1. Realize that you are worth being treated well.
2. Realize that you must be the one to protect your boundaries.
3. Learn the steps to stand up for yourself.

Through this kickboxing class, all of us went through this transformation. It wasn't a linear process. Sometimes it was straightforward: We found a sense of our own worth and decided that we were worth protecting, and then we could focus more on the technique. Sometimes it was backwards: As we learned the steps, we felt stronger, and then realized what we were worth. But the more our self-view changed, and the more we learned how to protect ourselves, the stronger we became. Now I tell you what: We are a bunch of jab-cross-uppercutting, side-sweeping tough cookies.

Fighting workplace abuse requires the same three steps: Realize you are worth defending, Realize it is up to you to stand up for yourself, and Learn the steps to fight the abuse. This book is focused on part three: teaching you the steps to stand up for yourself and making a change. But please realize that this might not be enough—you might need to find resources to help you with parts one and two—creating the mental and emotional strength. You can find this through your community, support lines, or a variety of other books.

Another technique for helping you through steps one and two is naming the type of abuse. There are some types of abuse that you can address through the steps in this book. But if someone is abusive with no signs of change, it is important to diagnose that early so you know how to respond. Realize that bad people are not limited to TV shows. If someone is making you feel small, worthless, less than, trying to dominate you or show that they are somehow better, then you are likely dealing with some form of abuse. As you identify it, then you will be able to find a more focused resource for helping you. Is it racism? Ageism? Sexism? There are fantastic resources out there to fight against these types of abuse. Start by calling the EEOC. Utilize their mental and emotional resources to guide you through this process.

Not all conflicts can be resolved by having a conversation—if you are dealing with insidious wrong, then you will probably need an additional support. Your HR, manager, counsel, or ombuds will be able to guide you through this process. Use the techniques in this book to identify what is wrong and what you need to change, and then reach out for help. If you can't find a resource to help you, please reach out to mediate.com. The staff there is trained to triage and connect you with a guide.

If you feel that you might have been abused, discriminated against, uncovered something untoward in your office, or your office is not providing reasonable accommodations, your first course of action is to document it, then go to HR. However, if HR is not being supportive or if this is a whistleblower case, you might want to file a claim with the EEOC.

In part II, focusing on resolving your conflict, I'll go into more detail about how to approach and resolve workplace abuse.

Neurodiversity

22

LIFE WOULD BE BORING IF WE WERE ALL THE SAME

Understanding Neurodiverse Coworkers

This chapter is clearly different from the others. Whereas other chapters have highlighted difficult behaviors that need to be improved, this chapter highlights unique personalities that might need to be better understood. This chapter takes a break from the negative behaviors we have looked at and examines conflict by building on the diverse strengths of those around you. Just as we are examining conflict through the lens of gender, we are also examining it through neurodiversity and later through spiritual diversity.

"If you've met one person with autism, you've met one person with autism," says Dr. Stephen Shore.[1] "Autism is one word attempting to describe a million different stories." This chapter will try to provide advice and tips from those in the community, but it simply cannot address the complexity of every person.[2] It would be like trying to identify the personality behaviors of everyone who wears a blue shirt. But neurodiverse coworkers may have a different type of frustration in the office, and this chapter discusses some of the more commonly reported frustrations from our neurodiverse coworkers and looks at how we can support each other. The main point here is to remember that we are people, we are not our issues. Putting that in terms of workplace concerns: identify the behaviors, but don't allow the behaviors to identify the person.

A friend of mine described this classroom scene of her son: RJ sits in the back of the classroom, vaguely aware that the teacher has called on him. He can see the walls pushing against the floor and the ceiling desperate to push closer into the room. He can feel the sounds tumble into his eardrums: the ticking clock, students clicking their pens, the lawn mower out on the field. He knows the teacher is asking him a question, but the cacophony of other sounds have not left any space for her voice. And the longer he sits there, the bigger the other students become. Big eyes on big heads on towering bodies. Waiting and watching. The lights get brighter. The clock gets louder. RJ bolts out the door.

Thank goodness schools have learned to identify autism signals in students and provide a more supportive environment. But how can workplaces support neurodivergence when most workplaces were designed for the neurotypical?

First, remember what it was like when you were in a situation where you weren't comfortable. A coworker played the radio too loud, wore too much perfume, or talked too aggressively. Or you were depressed, going through a divorce, and you had a hard time staying focused or motivated. If you weren't in sync with certain aspects of the job, how would you want to be treated? For instance, if lights or sounds or certain types of conversation were hard for you in the office, how would you want people to treat you? The answer probably looks something like you want to be treated as someone with great skills that you bring to the office.

Second, ask your coworker what would help him succeed in the workplace. How can you be supportive? Autism Speaks shares that some studies say 90 percent of those with autism are unemployed, simply because they are finding discrimination and a lack of support in the workplace. Many companies, such as Microsoft, SAP, Walgreens, and Zenith Optimedia, have created specific autism-hiring initiatives. They are specifically trying to understand what supports those with autism in the workplace. They are also focusing on the strengths those with autism might bring to the workplace, such as out-of-the-box thinking, attention to detail, organization skills, and lower turnover rates. In order to attract workers with autism, they are simply asking the question: How can we support you?[3]

Third, review these suggestions from other workers, and see if any of them might be helpful in your office. This list was compiled from neurodiverse employees, stating what they wished their coworkers knew.[4] This is not an exhaustive list, and it might not even apply to your coworkers. Perhaps one or none of them are relevant. Perhaps review this list with your coworker, if they have already invited you into that conversation.

- Avoid irrelevant small talk (or take cues—some people might prefer a bit of small talk, for others this can be a high-pressure, frightening, or frustrating experience).
- Try to avoid harsh, bright lighting and quick changes in lighting.
- Try to avoid loud music or a setting with multiple people talking over each other.
- Avoid perfumes or strongly scented body-care products. What smells lovely to you can be causing your coworker vertigo.
- Use smaller hand gestures, facial expressions, and vocal range. This will make it easier for your coworker to stay engaged in the conversation. (Some workers said this was a dumb suggestion; others said this was golden. So, check in with your coworker to find out what would be helpful.)
- If you know of a disruptive situation (fire alarm drill, surprise birthday party, etc.), kindly give your coworker a heads-up and an option to participate from a more comfortable distance.
- While some neurodivergent people can shift from one project to another, many people report a preference for focusing on a single task and not having to deal with major schedule changes. The same daily schedule with consistent breaks and routine has been identified as calming and reassuring, allowing the coworker to better focus on the rest of her job. However, for someone with ADD or ADHD, the monotony of the same schedule can be disastrous. Allow these coworkers the freedom to take short, frequent breaks, so that they can return and engage at a high energy level.
- Giving people with ADD or ADHD concrete deadlines and time to work without distractions was a common suggestion.
- Assume that your coworker on the spectrum is telling the truth. Lying, sarcasm, deceit, and manipulation are less common from many personality types. And this is another huge generality, so again—reconcile this information with what you know about your coworker.
- Since your coworker is prone to telling the truth, they will likely assume you are always telling the truth. This means that they might not appreciate your jokes involving trickery or sarcasm.

- Even if your coworker is being blunter than you are used to, don't assume they are trying to be offensive.
- Remember that people on the spectrum are people! They want to be liked and to be kind and to do the correct thing. If your coworker is doing something inappropriate or offensive at the workplace, kindly, clearly tell them what the action was, why it was inappropriate, and what would be a more appropriate action. The exact same way you would want someone to do for you.
- And the main one? Instead of assuming, ask your coworker to describe the workplace environment and situations best suited to their peak productivity.

Is this a whole list of generalizations? Obviously. A list that people with different anxiety disorders or on different ends of the spectrum have said they wished their coworkers knew. The resounding takeaway I heard from many frustrated coworkers: *Autism doesn't hold coworkers back in the workplace; discrimination does.*

I also wanted to understand a bit about how different brain processes work. In many autistic brains, for instance, research suggests that the brain places less importance on reading the social context cues and puts more of a focus on deciding what to do. As described earlier, the temporal lobes, which observe and interpret social context cues, are less engaged. In response, many workers with autism said that they preferred jobs with a clear set of instructions where they did not have to rely on reading social context clues.[5]

According to another site, anxietycentre.com,[6] anxiety affects almost a fifth of American workers. This means that for one out of every five people you work with, there is probably some part of the job that is overwhelming, and maybe causes them overwhelming dread. With so many flexible work structures and daily technology innovations, it would be worth it to brainstorm options with your coworker. There is most likely a way that she can both effectively do her job and cope with her anxiety. Also, remember that there are a variety of employee assistance programs (EAPs) that are well-versed in brainstorming solutions. Some of the anxiety could also be coming from you. If your coworker senses that you are expecting them to fret and fruff over an upcoming presentation, this will make their anxiety even worse. This is all to say: Treat your coworker with support.

I recently read a story from the amazing Brandon Stanton. Brandon is a photographer who began taking pictures of New Yorkers and asking them for their story, turning him into a well-respected "social media-ite master" and *New York Times* best-selling author, from his website Humans of New York. He described a man who was the assistant director of a middle school and had a medical condition: clammy hands. The man described how embarrassing it was growing up. But being up front about his condition has helped those around him to be up front and normal with him. He has turned it into a humorous superpower. For instance, whenever they need to open a plastic bag? They come straight to him!

If you are awkward and anxious, people will likely feed that anxiety back to you. If you are open, honest, and kind, chances are good that you will get kindness in return.

Fourth, if you are in a position to do so, and if your coworker has invited you to help, find out if there are any reasonable accommodations that your workplace could make. Could communications be handled more via email instead of impromptu chats? Could presentations be prerecorded? Is telecommuting an option? Would asynchronous communication be preferred? If your coworker has autism, their condition is classified as a disability. It is covered under the Americans with Disabilities Act (ADA), mandating that workplaces are required to make reasonable accommodations to support their working needs.

Fifth, realize that many people on the spectrum or with some type of an anxiety disorder born before 1980 have a lower chance of having been diagnosed. This means that they might not have had a chance to develop any coping mechanisms or to determine their preferences. Opening the door to an open and respectful conversation to determine their preferences could prove insightful for both of you. It also means that they might have had a history of confusing or hurtful social situations. Make sure that does not continue in the workplace.

Sixth, remember that those on the spectrum and neurotypicals all carry their own strengths and weaknesses. You have needed to figure out what you are good at. You should also figure out what your coworker is good at. What are specific skills or projects that your coworker excels in? Spend your time acknowledging those benefits. As an example, many people with Asperger's mentioned their abilities to focus on a task without being distracted—for 14, 16, or 18 hours straight—with the ability to adhere to high quality standards. They often have very high IQs and the ability to solve complex problems. What an incredible asset to your team! But again—everyone is different! So, get to know your own coworker and don't rely on my generalities!

DON'T

Don't avoid someone because you are not sure how to support them—you would be missing out on wonderful relationships! Instead, find out how they want to be treated and be clear, kind, and consistent in how you need to be treated.

Also, stop assuming that everyone with autism, anxiety disorders, OCD, and so on are exactly the same. Talk to them and find out their preference for a work environment. What if someone read an article about you that said *all brunettes prefer to work in a quiet, monotonous job*, and they made changes to your job responsibilities and your workplace settings without talking to you first? You would be furious, right? Insulted? Don't make the same mistake with your coworkers. Talk to them about their preferences and how to support their job.

Finally, don't assume that everyone with these characteristics has autism, anxiety, or something else. And, because these are medical conditions protected by HIPAA, you cannot ask anyone directly if they have them. Instead, address specific behaviors. If they have been diagnosed and if they share that information with you, they have given you a privileged gift that you should protect. That's a nice way of saying, "Don't share their secret!"

DO

Prepare yourself for frank conversations. Be honest with your coworker about their strengths. Be forthright about how you need to be treated. Be consistent in standing up for your comfort in the workplace as well. Remember that people on the spectrum often do not have the same social norms and might come across as blunt or inappropriate. To them, if you are sarcastic, you might be coming across as crass or untrustworthy or dishonest. Simply let them know what makes you uncomfortable and what is appropriate, and invite them to share their needs with you. The same advice as for almost every other behavior: Share your interests and listen to theirs.

IS THIS YOU?

If you are on the spectrum, have PTSD, or are otherwise neurodivergent, realize that your coworkers want to know how to honor you. The more up-front you can be about your needs, the better they can be about meeting your needs. The more you can acknowledge the strengths you bring to the workplace, the better those strengths can be utilized. This doesn't mean you have to share confidential or personal information. It simply means that you can be honest about what behaviors would support you to be the best employee.

STAY OR GO?

So, if you are not on the spectrum, but your coworker is—what do you do?

Well, stay. Duh. You have the honor of working with someone whose brain operates differently from yours, and who can be a great complement to how you think. You are lucky to have a coworker with a different outlook to round out your team.

My daughter learned this recently. She was giving swimming lessons, and there was a four-year-old boy in her group with almost nonverbal autism. The rest of the kids were learning the front crawl, and she explained it to them using abstract concepts such as swirl your arms like a windmill and cup the water like an ice cream scoop. This boy was becoming lost and defensive. The instructions were not registering with his brain, and so he wanted to withdraw. The rest of the class weren't sure of the best way to interact with him. My daughter (who is just amazing) spoke with the boy's mom. She explained that her son didn't appreciate the abstract concepts and wanted something clearer that he could relate to. So my daughter brought in a pink diving ring and told the boy that he had to twirl his arms in a circle like the shape of the ring. He looked at the shape, nodded, and instantly got it. Then, he was able to watch the other students and point out where their arms were not forming a circle but were sloping off to the side. Once his brain received clear instructions in a way that he could process, he could immediately understand, master the stroke, and help the rest of the class to improve their stroke. She changed the way she worked with him slightly, and by doing so he was reengaged and could also help his team.

TAKEAWAY

Trying to provide a list of common characteristics for someone who is neurodiverse is like trying to list characteristics of people who live in blue houses. Every one will be unique with their own accommodations that will make them effective in the workplace. The best way to find out what will help someone at work? Ask them.

Feminine Response

Interacting with a variety of personality types is typically where women excel. They are able to pick up on micro expressions and quickly adjust their response to make sure the person feels comfortable.

Another common feminine strength is being able to describe behaviors, without necessarily labeling the person. The majority of therapists are women, simply because it seems that a common feminine strength is to understand what people are going through.[7] No one in an office wants to be labeled. Instead, it is helpful to respond to every person you work with based on their behavior. Be careful making an assumption about labels or jumping to conclusions. Just be content to support that person for how they contribute to your office.

All of these chapters have the same tip: Talk to the person. Find out what they want, instead of assuming what they want or why. Then tell them what you want. And then come up with a plan together.

Part II

ARE YOU PREPARED TO RESOLVE YOUR CONFLICT?

TYPE	*I work with:*	*My response:*	*I can be a:*	*What I will do:*
Clueless Carls				
Snappy Sallies				
Bad Brads				
Meany Minnies				
Quiet Queens				
Chatty Patties				
The Dude				
The People Pleaser				
Inappropriate Ingrids				
Micromanagers				
The Hulk				
High-conflict Personalities				
Busier-than-Thou				
Honey Badgers				
The Passive-Aggressive				
Rude Coworkers				
Family Businesses				
Dismissive Bosses				
The Boxer				
Abusive				

Conflict Personality Worksheet. Source: Author

23

WORKPLACE ABUSE—AND WHAT TO DO ABOUT IT

Never doubt that a small group of thoughtful, committed, citizens can change the world. Indeed, it is the only thing that ever has.

—Margaret Mead

Between 2008 and 2010, 43 top employees at France Telecom died by suicide. They had cited extreme verbal harassment from their management. The French government produced a report with 107 recommendations and a strong push to ensure that there was a follow-through of immediate and radical change from the leadership. Eventually, safeguards were put in place to monitor employees' psychological health, a team of internal mediators was deployed, and in 2010 nine members of the management were jailed for their abusive behaviors. This was a landmark case, proving that people needed to be held accountable for workplace abuse.[1]

Over the last few decades, more people have become willing to discuss workplace abuse. People are ready to finally change the noxious behavior in their workplace. What this means for the employees who are in an abusive situation is that there is a clearer path for addressing abuse. It also means that there are protections in place for those who bring to light workplace abuse.

Organizational ombuds, who document workplace conflicts, have identified an increase in conflicts reported. Initially, this seemed to mean that the number of conflicts in the workplace was increasing. But after researching it, the ombuds reported that it is actually the standard that is changing. Employees aren't putting up with as much. They are beginning to report conflicts that otherwise they would have tolerated. The conflicts have always been there, just existing under the surface and causing tension in the workplace. Additionally, employees are saying that they are ready to deal with the latent conflicts and bring them to the ombuds office for help. What is wonderful is that after seeing an increase in the number of conflicts reported, offices are also reporting an increase in morale. This means that as people are bringing up issues, they are satisfied to have those disputes resolved.[2]

WHAT IS ABUSE?

Let's begin by defining workplace abuse (according to the Oxford Dictionary):

- Abusive behavior is repetitive.
- Abusive behavior is intentionally mean, intended to cause harm.
- Abusive behavior is a form of control. The person is using an abusive behavior to assert or reinforce a power imbalance.

Don't forget (according to studies on ending domestic violence):

- Abusive behavior is not acceptable in the workplace.
- People can change their abusive behavior.

Abusive behavior typically plays out in one of three ways:

1. In one possibility, the abuse stays the same. A person who abuses has likely found the balance of where they can mistreat someone and get away with it. What this means is that there is not any pressure exerted on the person to stop the abuse.
2. Abusive behavior can improve. A person who abuses might have realized the error of their ways. Or someone else might have reported them to the company, resulting in therapy, anger management, coaching, or a performance improvement plan where they are being strictly monitored. The *Wall Street Journal* conducted a study showing that for those who intentionally tried to change their behavior and had help/classes/training, 70 percent

were able to make permanent changes. (This was a study on domestic abuse, and not workplace abuse. And it is important to note that the study focused on those who were involved in a training.)[3]

One situation where a person may become abusive is when they have encountered something that is outside of their "Window of Tolerance," a model developed by psychiatrist Dan Siegel in 1999 that outlines what we can handle effectively. Anything outside of that window causes us to respond ineffectively, such as panicking, withdrawing, or attacking. And for those who have observed abusive behavior, this might mean that in times of stress a person falls back on abusive behavior. For instance, a boss might yell at her employees when she is going through an extremely stressful situation, one unrelated to the supposed reason for yelling. Then if that situation is resolved, or she learns more appropriate ways of managing the stress, her behavior improves. The person is resorting to abusive tactics because in certain stressful situations that behavior is familiar, but they may not typically be an abusive person. If this is the case, there is a chance that through counseling and exposure to more appropriate behaviors, the person might be able to change. None of this excuses abusive behavior, it just helps to property identify it and know the best way to handle the situation for all involved.

This doesn't necessarily mean that you should stay in the situation while the person is going through steps to change their abusive behavior. There is no guarantee that people who abuse will change for the better and no predictable timeline for that change. Above all, keep yourself safe.

3. In the worst scenarios, the abuse escalates. The person acclimates to a certain level of abuse and the behavior may increase. Almost like a drug addict, what was first an acceptable fix becomes insufficient. The high (from norepinephrine and adrenaline) that some people get off of the control is addicting. If you see this trend, please be careful. Begin looking for an exit plan immediately. What was an occasional sneering remark at first can escalate to torment and bullying. What was just inappropriate in the beginning can escalate to verbal and then physical abuse. If the person is not forced into a training, with clear boundaries and guidelines, and a motivation to change, then the chances of them making permanent changes are slim.[4]

Action Steps

1. Determine if it is abuse (repetitive, purposefully unkind, designed to be hurtful). If you determine that this situation should not be categorized as abuse, move to the next section, "What Is Not Abuse."
2. When appropriate, let the person know that the abusive behavior is not acceptable. In an ideal situation, you tell them exactly what behavior is unacceptable, what behavior you would prefer, and then they use that information to change their behavior. This is giving the person a chance to improve and it is also giving them the benefit of the doubt, assuming that they just needed information to change. However, plan this conversation carefully. Make sure that the person is in a relaxed mood, that you have time to talk through this, that you can have the conversation without anyone overhearing but also in a public space in case the conversation becomes violent. Plan out specific events that you want to discuss, the reason why the behavior was inappropriate, the effect on the office, and the desired improved behavior. Try to state this as calmly and nonjudgmentally as possible to improve the chance that the person can hear what you have to say without becoming defensive. However, if you are concerned for your safety, avoid this conversation and skip to the next step.
3. Alert the company authorities. This will typically begin by speaking to your HR office, which will put your company on notice that there is an abusive situation. This means that your company now has a responsibility to respond to the situation and to protect its employees. If there is an imminent threat, contact the local authorities, such as law enforcement.
4. If your company is not responding quickly, or if the situation is continuing, then it is likely time to leave the company. If you decide that you need to go, plan out your exit.

    a. First, you probably want to begin looking for a new job.
    b. Second, alert others outside of the office.
    c. Third, alert someone in your office if you feel it is safe and you are still protected, such as an ombudsperson.
    d. Fourth, you may decide to tell your supervisor the reason for your leaving when you give your notice. There have been cases of the supervisor putting the person on leave until they received help and stopped the abuse.

e. Fifth, protect yourself. Write down the unkind things and actions that have been said. Print out emails. Save voicemails. Keep all of this in a safe place (not at your office). Write out your physical exit. I wish it weren't true, but there is violence in the workplace. What can you do to ensure that the two of you aren't alone in the office? On a business trip? Alone in the bathroom? The parking garage? Remember, you are the person who knows this situation better than anyone else, and it is up to you to protect yourself.

Planning your exit also helps you get through the situation while you are still in it. When someone is rude to you, knowing that you have already started on your exit plan might be enough to motivate you to stop putting up with the abusive behavior. This is not the time to use the principle of just get along, "don't rock the boat," or "turn the other cheek," which can actually invite more abusive behavior. This is simply saying that until you can extricate yourself from an abusive situation, do what you can to prevent the abuse from escalating. You are not a doormat. You do not have to put up with abusive behavior. You need to get out of there before you are injured. This could be physically—but it could be emotionally or mentally as well. You also do not have to respond to it in a way that you will regret. Simply plan to get yourself out of there, keep your head down, and repeat in your head, "I have an exit plan. I have an exit plan."

WHAT IS NOT ABUSE

While we are discussing this topic, let's take a moment to make sure we are correctly identifying these behaviors. Unfortunately, when a behavior is wrongly categorized as abuse, it will not be appropriately addressed. This mischaracterization often occurs because many people do not understand what constitutes abuse. Or, they casually misuse the word for storytelling flair or to gain sympathy.

One reason this is a problem is the Never-Cry-Wolf scenario. If someone complains consistently about abuse when there is no abuse present, they might not be taken seriously when they really are in an abusive situation that requires change. It also means that a company has to investigate the situation and perhaps put those involved on legal notice, which could delay the process of resolving the real conflict. In other words, if two employees are involved in a difficult situation that needs to be mediated, but the situation is incorrectly defined as abuse, then the two employees will be put through legal delays and red tape and investigations before they are allowed to talk through the matter and resolve it. As soon as an allegation of abuse is presented to management or the HR office, the company is required to take time to investigate.

Let's look at specific situations that are not abuse.

Annoyances Are Not Abuse

There are some things that you just have to put up with that are annoying but are not categorized as abusive. Susan's halitosis, for instance, might be one of those chronic annoyances that you will just have to deal with. A boss who is a micromanager is frustrating—but not necessarily abusive. A coworker who is an Inappropriate Ingrid or a Chatty Patty around clients. An employee who Honey Badgers you and steals your ideas. An employee who is Busier-than-Thou and thinks they are overworked and feels sorry for themselves. Frustrating and annoying, sure, but this is not causing you to be afraid and is not abusive.

An annoyance is typically not an abuse. However, an annoyance can advance to the point where it becomes detrimental, and you need to take action to care for yourself.

Everyone has a different 10. We are all built differently, with different skill sets, personalities, and sensitivities. Thank goodness—could you imagine if we were all Kardashians? What that means, however, is that we all place things differently on a scale from imperceptible (0) to tragic (10). A mild annoyance (3) to you might be a deal-breaker (8) for someone else. And vice versa.

REAL-LIFE EXAMPLE

Jason told me about a time when he was trying to get a coworker's computer to connect to the office internet. And her computer was stubbornly not complying. The longer it took the more and more upset she got. He knew she was on a work exchange visa and thought to himself maybe this was indicative of her culture. He updated, installed, and rebooted. She finally turned to him and screamed, "What is wrong with you? Don't you know how to do anything?" *Wow,* he thought to himself, *glad she was on a temporary visa and not a permanent worker.*

> *We really dodged a bullet with this one.* "Hey," he told her, "if I don't get this working quickly, you are welcome to go across the ocean back to your family." She ran sobbing from the office. What he assumed was a minor annoyance, like a 2, she was treating like a full-scale 10 on the pain scale.
>
> Jason told me that he found out later that afternoon that she had just suffered a miscarriage and had been trying to email her husband to tell him. "I carry that painful example with me now, and it is a constant reminder that when someone overreacts they might have a really good reason for it."

So, what are the office implications of this? It means that when an employee is having a difficult time, our response cannot always be, "Get over it." Sure, you might think that silently in your head, but you have been reading this book and you have more tact than that by now, so what you actually say out loud is, "Tell me why." Approaching situations like this with curiosity instead of criticism helps you to understand why they are experiencing something as a 7 when to you it is clearly a 3.

Do you know why you do nice things to your coworkers, like employ curiosity, keep your mind open and yourself in check, and extend the benefit of the doubt? Because of the Golden Rule! Treat others the way you would like to be treated. In other words, model the behavior you desire to come around to you when things go around. Because when you are having a difficult time in your office and you bring it to a coworker's or supervisor's attention, it would be crushing to hear, "Get over it." Rather, if you summon up the courage to raise an uncomfortable conversation, your hope against hope is that someone will respond to you by saying, "Tell me what's going on."

There are some situations that will be extremely difficult for you but easy for others. Dealing with frustrating people or circumstances may not be a viable, healthy, long-term situation for you, but that does not constitute abuse.

Some people have no social skills. Earlier I mentioned the difference between bad communication and mean communication. Bad communication simply means that a person might be saying things that are frustrating, annoying, or even hurtful—but is not intended to be. Whereas mean communication is intended to manipulate, denigrate, upbraid, humiliate, and generally have a negative effect on the recipient.

Unfortunately, until we can master the Vulcan mind meld, there is simply not an easy process for determining intentions. But here are a few things to consider:

- What has been your previous experience with this person? If they are typically kind, could it be possible that they just snapped at you this morning because of an exceptionally bad day?
- How is your day going? Unfortunately, our expectations often affect our perceptions. Have you ever noticed how people become exceptionally annoying when you are tired? This is not a sign that the entire world plotted to get you. It is simply a sign that you have less of a buffer, less forgiveness than you normally would. If someone says something particularly irksome, ask yourself if it would be wise to wait a day to do something about it. It is possible things will look very different after a good night's sleep.
- How do they typically treat others? Do you observe them treating others badly? Have other people complained to you of unkind behavior?
- What is the context? In our house I lovingly call my son "crazy." As in, "come here, you crazy little monkey." He got in trouble in kindergarten for "calling another boy names on the bus." Which meant, of course, he called the other boy "crazy." Out of context, the bus driver was right. My son called the boy a name—crazy can absolutely be meant as an insult. But if you look at the situation closer you realize that my son was actually trying to speak kindly to his friend while they were playing Spiderman together. The context shows us that this was simply bad communication—an unkind word, but spoken in a kind context with kind nonverbals. (We can also learn from this situation that I clearly need to stop using the word "crazy" so lightly and I need to find a better term of endearment for my children!)

Chances are you are not playing Spiderman with your coworkers, like my son was with his friends. In this context of friendly banter, you realize that insults might be said playfully. (If you are running around your office playing Spiderman, it sounds like you have an awesome relationship with them and don't need to read any more.) But if you are not playing with pretend web shooters and hopping from cubicle to cubicle, there might be other nonverbal cues that indicate their intention. If they are repeatedly using offensive, bad communication, you are wise to let them know that it is bothersome.

In summary, abuse is not:[5]

- something that is just annoying,
- a one-time outburst,
- bringing up a conflict, concern, or a criticism of work,
- viewed as abusive by one frustrated person, but acceptable to all other informed coworkers, or
- bad communication.

HOW CAN PEOPLE LEARN TO STOP ABUSIVE BEHAVIORS?

- *They need to be made aware of their actions*. Abuse is often a learned behavior. If you were fortunate to grow up in a respectful home, with fairly functioning parents who taught you social skills, be grateful. A lot of people never had that opportunity. (This knowledge is only to help you understand—it is not a substitute for action. Understanding the reason why someone is abusive should never be an excuse.) Being made aware of their actions, how unacceptable and how detrimental their actions are, probably cannot come from you. It will likely need to come from a supervisor or a group of managers.
- *They need to have a way to learn new behaviors*. This might be an anger management class. They might need more in-depth counseling. They might need to start going on walks. They might need constant reinforcement of what is acceptable and what is unacceptable in order to create lasting change. This does not mean that you continually drag their nose in the mud—this can become too discouraging and cause people to give up. It can also be infuriating, not a good choice for someone who can be abusive. Instead, I prefer a simple, "Ouch!" This is quick, fast, and doesn't ask for a response.
- *They have to decide to change*. You can do everything right, but if the person doesn't decide for themselves to change and stop the abuse then you can't make them. There is a wealth of resources on this topic; try Lundy Bancroft's[6] work. If you are facing an abusive person, please educate yourself about the best way to proceed.

What Are Signs the Behavior Is Changing?

- They are taking responsibility for their actions.
- They are making up for the wrong they did.
- They have incentive and time to change their habits.
- They are no longer minimizing your pain.

DON'T

Don't confuse understanding with enabling. It is great to understand why your boss is a sadistic pile of poo, but that understanding doesn't mean you should put up with it. "She is a single mother with a lot of stress that she brings to work." "He is like that because his dad was." "He has a short fuse because he doesn't have a lot of time to listen to excuses." "She shames people in the office because she feels bad about herself." Just because you understood that someone was having a bad day, say they spilled their coffee in the morning, would you let them punch you in the face? No! Not even if it was an uber-expensive soy vanilla extra-unicorns latte. You wouldn't let someone inflict physical harm on you because of a silly excuse; don't accept verbal abuse either. Both physical and verbal abuse are damaging. Both are unacceptable. And verbal abuse can often have longer-lasting consequences.

Don't expect another person to know what you want. You have to make it clear what type of specific behavior you expect. Many of my mediation agreements go into meticulous detail to explain ambiguous terms like "respect." Instead we would define the behavior that signifies respect, such as, "When I am speaking in a meeting, I expect to finish my sentence and not be cut off with frequent interruptions, sighs, or eye rolls."

Don't expect a change overnight. Abusive behavior is a bad habit that has been taught and then reinforced by years of practice. This takes a long time to change. With pressure and coaching, you can see changes in a month. Or it could take years.

DO

Have a conversation with the person about the abusive behaviors that are not helping your relationship and ways that you would like to see change.

Document your abusive interactions. Report them to your manager. Report them to HR.

Realize that this person preys on the kind, the flexible, the supportive, the team player. All of the things that you probably value in yourself. Don't let them harden you or diminish those qualities. But realize that their abuse is their own flaw, not a sign of yours.

IS THIS YOU?

If you are seeing ways that you have been abusive in the office, it is your responsibility to make changes. Find ways to relieve immediate stress before you come into a trying situation. Go for a run. Take a bath. Cook. Wrestle with your dogs. Even take a moment to order llamas for your party. But do something physical that helps your body to work through the stress and adrenaline. This will help you to be prepared to come into the stress of the office. Then when you find yourself ready to yell at someone, be honest. "I'm starting to get really upset because somehow you have been late 17 times in 16 days and I can feel myself losing my temper. But I am working on changing how I speak, so I want to call you a lazy worthless slob, but I won't. Instead, I will just say you have one more chance before HR places you on disciplinary leave."

These short-term steps can help in the moment, but it is important to also make long-term changes. Your HR office likely has communication resources. You can also see if your insurance has an employee assistance program (EAP) that will cover therapy or counseling to allow you to find better ways to manage anger and stress and to improve your communication with your coworkers.

STAY OR GO?

If you are working with someone who is being abusive, you need to make some big decisions. I have a few questions coming up in the next chapters that can help you decide what to do.

It depends on the severity of the abuse and whether or not the person is receptive to change. If the abuse is severe and persistent and if you have made attempts to point out the behavior to the person and HR and they are not changing or HR is not responding, then go. Life is too short. You have but one life to live. YOLO. Anyway, get out. There are a lot of other jobs out there and companies that will not tolerate abuse.

TAKEAWAY

Workplace abuse is often overlooked, excused, and perpetuated. "They had a bad day, they don't know any better, I made a mistake so it's my fault, I'm too scared to say anything, what if I get fired, what if I'm overreacting." Unfortunately, these are all excuses, which will perpetuate the abuse. Workplace abuse is the fault of the abuser. Only. Not your fault. And it is likely that it will continue and perhaps escalate unless you do something. So, face your fears and excuses and make a plan for protecting yourself and ending the abuse.

Feminine Response

Women statistically have put up with more abusive behaviors than men do. Which is why approximately 85 percent of abuse victims are female.[7] They justify it. They explain it. They understand it. They accept it.

They enable it.

They enable it because they want to make sense of a senseless situation, and by allowing the behavior to continue, they are indirectly condoning it.

They can sympathize with someone's rough past, work stress, and difficult home life. Sometimes women might even think that their contribution to the office is to allow this person to vent. Women pride themselves on the ability to handle these hard conversations.

But putting up with abuse means that a) the person isn't going to change or stop the abusive behavior and b) your office isn't getting the employee they hired. Stop justifying the reasons. You weren't hired to be a whipping boy or a punching bag.

Here is an instance where I say start the conflict. Fight the fight. Confront the unacceptable behavior. Escalate it if you need to. Protect yourself and your boundaries and call the person on being a raging jerk. Do whatever it takes—talk to the person abusing, or HR, or management, or general counsel. Hire a mediator or an attorney. Stop this before it gets worse. Or escalates to someone else. You wouldn't let anyone treat your mom this way. Or your kids. So don't let anyone treat your mother's daughter this way.

24

KEEPING YOURSELF SANE AND SAFE

The last chapter on abuse gave a few suggestions for keeping yourself safe. This chapter is going to cover some more thorough suggestions for getting through difficult situations that may or may not be abusive, without going berserk. Keep yourself sane and safe by assessing, planning, and acting.

ASSESSING

Let's begin by assessing your personality type when it comes to responding to difficult situations. There are just as many personality types as there are people, but for the sake of simplicity we will be focusing on only two examples: The People Pleaser and The Boxer.

When you have dealt with overbearing personalities, did you typically put up with them? Did you freeze? Did you challenge them?

CONFLICT RESPONSE WORKSHEET

When faced with overbearing personalities, I:

When you begin to feel the stress of too much work, do you snap at your family? Do you lord it over your coworkers?

When I am overstressed, I:

Look back on other situations where you felt as if you could barely hold your head above water. Were you typically just fine in a day or two? Or did you try to take on too much without asking for help and then barely get by?

Are your coworkers and friends more likely to tell you to "get a backbone and stand up for yourself" or "to calm down and get over it already"?

Examining your past reactions to similar situations and similar personalities might not explain exactly what is happening now, but it will help you to be aware of your habitual responses to that situation.

IN THE RING WITH THE PEOPLE PLEASER AND THE BOXER

Remember The People Pleaser and The Boxer from earlier in the book? Let's use them as an example to see how we can help two very different personalities to get along. Consider The Boxer more of a vinegar personality. It adds some tang, some depth, and can make boring work projects more exciting. The People Pleaser is more the oil. The People Pleaser wants to go with the flow and smooth things over. Both are necessary elements in a work environment—elements that often do not naturally gravitate toward each other.

How can you mix oil and vinegar? You've gotta keep shaking things up. When you grab salad dressing that has separated and you want the ingredients to reincorporate, you shake them up, right? In other words, when you have two drastically different personality types such as The People Pleaser and The Boxer, don't let them settle into unhealthy patterns. Shake things up. Continually shift around projects, introduce new schedules. Give The People Pleaser a chance to continue to assert their interests, and give The Boxer a chance to understand the feeling of being unsure.

Creativity helps. Working together on a project helps. Attacking the problem instead of the person helps. Creativity helps with both The Boxer and The People Pleaser personalities. Encouraged creativity and judgment-free brainstorming frees The People Pleaser from self-doubt, while it often calms down The Boxer and focuses them on something other than The People Pleaser.

When assessing a conflict, you have to look at your own contribution as well as the other person's. Do you purposefully egg them on? Do you continually hide your feelings? Have you become such a People Pleaser that no one knows what you want? Have you become such a Boxer that people are afraid to get what they want?

You might not have the responsibility in your office to shake things up by shifting around projects or schedules. But you do have the power to change how you interact with people. If you are working with someone who boxes or people pleases, then shake things up. Be willing to be creative, try out new ideas, try interacting with them in new ways. Try being funny, or listening, or brainstorming, or bring in another person so the three of you can plan out a project. Just don't let them fall into habits that aren't healthy for you. Shake things up.

PLANNING

Plan Your Approach: Serious, but Not Aggressive

Understanding your typical role and response is only the foundation for action. You wouldn't be reading this book if you didn't see an opportunity for improvement. There is a situation that needs to be improved, now you just need to decide how to do that.

While there are many possible next steps, your first one is to decide how to respond safely. For People Pleasers, preparation will help you feel prepared for a difficult conversation. This will allow you to be open to hearing what the other side is saying and still be able to speak your piece. For Boxers, preparation will help you speak in a way that the other side can hear what you are saying. In other words (words, it's punny—get it?), preparation will allow you to have an effective conversation. Effective conversations means that both sides were able to speak and hear the other. A fantastic mediator and president of Lipscomb University, Randy Lowry says that if you want to have an effective conversation with someone you need to hang the meat low enough so the dog will bite. In other words, present your issue in a way that the other person understands you are serious without making them defensive. This means speaking respectively but assertively. Maintain eye contact. Leave lots of personal space.

You might also want to think about location. Is there a place that is private, that also feels safe? A conference room? A back corner of a lunchroom? One of my clients told me that after her first argument with a coworker, she did not want to be alone in a room with her. I discussed this earlier—and mentioned that it got to the point where she had an informal restraining order on her coworker. She always made a point to be the last one to arrive at meetings and the first one to leave. A year later, when the coworker was ready to discuss the disagreement, they found an open lobby. This was not a confined space, but also a place where no one could hear them.

Plan for Your Health

When going through a conflict, you need to take care of your body, your family, and your brain.[1]

- *Taking care of your body*. Difficult workplaces find subtle ways to eat at you. Studies vary based on the type of dispute and the type of workplace, but all employers agree: Extended employee conflicts are bad for business. Employees in conflict are more distracted at work, less eager to return calls, and spend longer gossiping with other employees at the watercooler. Eventually they begin calling in sick. Employees in my study pool reported two main reasons for calling in sick. The first was that the employee faked being sick. Typically, this was due to being fed up with work or too nervous to come in and face a difficult coworker. The second reason was the employees were actually becoming sick because of the workplace situation. They were not resting well. They reported stomachaches, headaches, shoulder pain, and decreased immune systems. Internalized stress seems to attack people in different ways, but it can often be a cause of otherwise unexplained chronic conditions. The physical stress of a difficult workplace over time takes a severe toll on your body.

  THOR (The Health and Occupation Research network, but it's more fun to say THOR) released a study in which they examined 81,865 sick days and found that 55 percent of them were considered mental health days. The reason the number is so high is because mental health is not like a flu, which runs its course over a few days. Ten percent of these mental health sick days were due to bullying/harassment, 35 percent were due to workplace factors/systemic issues, and 24 percent were due to difficult interpersonal relationships.[2]

The stress also takes its toll on the rest of your life. Gossiping and complaining every day is not a healthy approach to parenting, friendships, or marriage. Grabbing a beer or a glass of wine every day when you get home from work? Also, not healthy. We all know that—so why do we do it? Chronically complaining about work, self-medicating, and lack of interest in other fun hobbies are signs that the stress of work is eating at you. When you have to be on your guard all day at work because you feel like you are under attack, have to listen to cruel jokes, feel the rush of adrenaline every time your micromanager boss walks by, and the like, then your body chemistry simply goes out of whack. Our bodies aren't prepared to live in a war zone. We are prepared to deal with short conflicts, and then flush the toxic stress out of our system and return to a healthy set point. But when you spend your day in a stressful office and then you also bring that stress home and perpetuate that level of strain—well, your body is simply not equipped to handle the demands you are putting on it. Which is why we vent at each other, or have a beer, or two, when we get home: Our body does not have the time to decompress naturally and so we are trying to help it out.

But, imagine you are trying to grow a fern. You keep dousing it with root beer and wonder why it isn't growing like you expected. You are pouring more acid onto the fern than it is able to flush out. It has to spend its time in self-care and isn't able to take the time to grow. At some point it will need to push all the toxins out, slurp up some healthy clean water, bask in the wholesome sunshine, and take in the nutrients that will allow it to thrive.

Taking a vacation or some time off is always a good start when you need to reset, but unfortunately, unless you have the best boss in the world (and if you do, I want her number), we cannot live permanently on vacation. Rather, you need solutions for taking care of yourself while you are in the midst of this conflict. The first answer is that we should avoid a lot of the stuff that feels so good in the moment. Put down the wine and chocolates (or at least, put some of them down but maybe not all—let's be real), and give your body what it needs to stay healthy. Plenty of water, exercise, nutrients, and sleep. But there are a few other things you need to do too during this time.[3]

Realize that your body is handling more stress than it should, and you need to get that stress out before it starts having a negative effect (insomnia, irritability, headaches, difficulty focusing, etc.). Before we discuss how to tackle the workplace situation, prepare your body for this challenge. It is hard work resolving conflict, and you need to be physically prepared. Give yourself the nutrients you need to detoxify and support your immune system. Also give yourself time to rest. Lots of sleep, of course. But more than sleep, give yourself permission to relax during the day. Take a weekly bubble bath, read a book, play catch with your kids, go out for Taco Tuesday with some buds, get a massage, or get up 10 minutes before everyone else so that you can have some peaceful time alone with your coffee.[4]

- *Taking care of your family and friends.* Second, your relationships are withstanding more stress than they should. Your spouse, your kids, and your friends are not working in your office—you are. It is not fair to them to ask that they continually absorb your stress from your job when you want to complain or are irritable—or are just not the fun person you want to be. Your family and friends have their own stresses in life. They have their own struggles for which they probably want your support. Sure, they are supportive, but you also need to understand what you are asking of them is to hear your venting on repeat and then to try to build you back up. This is not a long-term solution. Do what you can to minimize it. Take a couple of extra minutes in the car or your walk from the train, take a few deep breaths, and plan your entrance. Choose to ask people about their day when you get inside. Put a time limit on your venting. Say to your friends, "I need five minutes to get this off my chest so I can relax for the night, and then I'm done." Acknowledge what is going on. "This coworker/situation is making things really difficult for me right now. You have been very supportive. I just wanted you to know that I see it and I appreciate it. I am trying to figure out a solution, but I would like you to bear with me just a little bit longer. Please let me know, though, when I'm asking too much or when you need a moment that is about you. Okay?"
- *Taking care of your brain.* Third, your brain is withstanding more stress than it should. This can have long-term negative effects on the way your brain is wired. That could eventually mean a shorter reaction time before you escalate conflict. It might be

increased anxiety and irritability. Extreme situations could lead to PTSD. No job is worth that. The greatest way for your brain to deal with such stress? Give it hope. The next part of the book will talk about the specific action you can take to get out of a difficult situation. Once you have your plan in place, continue to remind yourself that it won't be like this forever. Remember, to protect your mental health requires clarity, pride, and hope. Clarity means that you have a plan for resolving the conflict. Pride comes once you have begun to take control of your conflict. Hope comes from tackling a conflict and knowing that you will be able to solve whatever else comes your way.[5]

HOW I WILL PREPARE FOR CONFLICT WORKSHEET

Body
One short-term splurge I will give myself:
One long-term change I will make to be healthier/stronger:

Family
One request I will make of my family to support me:
One request they will make of me/one thing I can give them:

Friends
How I will ask my friends for support:
One fun thing I can do for my friends:

Brain
Clarity: The exact reason why I am making this change:
Pride: What this change tells me about myself:
Hope: What success will look like:

ACTION

After you have *assessed* the situation and *planned* for a response, you are ready for *action*. Begin by assigning a date, a "Freedom Day." This is the day when you will start to be free of the weight of this conflict because you know you are starting to do something to make it better. You're marching in the right direction. You might say, "By the end of this month, I am going to have a conversation with my coworker. If things are still getting worse by the end of next month, I'm talking to my manager. No changes by the month after that? I'm looking for a new job." Write down specific dates and what you need to do to prepare for them.

Conversation Starters

This is hard. Having a difficult conversation with a difficult coworker is, well, difficult. It is difficult because you want to avoid coming across . . .

- too meek, and your request won't be taken seriously.
- too strong, and the other person is already defensive.
- too whiney, and you sound like an Eeyore that will always be a sourpuss.
- too accusatorial, and you sound like a victim who enjoys playing a martyr.
- too exaggerated, and you sound like a drama queen.

Your approach determines how the other person responds. People say that the only behavior you can control is your own, but you can definitely have an effect on other people's behavior. And right now, you want to have the effect where your coworker is willing to have a conversation with you.

There are no outs here. There is no role that you can slip into or mask that you can hide behind. The only way through it is just to do it. So, figure out what you are going to say, practice a few times, and walk up and say it.

- *The invitation.* Invite them to have a conversation, don't just launch into an attack. A gentle invite might be:

  - "Do you have a few minutes?"
  - "There is something I would like to talk about. Do you have some time this morning, or would this afternoon be better?"
  - "Can we grab a cup of coffee at break?"

  All of these statements are allowing your coworker time to get their bearings and realize that you are not being a threat. These statements are also asking them for a commitment. This whole package helps your coworker to come into the conversation more willing to talk.

- *Problem statement*. State the why. This typically begins with the word "I." "I have been wondering about . . ." "I was hoping we could find a better way to communicate." "I have been feeling like we are not seeing eye to eye." "I was thinking that maybe we got off on the wrong foot."

  The goal here is to attack the problem, not the person.[6] "I was wondering if we could brainstorm together on how to improve communication." You have invited them to do something together. This is a much easier request than attacking them and expecting them to hear you.
- *Be curious*. Ask them about what they think has been going on. And really listen. Maybe clarify what they said, as with repeating back or a paraphrase: "So you think . . ."

  Then, with the same openness, state what you think has been going on. Finish with an invitation for them to be curious in return: "What do you think about that?" "Does that seem right to you?"
- *Planning a solution*. Work with your coworker to plan out a solution. This has to be a melding of both of your interests for it to work.
    - Listen to your coworker and their interests.
    - Voice your interests.
    - Develop a solution that incorporates both.

This means that your coworker might have to give a bit to meet some of your needs, and you might have to give a bit to meet some of their needs. If you are the one who initiated the conversation, fair or not, you might have to be the one to give in first. I'm not saying it is right, I just want to prepare you for that possibility. Also realize that you have had a long time to think about this conversation, and your coworker has just had this sprung on them. They might need some time to think about this. If they need space, give it to them and make sure to plan out the next time you will speak.

Once the two of you have agreed on a solution, thank them and end the conversation, paving the way for a better future relationship as you do so. End on a joke. A compliment. An acknowledgment that this has been hard, but you are glad that the two of you are going to be able to work together again. Or go down some nachos together at the next Taco Tuesday.

TAKEAWAY

Assess the situation to determine the best course of action, and then plan out your next steps. What are you going to say? Be direct, but not aggressive. Give yourself a specific date and venue for the conversation—and get excited about it! This is the day that things will start changing!

25

THIS IS YOUR BRAIN ON CONFLICT

Our response to conflict can be blamed on nature and nurture. This means that some of your response to conflict can be blamed on your DNA, but some of it you learned from family and friends.

Picture a lovely caveman family. Let's call them the Waks. Imagine that everyone is snoring in their lovely cave, in front of their lovely fire, on their lovely bearskin fur. Suddenly Papa Wak hears a twig snap outside. He immediately recognizes danger. His body is on full alert, ready to protect his family and wrestle that cougar with his bare hands. There's a danger to *recognize*; Papa will *react* to it and assume a *role* in this danger plot.

RECOGNIZE

Our first response is to recognize conflict. This is a physiological response designed to keep us alive. It is our body's instinctual way of protecting us. Let's look closer at what is happening.

- *Eyes*. In a normal state, our eyes are focused on what is directly in front of us. Our brain is placing importance on the image it is receiving from the center of our field of vision. Peripheral information is blurred and ignored.

In a heightened state, such as when we sense conflict, our body tries to protect us from a stealthy cougar. Our brain immediately pays more attention to the information it is receiving from the periphery of our vision (yup, our brains are awesome). This means that when we are in conflict, our eyes blur out the face in front of us and focus on threats from the outside (*hyperopia*[1]).

- *Ears*. Our ears undergo a similar change. In a normal state, our brain is focused on the information it receives in the middle register of tones. This is typically the level used for human conversation.

  In a heightened state, our brain places more importance on the outlying tones than the middle tones.[2] Our ears are now perked for the low growl of an approaching cougar or the shriek of a baby's cry. Our brains are essentially ignoring sounds in the range of a normal human voice and are hyperaware to threatening or whining sounds.
- *Muscles*. In a normal state, our muscles are focused on absorbing nutrients and circulating blood and oxygen. They are relaxed.

  In a heightened state, our muscles became tighter, stronger. You know the reports of a woman lifting a car off of her baby's car seat? Not impossible when your body is tightening your muscles and loading them with extra blood and oxygen. Your body is also pumping full of adrenaline and noradrenaline, which prepare your body to move quickly. After the threat has gone, it takes between 20 and 60 minutes to return to our previous relaxed state.[3]
- *Digestion*. Some people complain of a stomachache during a fight. This could be due to the skyrocketing stress levels.[4] For some people it is indigestion. But another reason could be that your body is grabbing available energy as quickly as possible so that your muscles are ready to fight off that cougar. This means that it doesn't waste time digesting your last meal, but instead breaks down existing fat stores in order to have a quick burst of energy. When I fight with my husband, I tell him it's just my new diet plan to quickly burn fat. He doesn't buy it.

How do these physiological changes affect us when we are arguing with someone?

Papa Wak is perfectly primed to wrestle with a cougar at this point. But then he realizes that it wasn't a cougar at all; actually, his mother-in-law just stepped on a twig. His body is primed for a fight. His mother-in-law came out to talk to him, and he is in the worst place to argue with mama-in-law Wak. Everything his body has done to prepare him for a fight has also made it fairly impossible to have an effective conversation with another person.[5] The nonverbal cues that we rely on to tell us if a person is being kind, the micro-expressions that flit across a person's face when they smile, are less perceptible when you are arguing. Your eyes are taking in less information from in front of you (the person's face). Instead, they are hyperaware of peripheral movements (such as mama-in-law's gesturing arms). Papa Wak's ears are cued to listen for a cougar, and they are barely registering the actual words his beloved mama-in-law is saying. Primed for a fight, he isn't trying to understand what she is saying—he is looking for the fight in those words.

Let's focus on that:

When we are in an argument, we are not always trying to understand the words someone is saying; we are looking for the fight in those words.

When someone is super geared up, you are probably not going to make much progress talking with them. Which probably means, crazy thought that this is, when you are geared up you might not be operating completely rationally either. You might be overreacting to the conversation and missing out on some logical statements.

Nah, that can't be right. An argument can't be my fault.

Nope, not your fault, it's your brain's fault.

So . . . Blame it on the brain, *oo-ooo*.

REACT

The next step is Papa Wak has to react or decide how to react. This reaction is a combination of nature (what his body is primed to do) and reinforcement by nurture (what he has seen others do and what he has done in the past). His body will most likely respond in one of three ways: *fight*, *flight*, or *freeze*.[6]

- *Fight*. When Papa Wak thought he heard a cougar, his instinct was to fight. His level of aggression went up. His brain surged with oxygen and blood. His adrenaline levels rose. He was ready for a good cougar-wrestling.

Fighters can also remember details of a conversation with extreme clarity. Things almost seem to slow down for them. Have you ever watched those courtroom dramas where the lawyer is just tearing apart a poor witness? The lawyer is making eloquent speeches with spitfire speed and making connections that the rest of us didn't notice? The lawyer is operating with heightened senses.

People who respond to conflict by fighting often notice a surge of energy. You might notice them smiling. It's not that they enjoy arguing—it's that they feel good! This is your body's way of reinforcing your urge to fight a cougar. Some people whistle or hum unintentionally while they are arguing.

- *Flight*. The flight response is similar to the fight response in that it usually follows a surge of testosterone and a surge of adrenaline. This means that your body is amped up and ready to do something. In this case, though, fleers do not usually get the extra surge of oxytocin (that feel-good brain chemical) that fighters get, meaning that they are not enjoying this process. Instead, they get a cortisol surge and feel stressed. They just want to get away. This is wonderful if we are fleeing from a cougar. Less helpful if you are trying to have a conversation with someone and then you inexplicably bolt out the door to get away.
- *Freeze*. The freeze response is another one of nature's ways of protecting us. The freeze response is invoked in the common wisdom to play dead when encountering a bear. The technical term is Playing Possumatosis. Just kidding. The term for when animals freeze around predators so that their movement is not detected and they are not seen as a threat is *thanatosis*. Frogs, possum, and moles have all perfected this method as a great way to stay alive around predators. It has also become a survival technique for many of us in the workplace. When your boss is on the warpath some of us instinctively avoid eye contact and don't make any sudden movements. When taken too far, however, this Playing-Possumatosis response can prevent you from dealing with problems. The freeze response can inhibit you from growing and strengthening relationships.

This list further explains these behaviors.[7]

Fight	*Flight*	*Freeze*
Thinks logically	Feels helpless in an argument	Feels overwhelmed in an argument, as if walking through a washing machine
Thinks clearly	Inability to set boundaries	Lack of motivation
Difficulty sleeping; brain won't calm down	Burst of energy, then tired	Lethargy
Makes conscious choices	Automatic obedience	Dulled capacity to feel
Wide range of emotional responses	Wide range of emotional responses	Nonexpressive
Hyperalertness	Listless	Listless
Heightened senses	Heightened senses	Diminished senses
Feels grounded	Heightened capacity to feel fear	Can look disengaged in office
Seems "manic," or excited	Emotionally constricted	Depression
Able to look others in the eye	Shifting eyes, short conversations	Able to look down
Can be charming, confident, or pushy	Avoids social settings	Difficulty forming office relationships
Aggressive, confident	Fearful, can shift to "caged animal"	Seems to have sunk inside
Quick decision-making	Slow decision-making	No decision-making
Excessive motor activity	Bursts of activity	Reduced activity
Overly confident to irritable	Easily overwhelmed	Shrinking
Overwhelms others	Disorganized	Unable to set boundaries
Increased heart rate	Increased heart rate	Decreased heart rate

Fight, Flight, Freeze. Source: Author

By contrast, if we are able to move past these responses, push past our defensive role and instead face the conflict, we tend to find these responses. This list is compiled from my observations of mediated conversations, when I watch people change their responses.

Facing Conflict Peacefully and Firmly
Think logically
Think clearly
Make deliberate choices
Connect choices to past and future implications
Make eye contact
Stable heart rate
Controlled uninhibited movements
Feels grounded
Notices calming breaths
Communicates interests and concerns clearly

Firm Responses. Source: Author

ROLE

Another way most of us react to conflict is by sliding into a role. It isn't fun in conflict to be vulnerable and transparent and explain our feelings. No way. That vulnerability requires trust that must be earned. Instead, we cover up what we are really feeling by playing the Superhero, Victim, or Dragon.

According to Ken Cloke and Joan Goldsmith (conflict resolution authors, peacemakers, workplace mediators, and the closest people to Yoda that I have met on this earth),[8] these are learned behaviors. I point that out because if we learn a behavior, by intentionally changing our reactions, we can also unlearn these behaviors (known as neuroplasticity: the ability of the brain to reform after a learning experience).

For a more thorough presentation of the Superhero, Victim, and Dragon roles in conflict, please read the book Mediating Dangerously *by Ken Cloke, along with Joan Goldsmith.*[9] *Probably the most insightful authors on conflict resolution, they have written numerous books that address personal, workplace, and family conflict.*

It is 4:30 a.m. in the San Diego airport. There is one—that's right—one coffee shop in our entire temporary terminal. And the woman who normally opens up did not show up to work.

It is now 5:00 a.m. in the San Diego airport. Okay, I'm going to be fine—another worker showed up and is slowly starting to open up the coffee shop. We don't board for another 45 minutes. Everything will be fine.

5:30 a.m. Passengers are beginning to drool and twitch. It's beginning to remind me of a commercial for *The Walking Dead*. The young woman behind the counter calls out, "I'm sorry. The main barista didn't show up. I'm doing the best I can. I'll open soon, just please be patient." Her boss, a portly man with too much cologne for this enclosed space—well, too much cologne for any place other than a New Jersey Mafia meeting—walks over to the barista behind the counter and says, "You need to hurry and open up your till." She looks at him with eyes that say, "Oh, gee, I had no idea. Thank you so much, because I was just standing here with my key in the till trying to figure out what in the world I should do today."

5:32 a.m. The main barista finally shows up. She is an older woman who looks like she has already had way too much of a day. She seems to be a chain-smoker needing to light up at any moment, which makes me nervous since the amount of hair spray on her hair is clearly a potential fire hazard. She adjusts her leopard-print top and mumbles that the "dang babysitter didn't show up to watch the dang kids." She unlocks the till and the caffeine-deprived passengers storm the counter in a red-eyed horde. The younger barista looks up timidly and begins taking orders. The boss comes in again and says, "Let's speed it up, ladies. These people have a plane to catch." The older woman tries to get mochas churned out as quickly as possible, handing caffeine fixes to the impatient customers. As she is moving the drinks, a caramel frappuccino spills on the counter. She looks at it for a moment, decides she can't deal with anymore, says, "Screw it," and walks away.

On the downside, they haven't made my latte so now I don't get to sit and sip an overpriced coffee. On the upside, we now have the three characters needed to illustrate the roles people take in conflict. (And, I still have two free hands to type. Really wish one hand was holding a coffee, though . . .)

THE THREE ROLES IN CONFLICT

Every story has a Superhero, a Victim, and a Dragon.

Superhero

The boss in this scenario was clearly the Superhero. He bustled in late, did very little work, and "saved the day." Or, at least, he thinks he did. He gave orders without fully assessing the situation, did little to help, strained relationships, is disappointed in the performance of the other workers, and reinforces his belief that he is "the only one who can get anything done around here." If you and your team have been working on a report for a month, the Superhero is the one who storms in frustrated, sweeps up the report with a sarcastic "looks like I'll have to finish it myself—again," and then walks the report to the boss. He might add a finishing touch or two but is oblivious to the month of research and editing that it took to get the report where it is. Any explanation of that work is interpreted as whining and excuses.

The Superhero can be a valuable asset to a team that has stalled. They make quick decisions, are confident, and enjoy finishing projects. Superheroes enjoy recognition. They prefer to be the leader on a team. They are typically big-idea-thinkers—and small-detail-avoiders. Superheroes are task-oriented, not relation- or process-oriented. Working with them effectively means assigning them a job that they can completely fulfill. Superheroes are task-focused.

Stay or Go? Working with a Superhero can be infuriating and insulting. The most frustrating part is that those who work closely with him see him as being rude and adding little to the project. Management often sees him as the one who gets a project done.

Before deciding whether you want to stay or go, see if you can help the Superhero to be relationship- or process-focused. The next time they try to grab a project, challenge them on it. "Hey, I have been working on this for a month now, and I can finish it up by tomorrow just fine." Or "I already know how it is going to be presented, but if you can help, I would appreciate you getting the final budget from upstairs. Thanks." Or "I appreciate your offer, but I've got this."

Remember, it will take time to change habits. It will take time for you to change how you react to a Superhero, and it will take time for them to change how they react to you. If changing behavior and time do not help, you still have other options before you decide to go. Begin writing down your contributions to projects, and the Superhero's response. Document different projects and who was given credit. Make sure to document the effect this behavior has had on office morale and teamwork. Request a conversation with the Superhero, with a manager or a neutral in the room. Present the facts and the consequences, and be prepared to provide simple suggestions for new behaviors.

Victim

The Victim in this scenario was the younger woman. She must have stated a dozen times that her other coworker did not show up, making sure everyone knew that she was the innocent Victim. Clearly, we should all stop pressuring her for coffee, as she really deserved to be lounging in her tower. She felt betrayed and abandoned. She has clearly set the stage for our charming Superhero to come rescue her. She was running around the coffee shop in a tizzy but accomplishing little. She was too busy blaming her other coworker to take any responsibility. And yes, she was in a frustrating situation. But she was using that as an excuse for her own bad behavior. She was costing herself peace and pride in her work.

A victim role is relationship-focused. If the relationship is not going well, she jeopardizes the process and the task.

Stay or Go? To work effectively with a Victim long term, they will need to stop blaming others and take more personal responsibility. You cannot force them to make this change—but you can take steps to support this change. The Victim, just like the Superhero and the Dragon, is justifying poor behavior because of other people's poor behavior.

Sometimes the Superhero, Victim, and Dragon are truly in a horrible situation, and the wrong that was done to them needs to be discussed:

- Ask the Superhero, Victim, or Dragon in front of you about the original wrong. "You seem a bit out of sorts today—everything okay?"
- Validate their feelings. "Sheesh, that would be really frustrating!"
- Encourage your coworker to take a positive action. "Well, sounds like you have to clean up someone else's mess. How are you going to do that?"

Dragon

You have probably noticed that some of the most intriguing shows and movies nowadays do not have a clear good guy and bad guy. Rather, the characters are complex and multidimensional, with understandable motivations for both their good and their bad actions. (Think about Hulk, Doctor Strange, Batman—complex characters with good and bad sides.) These shows are intriguing because we recognize their characters as closer to reality—there are few people who are truly good or bad. We have all been in situations where we just get fed up, sick of being portrayed as the bad guy so often that we just decide to give up trying to be nice, go with the flow, and become the Dragon.

This was how the older woman at the coffee shop responded. She tried to fix things and take responsibility for getting the shop opened quickly. As time went on, other people messed up, and she was continuously treated disrespectfully. The customers and the younger barista made it painstakingly clear that she had messed up by being late. She reached the point where she said, "Screw it." Which translates to, "I just don't care anymore. Being nice didn't work. Nobody else is being nice, so why should I? I have reached my limit of this feeling and caring stuff. If you back me into a corner, then it's your fault that the claws came out. Being the Dragon gives me back a little bit of the power that I lost—and it feels good."

The Dragon is process-focused. The Dragon has withdrawn from the relationship and doesn't care as much about the end product anymore. She wants to make sure that she is treated fairly during that process and not taken advantage of. She just wants to get things done, without having to worry about everyone's feelings around her. She probably has enough stress that she just can't take on anyone else's stress. Even if she hurts people in the process, she is going to get through that process, regardless of who is in her way.

Stay or Go? To continue working with Dragons, you have to give them space to process their frustrations. Afterwards you can find out what was so upsetting to them. If, eventually, they can see the consequences of their actions, they might be able to change, and then you can probably stay.

WE ARE ALL THE SUPERHERO, VICTIM, AND DRAGON

In the above example, the Coffee Catastrophe, I used a male for the Superhero and females for the Victim and the Dragon. We often have a preferred role, but I do not see those roles as being gender specific. Every one of us has assumed every one of these roles at some point. We want to be the hero. We, victim-like, want to show how wronged we were by the big, bad Dragon. Or, we have been pushed so far that to self-protect we take on the role of the unfeeling, fire-breathing Dragon. Similar types of situations often produce similar results, so you might find that you are often, for example, a Victim at work and a Superhero at home. The important thing is to recognize that we have all adopted our own ways of dealing with conflict.

This is loosely based off of the Karpman Drama Triangle, which says that the three roles we play in conflict are Persecutor, Rescuer, and Victim. This Drama Triangle is important as it shows how all three roles in conflict can be destructive toward the other. In other words—in conflict, we all have a contribution and are very rarely completely innocent. Even if we think we are completely in the right, good ole Karpman says that we probably played a part in getting into conflict.[10]

FORGET THE FAIRY TALE; THIS IS REAL LIFE

Adopting a role of the Superhero, the Victim, and the Dragon all boil down to the same thing: a comfortable excuse for irresponsibility. If you work with someone who often falls into one of these roles, or you recognize any of these in yourself, come back to the question of how do you, how does anyone, take responsibility in your office. I have found that a written agenda and task list at the beginning of a project is one method for keeping everyone accountable.

Another method is by asking questions. Be wary of "why" questions, as these often come across as accusatorial. They end up reinforcing someone's beliefs, instead of helping them to change their beliefs. Instead, ask clarifying questions (What? How? When?) or open-ended questions (What do you think about . . .? What's another way to . . .?). Look at more examples of these types of questions below and consider how they can help you and your coworkers accept responsibility and not fall into a fairy-tale role.

Questions that inspire curiosity, not criticism:

- What do you think is your biggest contribution to this project?
- How do you want to handle hiccups, such as if someone turns in their piece late?
- When do you need this piece handed to you to ensure you can have your piece turned in before the deadline? What steps can we take to ensure that happens?
- How do you think you will best be able to contribute to the group? What about the other people in this group?

- When there is confusion or disagreement, what is the best way for us to communicate that? Email? Quick meeting?
- If no one communicates that there is a disagreement, can we all assume that things are going fine?
- Any other concerns to review before going forward?

TAKEAWAY

Our brains are primed to protect us, especially when they sense danger. Unfortunately, sometimes that protection is pushing us further into conflict. If your brain keeps telling you that you are not at fault, or a situation is too hard to face, or it isn't that bad so let's just ignore it, these are common deflections where your brain is trying to protect you from dealing with the real conflict. It is helpful to do some self-analysis to be able to identify some of the steps your brain takes that keep you in conflict. Recognizing your brain's deflection helps you to step out of that role and be able to face the conflict.[11]

RECOGNIZE, REACTING, AND MY ROLE IN CONFLICT WORKSHEET

When I recognize that there is a conflict, here are the physical changes I notice in myself:

When I react to a conflict, I usually:
____Fight _____Flight _____Freeze

The changes that I notice in my thinking, my muscles, and my instincts (to run, to talk, etc.):

In conflict, I usually take on the role of:
___ Superhero ____Victim ____Dragon

This means that when I am grounded, my core value is (being helpful, supporting others, taking responsibility when things are difficult):

In conflict, I need to take responsibility for:

I need the other person involved to take responsibility for:

Part III

THERE ARE SOLUTIONS!

Part I focused on diagnosing conflict. Part II focused on preparing yourself to resolve conflict. Part IV discusses being at peace with your decision, and finally Part V shows you how to use these skills to prevent future disputes.

But now, for Part III, we will focus on resolving and preventing workplace conflicts. I will be presenting multiple specific suggestions. You have a bit of homework in this section; pick the resolution that resonates most with your situation, but also please prepare a backup in case the situation changes.

26

PREACHING TO THE CHOIR

The single biggest problem with communication is the illusion that it has taken place.

—George Bernard Shaw

When you have had just a splitting-headache of an awful day at work, do you cheerfully go home, joyfully make an excellent meal, and pleasantly serve your family, asking everyone else kindly how their day was and go to sleep peacefully dreaming of fluffy bunnies? Of course not! You return home to your favorite people and vent. You tell your spouse every excruciating detail. You call your friends, your mother, and your friends' mothers.

We all discuss difficult days at work, but let's take a moment and examine why and what are the effects of those conversations.

This venting is known as preaching to the choir. Instead of risking disagreement from an audience, the speaker preaches to the supportive, like-minded choir. The choir, of course, will dutifully listen and agree with the speaker. Call and response. When the speaker expresses outrage at a wrong, the choir will sing, "TralaLAAAA! The outrage! You have indeed been wro-o-onged!" For most of us, we do not have an actual choir following us around, but we do have a metaphorical choir. We call out our feelings of injustice, and our spouses, children, parents, friends, and often, our coworkers, dutifully respond with validating, righteous confirmations of our having been wronged.

WHY DO WE DISCUSS DIFFICULT DAYS WITH OUR PERSONAL CHOIR?

- *We get attention.* If we have been ignored or dismissed all day at work, then venting fulfills a need—negative attention is often better than no attention, after all.
- *We are able to process.* Remember, verbal processors feel the need to talk through something in order to be able to reflect on what happened.
- *Misery loves company.* Nobody wants to go through something difficult by themselves.
- *Talking can be brain medicine.* After a long day, nothing sounds better than a glass of wine and some chocolate. Okay, fine, I'll be honest, a good bottle of wine and a few boxes of chocolate. But this self-medicating, as easy as it sounds, does not do anything to help my brain deal with the problem. It is only delaying the problem. My brain is still screaming out saying, "Hey! I was wronged! You down there, put down the chocolate and listen to me!" And if that lovely brain of yours does not get some attention, it starts to force you to listen. Depression. Exhaustion. Bitterness. Talking through a bad day is actually a great way for your brain to know that you take this seriously, and that it can—should—expect better treatment in the future. If you keep ignoring the bad days and pretending like everything is fine, you are just gaslighting yourself. When many people feel the mental strain of conflict, they take a mental health day—TV, snacks, nap, venting with friends. All of these are fun for a minute, but they do little to alleviate the long-term strain of extended conflict. This must be dealt with for the anxiety to be reduced.
- *Choirs can be validating. (However, they can also be dangerous and misleading!)* When we need to vent about a difficult day, we're typically going to call that friend who agrees with us. The friend who will relate to what we are sharing and tell us what we want to hear. This, however, may not be what we need to hear. So, if we choose to call a particular friend because they will agree with us and tell us what we want to hear, at least acknowledge that. And keep in mind that they will not likely give you honest

feedback unless you press for it. They might also be projecting their own concerns, or working through issues with someone and trying to jump on your bandwagon (encouraging you to say or do what they wish they would have said or done).

ARE THERE POSITIVE EFFECTS FROM CONVERSATIONS WITH OUR CHOIRS?

- *Choirs can help you let go of bitterness and resentment*. Discussing a difficult day with loved friends and family might be all that you need in order to process a workplace hurt. Having a safe place to talk about your frustrations might prevent you from lashing out unfairly at a coworker.
- *Choirs can help you put things in perspective*. Preaching to the choir can also help you see things in a new, proper, or better perspective. Just hearing yourself describe a situation can be what your brain needs to realize that a situation is petty and not worth arguing about.

  To be careful that you are not overly hyping your side of the story, blowing something small out of proportion, you will need some honest feedback. Give yourself time to vent and complain. Once you have talked through it and calmed down a bit, you will likely be more receptive for feedback. Tell your friend, "Okay, thanks for listening. I'm feeling better. So, what do you think? Is it worth doing something? If I do something, what? Am I making a big deal out of nothing?"
- *Choirs can help propel you into action*. Sometimes when you are speaking to your choir, you realize that your situation is serious. You are not being petty, and you're not overreacting. Rather, you're in a workplace situation that requires you to do something. A good friend can help you brainstorm some possible options for next steps and consequences of those actions.

FROM CHOIR LOFT TO WORKPLACE . . .

Your ultimate goal is to be able to do your job effectively. If you have a coworker who is preventing you from doing that, then you need to find a way to work with them so you can get your job done. Yet, the most common responses we receive from our friends are about further punishing the difficult person or separating from them: "Tell the boss." "Don't approve any more of her vacation requests." "Quit—you shouldn't have to take that."

Very rarely will a friend offer a suggestion that requires *you* to change or discuss solutions with the other person. Collaborative approaches are simply not a common response to our calls for comfort from a friend. Instead, your friend is going to try to repair the pain that the other person caused by inflating your ego and insulting the other person. From there, your friend moves on to reinforcing your position on an issue. Speaking to a member of your choir may simply increase the divide between you and your coworker, making it more difficult to relate to them. A friend's job is to make you the good guy, which makes your annoying coworker, by default, the bad guy. It is like a teeter-totter, the higher up you look, the farther down it pushes the other. If they are the Dragon, you get to be the innocent Victim or the Superhero. And when you convince yourself that this is a good versus evil situation, well, anything is justified.

So, how do you stop yourself from going too far down that road? How do you prevent a small conflict from escalating out of proportion? One method is to put your choir's advice into context. Your choir is there to make you feel better, not to tell you the truth. Your choir doesn't know anything about your coworker except for the negative information you share with them, so they do not have a realistic picture. They do not have enough information to offer you worthwhile advice. You know the situation between the two of you better than anyone. You are the one who knows that your coworker is not always an evil person, and you might not always be very good yourself. And once you realize that this is not a good versus evil situation, you are back on track to developing real solutions. The kind of solutions that can produce lasting change and get you to working effectively with the other person.

My favorite solution is not one big thing that will make everything better. Instead, my solution is sewing. I worked with employees in Ukraine in the summer of 2022 as they were coming out of a war. Many were dealing with trauma and broken trust at not feeling protected or valued during the war. And I didn't have a magic trick to make everything better for them. But my advice is to sew with each other. You see, when we picture our coworkers as good versus evil, it is like tearing apart two pieces of fabric. And that hurts because every stitch that was ripped is a stitch that represents the trust, time, and respect that you put into each other. The only way to repair that rip is one small stitch at a time. This is not an easy fix—it really does take many months to repair that trust. But one small stitch at a time sews two people, or teams, or departments back together. And both pieces of fabric become stronger after being sewn together. These stitches are things like:

- Listening when the other person is speaking
- Listening with curiosity instead of judgment
- Validating their concern
- Saying that you are going to do something about their concern
- Actually doing what you say you are going to do
- Telling them/circling back to let them know you did what you said you would

These are tiny steps, but so powerful for uniting an office.

27

WHY I'M RIGHT AND YOU'RE WRONG

The solution described in this chapter examines how our brains reinforce the belief that we are right, even if sometimes we are not. By accepting the possibility that we might be the one who is wrong, then we can take responsibility for our part in resolving the conflict.

I grew up an only child, so I spent twenty years with the unshakable concrete certainty that I was right. Then I got married.

You, of course, are also right. Your logic is sound, you are smart, and goshdarnit people like you.

But why are you so convinced that you are right? Why do we, all of us, need to feel that we are right? One of the best theories to explain your confidence is something called *ingroup formation*, based on the Robbers Cave Experiments.

ROBBERS CAVE THEORY

In 1954, two researchers, Muzafer Sherif and Carolyn Wood Sherif, conducted an experiment[1] in Robbers Cave State Park, Oklahoma. I know, right now you're thinking, "Why is Clare wasting my time talking about a study that is so old?" I'm so glad you asked.

The researchers took 22 very similar 11- and 12-year-old boys to a 200-acre camp and studied them for three weeks. (And that is why there is not a newer, comparable experiment.[2] Could you imagine trying to conduct that same experiment today? "Hello, ma'am. May I borrow your 11- or 12-year-old son for three weeks and conduct experiments on him? Out in the desert where you have no access to him and you don't know what is happening to your son? Ma'am, please put the shotgun down!")

The Sherifs arranged the boys into two groups, the Rattlers and the Eagles. The boys began bonding with their group. Then the boys began disliking the other group. Then the boys began to feel that the only way they could succeed was with their own group. They had decided that their group was better. The interesting thing to note here is that since the boys were so similar academically and athletically and socially, there was *no truth* to thinking their group was better. The groups were equal. However, the boys' brains needed to think that they personally were in the right group. Our brains hate it when we are in limbo or when we have potentially made a mistake, so our brains squash such notions by telling us that we are in the right group.

The researchers identified the following phases when new groups/ teams form:

- *Ingroup formation*: The boys immediately bonded with their own group.
- *Friction phase*: The boys decided that their group was better than the other and they fought aggressively and competitively with the other group.
- *Integration phase*: The researchers proactively created exercises where the boys could only succeed by the two teams having to work together.

Whenever we make a decision (buy a coat, date someone new, start a job), we hope that it is the right decision. Our brain dislikes ambiguity and it wants to know that it is doing the right thing. This is why, just after a change, we go through an ingroup formation phase where our brain convinces itself that it is right. We are in the right group. We started the right job. We seek evidence to support our decision and ignore evidence that contradicts our decision.

A few years ago, I was considering buying a particular new car. I raved about the low cost, the color, and the terrific fuel economy. My husband showed up and pointed out the car's high cost of maintenance, the reviews showing low safety ratings, and how quickly its value depreciated relative to other vehicles. He showed me numbers that clearly pointed out this car was a bad choice. Yet I struggled with it for days—I needed to believe that I had made the right decision. I hadn't, but I was unwilling to let go of my belief that I was right. If I had made the wrong choice, it meant that my pride would be hurt and that I had to do something to deal with that. And, I would have to go find a new car, which was a difficult process that I wanted to avoid. We argued a bit, and we were not able to move past this conflict until I realized that I was stubbornly holding on to the belief that I was right. When I wasn't. I was wrong, but don't tell him I said so.

I spoke about this with Susan Terry, a fellow mediator. She said that this is similar to a child's magical thinking. They think that if they hold on to a concept long enough and wish hard enough, then they might just make it true. And dangit, she was right, that is exactly what I was doing.

INGROUP FORMATION

Now apply this concept to the office. Once you begin working at a new job, you will likely find a few likeable souls. Siya from the mail room, Larry from accounting, or the funny guy who brings the homemade gluten-free doughnuts to the break room. You move through the ingroup formation phase with them and decide that you are in the right place. You have bonded with them, you are wise, your brain is at peace.

But whoa, wait a minute. A new person joins the office and she is horrible. She tells loud jokes, she thinks she is really funny, and she doesn't like gluten-free doughnuts. Clearly, she is wrong. "You is smart, you is kind, you is important," your brain repeats to you. (If you don't get that reference, stop reading, go watch *The Help*, and come back. I'll wait for you.) You are in the right group, she is in the wrong group, that's why *we* don't like her.

Friction Phase

But let's go back and look at the Robbers Cave Experiment for a moment. Remember I said the researchers took 22 *similar* boys? Wait a minute! Does that mean that one group was not faster, smarter, funnier, better? Nope—they were equal. Then why would they think they were better than the other group? Because their brains needed to feel that way. Here's the kicker: It wasn't true. Let that sink in: Our brains will tell us we are right, even when we are wrong. In most cases, our brains prefer wrong information to ambiguity. So instead of waiting to see what this new person might be like, waiting to form a concept, and living in limbo, our brain prefers to fill in the vacuum (see the chapter on the horror vacui) with false information. We make a snap judgment that reinforces our betterness. Again, regardless of truth, we decide our way is the right way.

Integration Phase

The researchers were able to get the two groups of boys, the Rattlers and the Eagles, to work together and bond as a united group. Their notes on this process are very interesting. They pointed out that the two groups were unable to work together as one without an incentive. They also pointed out that simply having a common goal was not enough to get them to work together. Rather, it required two forces: pressure to work together *and* a common goal that united them.

How can this translate to your office? When you clearly know that you are right and have decided that the other person is cuckoo for Cocoa Puffs, it is going to take a concerted effort on two fronts to work together. First, there has to be pressure to work together. This might be pressure from you—simply a decision that you need things to change. It might also be pressure from HR, a manager, or coworkers pushing you to work with a new person. Second, there needs to be a common goal. Perhaps a group project, organizing a new product launch, making gluten-laden doughnuts, or a warning, "Work together on this or you're fired."

TAKEAWAY

If you know you are clearly right about something, chances are that you are right. Obviously, you are very smart since you picked up this book. However, there might be an infinitesimally tiny chance that you are wrong, or that you and the other side are both equal, like the Rattlers and the Eagles, but your brain is just helping you to feel that you are right. Here's the kicker: If your brain is telling you that you are right, then chances are your coworker's brain is also telling her that she is right.

Therefore, if you want to try to find a way to smooth things out in the office, shift away from figuring out who is right or who is wrong. You are simply not objective enough to figure that out when you are in the middle of it. Remember there are two things required to make opposing forces work together: pressure and a common goal. Apply some pressure to the conversation and find a goal that you both have ("we have to get this pitch finished up before Monday or we lose the account"). And know that by even attempting to work with this plebeian that you are probably getting some awesome karma points.

If you are unable to get along with someone, here are some suggestions:

- Don't isolate. Your negative feelings against them will be able to grow unchecked.
- Initiate a conversation. Don't wait for them. You need to take the first step. Because you are better informed and skilled at starting conversations. You have read this book.
- Ask if you can work on something together. A common goal might be the only thing that unites you and gets you both facing the same direction.
- Set realistic expectations. You might not be best friends overnight, but the goal is to open communication enough that you can discuss work.
- Celebrate little victories. Acknowledge, to each other, when things are getting better.

I was speaking with two clients just before writing this chapter, and I gave them this homework about two weeks ago. I asked them both to reach out to each other and find a project to work on together. Today was my check-in with each individually. They both said that things have been so much smoother. They are getting along and able to discuss schedules for the next year. They both said that their departments have commented on the improvement, and said that they are happier coming to work. What is funny is that neither of them had acknowledged it to each other. So I asked permission to share the feedback with the other person involved: Things are better! And I encouraged them from now on to celebrate the victory with each other and acknowledge that the trust is building. And this is the wonderful shift that happens when we stop preaching to the choir and we start talking to each other.

28

FREELANCE PROBLEM-SOLVING

> How wonderful it is that nobody need wait a single moment before starting to improve the world.
>
> —Anne Frank[1]

You are the hero in this movie.

Well, let's assume the movie is about workplace conflict and you are the one who's going to help find a positive way to resolve it—then yes, you are the hero.

(There are some employees who are perfectly content to be Alfred and are happy to let someone else be Batman. There is nothing wrong with that, it's just not what this chapter is about. These Alfreds might call in a mediator, ask HR to step in, tell the manager to fix it, go to trial, or take similar action. They know there are plenty of other people who can play the hero and that they don't need to play that role. Or, maybe Alfred knows that you have read this book and they can call on you to be a hero communicator to help resolve office problems. You. Are. That. Hero.)

Vigilante problem-solving assumes that you want to be the hero and you are ready to resolve things. Ready to fight this fight. You want to take the steps to fix the problem. You are empowered to resolve this dispute. Because now you have all the tools you need.

Let's review what awesome superhero powers you have picked up:

- *Nothing*. You can do nothing. Sometimes this is just a one-time problem and your best bet is to do nothing and let it blow over. And you know that because you have assessed the situation, identified that it was not abusive or repetitive, that it will likely end soon.
- *Quitting*. The other extreme? Quitting. You always have the option to run screaming for the hills and never look back. If the situation is abusive with no help in sight, or your mental health is taking continuous, severe blows, it is probably best to leave and find a greener hill somewhere else.
- *Confrontation*. So, what options do you have in between doing nothing and quitting? Confronting the person about their behavior. Letting them know why their behavior is unacceptable and how they have to change. This might be something as simple as a raised eyebrow, letting them know that their behavior was not respectful. Or it might be a shoulders squared, boots on, cowgirl hat pulled down, "Make that the last time you say that line to me, pardner."
- *Collaboration*. You can also ask the person in question to sit down with you and figure things out. Develop options together. Brainstorm together on how to get out of, around, in front of, or beyond this conflict. So stop. Collaborate and listen.
- *Curiosity*. Ask your coworker, with curiosity, what is going on—and listen. Then explain to them in a way that they can hear what this conflict is like for you. Huge success. Huge. You both approached the conflict with curiosity—now it becomes a shared problem instead of the other person's fault.
- *Improvement*. What if the problem is bigger than just the two of you? What if the company setup created this problem? If so, then it is probably creating the same problem for other people. Here is where you get to put on your most rugged superhero cape and undertake some serious improvement. What changes are needed? Office redesigns? Communication improvements? Better policies? Cultural overhaul? What if *you* became the office facilitator and *you* helped people to work through other problems? You have learned a lot working through this conflict, and you can probably help other people going through similar difficulties.

Whichever path you take, the important thing is that now you know you are not defenseless. You are an armed warrior attacking an invading problem. You have a variety of tools available to you, and you get to choose the best one for the job.

A vigilante problem-solver has the following tools:

- the wisdom to assess the situation,
- the knowledge to help people choose a resolution process,
- the patience to listen to other people's concerns,
- the courage to voice their own concerns, and
- the strength to do something about those.

TAKEAWAY

Freelance problem-solvers take responsibility for resolving a problem. They diagnose the conflict and then find the right resolution for that conflict. They can recognize that there is a systemic issue, a communication problem, a bad policy, or cultural quirks that are hurting the office. They are then able to make a plan for improvement. The real key here, what sets Batman apart from Alfred, is that they have the bravery to push for that change. Making small changes in your office should help you, but it should also begin to help those you work with.

After all, I'm not saying you're Batman. I'm just saying I've never seen the two of you in a room together at the same time.

29

KEEPING AN OFFER IN YOUR POCKET

I was adopted by a stray cat a few years ago. He was a bit skittish but quickly settled in and became calm and cuddly. He had bright orange stripes, which my toddler decided meant we should name him Toby. I didn't see the connection but decided against trying to get a logical explanation out of a toddler. Toby hung around with us for a few weeks, and it appeared he was going to stay, so I decided to take him to the vet for a checkup and to get his shots. Again, I had a toddler at the time, so I knew it wasn't long until the cat's tail ended up in my son's mouth.

I called the vet and made an appointment, gave Toby lunch, and put him in the cat carrier. We drove to the vet and when we opened the cat carrier door, a whirling dervish of hair and orange and spit exploded onto my face. Toby hissed and screamed and scratched. Toby locked eyes with me and I'm pretty sure he said, "Ask yourself one question, 'Do I feel lucky?' Well, do ya, punk?" Then he ran off. Vet assistants came out and tried to lure Toby inside—no success. After an hour of desperate searching, we all decided Toby's new residence was the vet's parking lot and I went home to disinfect my wounds.

What happened?

Toby had been such a calm, predictable cat. But I think something was triggered for him as we drove to the vet. He was boxed in. He couldn't get out. This family—which used to make him feel safe—had become his captor. He resented us. He feared us. He attacked us. He no longer saw us as providing things for him (food, water, hugs, etc.), but denying him of what he wanted (freedom).

When you first start at a new job, it feels like the land is flowing with milk and honey. The air is full of promise. You are getting a paycheck. You have new potential best friends right around the cubicle.

And then something happens. It could be that you didn't get an expected raise. You are pulled from working on a project you were excited about. You find out your partner is consistently late. Or you have to work late and miss out on a few key family events. The honeymoon is over. A seed of resentment and disenchantment creeps in. And once that seed is there, any little nuisance can water it into blossoming bitterness.

As resentment puts down roots, you begin to forget everything your job is providing you. Instead, you focus on all of the things your job is denying you. It might be that your job has cost you peace of mind. It might be keeping you from the pay raise you thought you earned, working on a project that you are interested in, working with people you get along with, or costing you the respect that you deserve.

What happened is that your perspective changed. Your workplace is no longer a place that offers you things you need (stability, satisfaction, respect, financial security, etc.), but it is a place that is caging you. You begin speaking in terms of "if only." If only I worked at a place where I was respected, valued, paid higher. If only I worked at a place where my coworkers had a clue, had manners, had an ounce of respect, took responsibility, stopped complaining, showed up on time, showed up at all, and so on. (FYI—marriage counselors say this is one of the most destructive things we can do to a marriage,[1] begin daydreaming the "if onlys." If only he picked up more, if only she was more romantic, if only she was funnier, if only he was Jason Momoa. Once our brain begins fantasizing about a different reality, we start losing the motivation to work on this reality.)

When you see your workplace as restricting you, you begin to feel caged, where everything you want is right outside the cage. Once you feel that your workplace has put a cage on you, it has become bad. Your workplace is now a battleground of good versus evil. And all is fair, after all, in war. So even if you do not consciously realize it, you begin to make little justifications. "Who cares if I show up 5 minutes late—Morenike is always 15 minutes late!" "It's okay if I don't finish up that project today. To put up with the things that I do in this place—I deserve a break." "They stuck me in this dingy cubicle, I at least deserve to take this Swingline stapler." And you have now become a suboptimal, less-than-effective worker because you feel caged.

GETTING A POCKET OFFER

The next logical step is to begin looking at other opportunities. As you read other job descriptions, they all sound perfect. You see yourself walking into a land of opportunities and experiencing the same honeymoon you did at your current workplace.

What happens when you receive an offer to work somewhere else? You now have a *pocket offer*.[2] A pocket offer is an offer for something else that you can keep handy—and you may or may not choose to take advantage of it. But notice now that you are no longer caged. Now you have the world at your fingertips. You are in charge. Instead of being denied what you want, you are now being offered what you want in two different places. You might decide to go to a different office, or you might stay where you are.

But here is the key: You cannot carry a pocket offer around forever. You can't live with one foot always out the door. You need to make a decision. So, let's say you stay at your current job. You have decided that even with your crazy coworker, you are getting enough out of that job that you have decided to put up with it. You decided that the benefits of your job are worth the downsides. You know you could go somewhere else whenever you want. But you have chosen, at least for now, that you are getting more from your current office.

Notice how different that feels. You are no longer trapped; you are in control. When annoyances happen, they are easier to deal with because you have opted to deal with them. You know that putting up with those annoyances is worth it to stay at this job. When you are working with an offer in your pocket, you are no longer the victim. You are invested and empowered in your current workplace.

TAKEAWAY

Even though it feels like it, you are not shackled to your job. (Unless you are physically shackled to your job, then please call me. I will gladly take your case.) Don't let your situation control you; you control your situation. If you don't like your job, stop being angry about it or being a victim to it—change it! Maybe that means changing your role, your tasks, or maybe it means changing companies. Maybe it means changing the communication patterns in your office, or designing a dispute resolution system. But don't let a bad situation result in a bad life—you deserve better.

Changing the communication pattern is completely possible. I worked in an office years ago that was built on gossip. The employees bonded by making fun of the boss. I began to feel uncomfortable with it, because I genuinely liked our boss. It was too disingenuous to be nice to him and then sit silent while people joked about him. I remember clearly one day, very quietly, I said, "I don't think that's true." After an awkward silence, the conversation shifted. It took one more time in a meeting where I disagreed with the gossip. And after that they stopped joking about him in front of me. I started taking responsibility to change the conversation and bring up something else that was funny. Perhaps they still made fun of him without me knowing, but I sincerely think it became less and less common. I felt a bit more peace and trust in the office. It was a really simple move, and I was nervous at the time, but looking back on it I can understand the power of putting your foot down and saying I don't want to have that type of conversation anymore.

Suavius cum difficultate is a Latin phrase meaning things are sweeter after difficulty. What this means is that we appreciate things more after we have had to work hard for them. So, yes, this choice might have been hard, but you made the choice to stay and go through it, so you are able to appreciate it even more.

30

DELEGATING DISPUTES

My husband and I decided to paint our house. I loved it. See, most of my work is very cerebral, spent hunched over a keyboard. So I relished the opportunity to move and create something. I grabbed my roller brush and can of paint and went to town. No taping off, no drop cloth—I had never really done this before, obviously—and I began putting Garden Stone Gray paint wherever I could reach.

While I was happily slapping away at the bottom half of the house, my husband's job was to paint the top half. We have a tall house, with some interesting nooks and crannies. Most of it he painted quite easily, hauling a 48-foot ladder all around our home. However, in order to reach some of those nooks and crannies, he had to be creative. And when it comes to heights and husbands and creativity, wives get nervous. What he rigged up was rather genius, but still too high for me to be comfortable with. To get to one particular high point, he constructed this amazing contraption that involved a tractor, the aforementioned 48-foot ladder, cable wires, a backpack filled with a paint sprayer, and duct tape. Because what dangerous project would be complete without duct tape? (I would share the picture of this gauntlet, but I don't want to tempt OSHA to descend with a list of citations.)

When the painting was done, we patted ourselves on the back for getting it done and for all of the money we saved.

And then he noticed my drips. And spills.

Did you know that paint is actually not that easy to clean up? Taking care of that mess took a long time. And this was time that I probably should have spent doing things like, oh, I don't know, feeding my poor children.

(By the way—my husband's painting getup of course inspired lots of other painting ideas on the street—by people who are less mechanically gifted than my husband. Many wives on our street doubled both their chardonnay intake and their life insurance policies on their husbands, watching them splashing paint around while climbing up their own Tractor and Duct Tape Tower of Terror.)

We agreed after this mess, that maybe he shouldn't use a tractor to paint, and maybe I should use a drop cloth. Or a contractor.

WHY WE DON'T DELEGATE

There is a certain pride and self-reliance that comes with taking care of things ourselves. I had a blast changing our walls to a soft gray. It was quite satisfying. And once my husband survived his death-defying-duct-tape feat, I think he also felt quite proud. In most of the previous chapters, I have suggested methods for solving problems yourself. You are, after all, the one who is most knowledgeable about the problem and most invested in the dispute. Most problems can and should be handled by your lovely self.

Consider some reasons why we prefer to do things ourselves:

- We want to know that it is done, and this gives us immediate knowledge and control.
- We don't want to take the time to bring in someone else.
- We don't want to pay someone else.
- We want it done the way we want it done.
- We take pride in having done it ourselves.
- We don't want a fuss. We don't want to make a huge, embarrassing hoopla over something that might already be embarrassing.
- Organizational culture rewards those who are proactive and take responsibility.[1]

WHY WE SHOULD DELEGATE

There are times, though, when solving a problem by yourself is not the right decision. What are some signs that we should delegate the dispute?

- You have already tried to fix it yourself.
- You have tried to discuss the conflict with the other person, and they have made it clear they are not willing to listen.
- You do not feel safe resolving the dispute yourself.
- Resolving it yourself is taking too much time away from your job or other responsibilities.

What happens when you resolve a problem that you shouldn't be resolving on your own? Just like with my painting attempts, when you get in over your head with too big of a problem, it

- makes a gigantic mess,
- is dangerous,
- is a huge waste of time,
- takes you away from doing what you should be doing, and
- doesn't address the problem well.

There's also this:

- Other people may have followed your lead and made their own mess—just like all of the other painting contraptions that started showing up on our street.

Most relationship communication problems can be solved by talking to your coworker. But let somebody else handle more complex problems.

What does your employer want you to be doing? Your job.

Did you know that when we are in a big conflict at work, some estimates, according to Dan Dana,[2] suggest that we spend about 25 percent of our time per week distracted by the conflict? Your mind wanders, you come in late, you spend an hour on your lunch break updating your coworkers on the latest gossip. This means people wrapped up in a conflict spend more than a day a week fixating on something other than their job. So crazy, but when you think about it—isn't it true? Let's say someone makes $50,000 a year, and they have been dealing with conflict for a year, then that conflict has already cost the company $10,000? Not to mention the time of everyone else they have looped into the conflict. And even when you are working, are you able to fully focus? When you are really upset at someone or about something, are you ever operating at full capacity? Or are you slow, wandering, erratic? Your brain is chugging away trying to fix the problem instead of doing your job.

Again, what does your employer want you to be doing? Your job. If the conflict has become so bad that it is eating up your time, and you haven't been able to make any progress by talking to the other person, it's time to tell your manager, "Hey, we gotta solve this thing so that I can fully focus on work." A few examples below:

- If the situation involves abuse or continued harassment
- If the situation is based on a perceived power imbalance or prejudice, such as racism, ageism, or sexism
- If you feel that you don't have the skills to represent your interests in this situation, or with this person
- If you have tried and you are not making any progress

Ask your manager to bring in someone, a mediator, a facilitator, a coach, and set aside a long lunch to go talk through it. It is usually worth paying someone to come in and mediate for a few hours so that the office can get back to work.

Many companies are able to cover the cost of hiring help through their EAP insurance. These employee assistance programs will often pay for a mediator or a facilitator to come in and help you talk through options and develop an agreement. You can ask your HR office, or call your insurance provider if your HR office is unsure of your benefits (or if you would like to explore options before discussing your concerns with HR).[3]

TAKEAWAY

Of course, our first step should be that we all make an effort to resolve the conflicts around us. But after multiple failed attempts, it probably makes sense to stop pouring your time into it. Bring in an expert to speed up the process, resolve the problem, so that you can get back to your life. Instead of trying to tackle the problem yourself and realize that all you did was make a huge mess.

31

OPTIONS FOR EMPOWERING YOURSELF

During my doctoral research, I worked with approximately 100 small businesses. One of the challenges common in smaller businesses is that they often don't have a separate HR department. That means that when an employee of a small business has a personnel issue, a workplace conflict, a typical initial response from their overworked business owner boss is something like, "Figure it out (yourself)." These employees often state that their crew is so close, almost like family, and they know their boss would provide help in figuring out the problem *if they really needed it*. But in order not to be another burden on a busy small business owner already wearing too many hats, the employees wanted options for figuring out conflicts themselves.[1]

The first thing that I would show these committed souls is the Conflict Resolution Continuum, which helps parties to visualize the options available to them. It also shows that as parties relinquish control over the process, they also relinquish control over the outcome.

The Conflict Resolution Continuum depicts options that are available to employees. These vary in the amount of money and time that it will take, and also in the amount of control that an employee has over the outcome.

OPTIONS FOR RESOLVING CONFLICT

- *Avoidance.* You try not to think about your conflict.
- *Negotiation.* You talk with the other person until one person wins.
- *Collaboration.* You and the other person talk through it together until both win.
- *Mediation.* Someone guides you and the other person through it.
- *Arbitration.* Someone tells you both what to do after each side explains their situation.
- *Litigation.* Someone tells you both what to do after each side's attorney states "the facts."

CREATING A POSITIVE OUTCOME

Initially, people often think they will have the greatest result with the least amount of personal responsibility if they "just sue 'em." In other words, they want to hand control of the conflict to another person, have someone else take care of it.[2]

The data from my study, however, showed a different picture. I examined which processes resulted in the most positive outcomes. The positive processes involved

- employees who understood the conflict,
- multiple face-to-face conversations with the other person,
- control over the outcome,
- a manager who supported those conversations, and
- access to help if they needed it.

I created a five-step guide for managers and HR offices to use to create positive conflicts. While you might not be in a position to implement all of this, perhaps you could suggest some of these. Maybe put these in a proposal, your boss is awed by your brilliance, moves you into management to implement these steps, and then you don't have to work around that Inappropriate Ivan or The Dudette anymore. Conflict solved. You're promoted. Win-win.

I distilled these steps into the TEACH[3] acronym:

- *Train.* Train employees in communication early. Employees and managers develop office communication and conflict protocols and revise them as needed. If employees have access to resources to understand what is happening in a conflict, they respond effectively instead of overreacting out of fear or anger. In other words, they are able to keep their logical prefrontal cortex engaged instead of shifting to a fight, flight, or freeze response that is controlled by their amygdala.[4]

- *Engage*. The happiest employees reported that their managers frequently engaged with them. Managers had frequent team-building meetings and relationship check-ins. This allowed employees to feel comfortable enough to talk to their supervisor about a conflict, and it gave supervisors enough trust in their employees to know that they would resolve it well.
- *Address*. When a conflict arises, managers must support employees in taking steps to address the conflict immediately and directly. This might mean an ombuds office, an anonymous complaint box, or even giving the employees an extra hour at lunch to go and talk through it.
- *Choose*. All employees involved in a conflict need to have a conversation about it, using effective communication techniques. Employees should be involved in choosing the process and designing the outcome. A manager's role is to provide a few choices for resolving the conflict that employees can choose from. The sweet spot is three to four choices. Less than that feels too limiting or constrictive, more than that feels overwhelming. This term is known as choice overload, or overchoice.[5]
- *Help*. Bring in an objective employee, then a staff mediator, then an external mediator if needed to help parties in resolving the conflict. Many employees reported that even if they didn't exercise the option, they felt safer trying to sort out the conflict themselves knowing that they had access to a dispute resolution expert if they needed one.

TAKEAWAY

Conflicts have a better chance of ending well if employees are able to design a process to talk to each other. The five-step TEACH process allows employees to know that they can go and talk to their manager when they need to and that they have support to work through a process.

32

RISING TIDES RAISE ALL BOATS

Coworkers gossip. It's a fact. No one plays the game of Operator or Telephone better than a whispering office.

Even if you have told only a few people about your office feud, chances are the rest of the office already knows. Office spats take their toll on everyone. The secretary is wondering if he should have both of you in the same meeting. The assistant needs to know if he has to seat you separately on your next business trip. It causes stress on everyone.

It is also the best entertainment. Let's face it—your clash is now the Super Bowl of office excitement. Everyone has popped their corn and is scrutinizing what play you will make next, and what counterattack your opponent will deploy.[1]

Most people listen to bad advice in such situations, advice that may have been given only to pump up the excitement and the ratings. Let's be honest—our friends may like us, but they might like us more when we entertain them. The simple fact is that most of our friends say what they think we want them to say, or say things that add to the drama. Typically, they are not giving us good advice for de-escalating the conflict. Instead, they suggest plays that only fuel the conflict.

Fast Company magazine put together these signs that your friends are giving you bad advice:[2]

1. The person isn't qualified. They don't have conflict resolution advice, or they don't know you very well or what your long-term goals are.
2. The advice is not specific to you. It might be something that they have heard or, more likely, what they wish they had done in a similar situation.
3. The person is giving advice but not really listening to your concerns.
4. The advice is focused only on the end result, and not the process. Many people will end up accepting a different outcome if they feel that the process was fair. So if you instead focus on developing a process that is fair, you might both end up with a more satisfying outcome.
5. The advice is charged. The person might have a stake in the conflict, and they are reacting out of their own self-interest.
6. The advice ruffles your instincts. The simple fact that you are reading this book shows that you have good instincts. Well, at least I think so. So, trust your instincts, and if your Spidey-sense is going off, listen to it.

Take a moment and think about what an opportunity you have. You are in a bad situation with a Honey Badger, or Snappy Sally, and you have every excuse to behave impolitely back. But what if you don't? What if you do something crazy like go for an unexpected two-point conversion instead of the one-point extra kick? What if you don't let your coworker hook you into their rudeness?

Well, you are really doing something incredible. Something that most politicians and reality TV stars have yet to figure out: It's okay to repay rudeness with kindness. It's more than okay; it's mind-blowing. It's game-changing. It's creating a new tone in your relationship with your coworker and a new standard in your office.

1. It can be as simple as not engaging in a mean conversation.
2. Or take it a step further, and if someone says something mean or gossipy, say, "I don't think that's true."
3. Or even one step further, and say, "I don't want to talk about her behind her back. I'm not comfortable with that."

Hopefully your coworker recognizes the change and responds back with thoughtfulness and magnanimity. Maybe they won't. That's on them, not you.

But if you are able to positively respond in an office conflict, everyone will know. You chose to respond maturely in a way that lays the groundwork for effective conversations down the road. And, by making that choice, you have just laid the groundwork for powerfully solving office tussles yet to come. (Yup, you definitely sound like a hero.)

This creates a precedent for good habits in the future. A blueprint for the new unspoken office culture: "Hey pardner—we don't tolerate unkindness around these parts."

And you can feel a collective sigh of relief take place in an office heading in a new direction on a higher road. Instead of the exciting Super Bowl of conflict, the staff is now tuned in to a feel-good Hallmark movie. The spice level of the entertainment might be dwindling down, but, more important than that, the office stress level is going down too.

TAKEAWAY

Office gossip is one of the most pervasive and destructive forces in tearing down a company.

When I am giving a training on the effect of office conflict, I hold up a clear glass of water. Then I put in one drop of food coloring. Just one. And I show them how quickly just one bit of gossip can spread to the whole office and taint it. Your office has changed. People can't fully relax or trust each other now.

You can tell if it is gossip if you are sharing information without a positive intent. And it can form a habit. And it takes you being aware of it to break that habit. But the more you take a stand not to allow gossip, you start to find that your own habits change. You start to see people in a more positive light. And this eventually becomes your new habit.

If you know that your office is guilty of it, own up for your contribution and take a stand to halt gossip going forward. There will be an awkward transition while you find new things to talk about, but it will be worth it. And as you take a step to raise the standard, then the standard will begin to rise for everyone in the office. And this rising tide will raise all of the boats around you. So that your one small step will slowly increase morale for all of your coworkers.

33

FAITH-BASED PROBLEM-SOLVING

For many, there is an additional, spiritual component to dispute resolution. And no, I'm not saying to buy a voodoo doll to torture your coworker or pray that he is mysteriously struck down by lightning! I'm pointing out that for the many people who follow an organized faith, they might look to their spiritual resources for extra wisdom and conflict training. This helps you to choose an option for resolving disputes that is in line with your value set.

BUDDHISM

Buddhism teaches that in order to understand conflicts, we must first understand ourselves. This helps us to understand our part in the conflict and that we must work together to resolve the disagreement. According to Ajahn Pasanno,[1] a distinguished Canadian Buddhist monk living and teaching today, settling differences is akin to everyone working together to prevent a ship from sinking. Everyone must recognize that they have their own part to play in the solution and, if they each take responsibility for their role and plug the holes or bail water, then collectively they can save the ship and sail on.

We will all encounter many people with different views from ourselves and situations that trigger us. Buddhism instructs us to realize it's our job not to become upset by this: When walking on thorns, it is our responsibility to wear shoes. By taking responsibility to keep ourselves at peace, we then are able to engage in fruitful conversations with many viewpoints and resolve thorny circumstances with greater ease.

CHRISTIANITY

In the Christian faith, the Bible advocates working through problems face-to-face. Matthew 18:15–17 tells us, "If your brother sins against you, go and show him his fault in private. If he listens to you, you have won your brother. If he will not listen, take one or two others along, so that every matter may be established by the testimony of two or three witnesses. It they still refuse to listen, tell it to the church, treat them as you would a tax collector."

What's interesting about this passage from Scripture is that it begins by clearly saying someone has sinned against you. You have been wronged! You should be compensated! You should go to court and prove your case; you could win a lawsuit! But, while you might win a lawsuit, you could lose your brother. So, even when you have been wronged by someone, the Scripture is saying that we should still go and talk to them one-on-one to try to work through it. It doesn't say to confront them or shame them or judge them for what they have done. Because the goal is to have them listen so that you can win the relationship.[2]

The other thing I like about this section of Scripture is that it gives you a plan. (1) Go and talk to them—take personal responsibility. (2) If that doesn't work, bring in help. Communal responsibility. As in, the company needs to take responsibility to solve this situation as well. Try to solve the problem on your own, but then the next step should be to bring in another person.

Another favorite concept of mine comes from the Catholic faith and is called agathokakological.[3] Mind you, I can't pronounce it, but it is still one of my favorite concepts. It means that every person is comprised of both good and evil. This has two important impacts on our understanding of conflict. First, realizing that there is rarely a "good guy" and a "bad guy." Rather, it is more likely that both people involved in the conflict contributed toward it escalating but also have valid points that need to be addressed.

The second takeaway is understanding that humans are complex beings, good and evil, with both self-interest and "other-interest" (if that term goes viral, I'm taking credit for it). It means that if I win, but I destroy you in the process, I won't be fully satisfied. For us to feel fully satisfied with the resolution of a conflict, both our self-interest and our interest in others must be satisfied.

Gamification/Winners Theory takes this one step further. When someone wins, they feel a rush of serotonin, the feel-good chemical. However, when they win as a group, or both people in the argument win, they experience a higher dose of serotonin. In other words, I feel better when I won *and* the other person won.[4]

ISLAM

The Qur'an 41:34 tells us to "repel evil for what is better; then you will see that one who was once your enemy has become your dearest friend." These words bring hope to even the darkest workplace. By improving our communication habits, halting office gossip, and taking responsibility for our actions, we can change the office culture. I often see that many office clashes are between people with similar personalities who just need to treat each other with a bit more respect. Indeed, someone who was once your enemy could even become your BFF.

Abdullah ibn Abbas, cousin to Muhammad and learned teacher, elaborates on this, saying, "If someone behaves in an ignorant way with you, you must respond to his ignorance with tolerance." This one is a bit tougher, as it requires you to be the bigger person. If someone is unkind, ibn Abbas is saying that we need to continue to be kind to them. This prevents conflicts from escalating. This part of the Qur'an says that by listening and being kind, we can replace storminess with a calm in our relationships.[5] Also, by you continuing to respond with kindness, you will likely be improving the office culture.

JUDAISM

"Waheb in Suphah."

This is a Jewish term meaning in translation, "There is Love at the End." Rabbi Sachs[6] tells multiple examples of conflict, for the sake of conflict, where people argued knowing that there was love at the end. "When two sides fight, not with weapons but with ideas, they recognize that their very disagreement presupposes an agreement; about the value of argument itself." Rabbi Sachs tells stories of scholars choosing to disagree over different interpretations of the

Torah because they felt that the arguing was bringing them closer to Heaven. Instead of blindly accepting something that was written, discussing the ideas helped them to better understand it and helped them to become closer to others in the conversation.

Rabbi Sachs says that there are seven requirements for these arguments to "lead to Heaven," and to preventing a heated debate that "would not lead to Heaven":

1. Respect different interpretations.
2. Listen with curiosity—try to understand the different interpretations.
3. Never use force, be it physical, psychological, or emotional force.
4. If the process is fair, you must be willing to accept a different outcome or idea than what you were expecting.
5. View the disagreement not as conflict, but as a collaborative activity in pursuit of truth.
6. Accept this is a holy and legitimate part of life.
7. Keep talking.

And if we all learned to follow these principles when arguing, I do believe that "There is Love at the End."

TAKEAWAY

If values—faith-based, community-derived, self-determined, or a mix—play an important part in your life, then these are a few initial suggestions for incorporating those values into your conflict resolution adventure.

34

CHANGING THE SYSTEM

In a previous chapter I discussed how rising tides raise all boats. In other words, if you stop the vicious cycle in your own office relationship, it will begin to trickle into other skirmishes and set a higher standard for other office relationships. The ripple effect.

But in attempting to unravel a knotty mess, you might have also uncovered something deeper at your workplace. While most office conflicts are disagreements between two employees (according to the International Ombuds Association, about 75 percent of the reported workplace conflicts were relational issues[1]), some are also due to systemic or cultural issues. A systemic issue means the system itself is causing people to have issues.

REAL-LIFE EXAMPLE

A large home improvement store was having a problem with squabbling employees and a large number of sick days. They brought someone in to examine the matter. This person began to review the sick days and the complaints of arguing employees and noticed they all seemed to occur the first week of every month. She began asking supervisors what might be different about that first week. They didn't have an explanation.

The neutral then asked employees about that first week and the source of the conflict—and they were more than ready to give an answer. Hourly employees were not paid until the seventh of every month, after the total intake from the month before had been calculated. This meant that employees were biting their nails the first week of every month, when their rent was due, and their student loans, and their internet bills, and so on. They just kept hoping that their paycheck would cash before their other checks bounced. This meant that for a week, most of the company's workforce was under extreme stress. The system had a flaw in it, and that flaw was putting unnecessary stress on the bulk of its employees. The company took a few months to move its invoices and accounts around and was able to begin paying its employees on the first of the month. This systemic change resulted in a systemic improvement. The entire company had a decrease in stress. Employees were able to focus more on their job rather than on their late rent payment.

Take a moment and think about what is going on in your office. Systemic issues are trickier to identify since they do not have a face or a name. If you think through the conflict in your office, you might find yourself saying, "I'm okay, you're okay, but our office is totally screwed up!" This is a sign that maybe something in the system is causing conflict in your office.

Managers report that about one-third of conflicts are systemic conflicts.[2] This suggests some small issues that employees are dealing with could actually be a symptom of a larger issue. The nice thing about systemic conflict is its impact: As soon as systemic conflict is diagnosed and people begin to resolve it, life for everyone in the company can improve.

WHAT DO YOU DO ABOUT SYSTEMIC CONFLICT?

Well, to be honest, the answer to this one might be nothing. If you are one person who is already busy with a full-time job, the best answer might be to alert someone in management about the need for change. But if part of your job overlaps with some of the company responsibilities, then you might be able to play a small part in creating change.

Ben Zander, the conductor of the Boston Philharmonic Orchestra, discourages his players from a sense of hierarchy. Some players had felt unimportant, that they were only a fifth chair violin, or a second chair flute. But Mr. Zander requires his players to "lead from any chair." He tells them that whatever position they are in, they need to take a sense of ownership. They need to be a leader for what they have control over. And I encourage you to do the same. You might be leading from your cubicle chair, or from the custodian's closet, but that is what you have control over. Bring a sense of peace from that space, and slowly you can change the system. I also recommend recruiting others and asking HR and management to support you in changing a toxic system.[3] As a reminder, your rising tide will raise all of the boats around you.

Office systems are complex. They require careful analysis, an understanding of the nature and habits of systems and how each particular system functions, and a commitment from everyone in the system in order to initiate change. So you will probably need to do some good convincing of the right people. To encourage the right people that a workplace system needs to change, you need to have an answer for how this will benefit them and the organization. You will probably need to speak with a few different people, and these people will all be motivated by different things.

Here are some suggested motivators for different audiences:

- *Small business owners*. Explain to a small business owner how resolving a systemic conflict will save your company money. For a specific breakdown of how much this conflict is costing your company, look at *Controlling the Costs of Conflict* by Karl Slaikeu and Ralph Hasson.[4] This book is a checklist that will help you to arrive at a specific number of how much conflict is costing your company. The quick summary is to figure out how much time you are spending each month thinking about the conflict, reacting to the conflict, and trying to clean up/fix the conflict. Then figure out how many people are involved. Then take a guess at how much those people make in a month (yeah, this part can feel a bit awkward). Multiply the time by the people by their salary. This will give you an estimate of what that unresolved conflict is costing your company every month. The main purpose is to show how much time can be saved by addressing conflict.
- *HR*. Show your HR department information outlining the cost of conflict to a company that calculates the amount of time people take off of work due to conflict and that conflict severely reduces productivity and quality. Explain how resolving conflict can also reduce turnover.[5] You can show your HR office the cost of

conflict in terms of financial implications, but also the emotional and mental consequences of sustained conflict.

- *Supervisor*. When you present the systemic problem to your immediate supervisor, come armed with a solution. If possible, also have a plan for how you can help to fix the situation. If your office, for example, had the issue I described where employees were being paid on the seventh of every month, you can show your supervisor what you discovered about the environmental/situational source of increased squabbles—and that it's not your coworkers. Then explain how you have already planned out a solution, perhaps you've written a draft of a memo to finance and HR, and how you would be willing to make a presentation to them about how these changes would create an immediate improvement in employee morale that would ripple far and wide across the organization. Your supervisor might have concerns that this new undertaking will distract you from your current work. Be prepared to discuss with her what you have already done at home and what you will need to do during office hours. You might need an estimate of how much time this will take, but follow up with a quick reminder of how much time and money this will save.
- *Coworkers*. Coworkers can become very defensive of their office culture. Even if the improvements seem obvious to you, don't be disheartened if your wisdom isn't immediately appreciated. Give people a few days and bring it up again. Point out specific examples of the systemic flaw as they happen. If people still aren't on board, get curious as to why. Your plan might need refining and your coworkers may have valuable suggestions. Even better! They will feel involved and invested! The coming cultural change will have been a group effort. These little shared victories build group cohesion and keep people motivated for moving forward.[6]

TAKEAWAY

Making a major change to an office involves time and planning, and likely some up-front costs. But if you are willing to do the work, then your office will benefit from the decreased costs and improved culture.

If you are interested in this work, I recommend beginning by reading Jan Martinez's work about system consulting and design, specifically her book[7] on dispute system design, and then reaching out to management or consultants for help.

Part IV

DECIDING TO STAY OR GO

35

IS YOUR GUT SAYING GO?

Deciding the situation is serious enough that you need to go can be a difficult decision. Paying attention to your reactions can help you decide if this is a temporary annoyance or a chronic problem. If your emotions continue to be strong and are affecting the rest of your life, this is likely your body telling you to get the heck out of there.

STRONG EMOTIONS ARE A CLUE

There are certain emotional red flags. Anger. Resentment. Depression. Withdrawal. Snapping at others. Bitterness. Smiling to your coworker's face, then mumbling "jerk" as he walks away.

These emotions and behaviors don't mean that you are losing it. It is your brain's way of saying, "Hey! This is wrong! Do something about this!" These emotions are valuable information. They shouldn't be suppressed or ignored. If you are noticing these misgivings bubbling up, pay attention to them. Your brain is checking in with you, "Hey I thought we had decided that we were worth more than this. Was I wrong? Is this really how we are okay with being treated?" And your brain is eagerly watching to see if you are going to stand up for yourself, or if your brain needs to reevaluate its worth. Maybe lower its self-image to say, "Oh, I guess things have changed. I guess we don't need to be treated that well." You have begun gaslighting yourself.

It's common for people to say, "I can handle this. It's not worth making a fuss. I don't want to be the one to cause trouble—what will they think of me? I just need to go home and grab a beer and forget about this."

If you have a day or two like this once in a while, well, that's life. There is no perfect job out there. Every job requires a bit of struggle sometimes. Every one of your coworkers is going to have a bad day from time to time, and perhaps take it out on you at some point—and you just might snap and take out one of your bad days on them at some point as well.

But if you start telling yourself this day after day, and you have a month of bad days, then it is time to realize something: *The conflict is holding you hostage.*[1]

- This is a chronic problem that is not getting better on its own.
- This situation is turning me into a bad employee—and my boss is not getting her money's worth out of me when I'm too focused on this situation.
- Life is too short to dread going to work.
- I am the only one who can create the job I want.
- If I don't say something, no one else will.
- I need to say it in a way that will make a change—not just hurt people.

And . . .

- If I have communicated that I need things to change and nothing is changing, then I have a decision to make.

SHOULD I STAY OR SHOULD I GO?

If you stay, what changes can you make? Can you move to a different office? Be assigned to a different project? Change how you communicate (more email and less face-to-face)? Can you change your attitude about the situation—remember that you chose to stay and you are not the victim? Can you set up clear communication standards about what you will not accept? Can you be specific about what your goals are? Write them down like this:

I want to get ______________________________ from my job
and I need ______________________________ to get there.

If you go, don't stay tied to this office. In other words, say what you need to but don't say anything you will regret. You don't want to walk into your new office with guilt. Make sure you are clear with yourself about what it was that led you to this decision, and make sure you don't walk into the same situation somewhere else. Be careful about complaining too much about your old office in your new office. This gives the impression that you are someone who might not ever be happy. Instead, find another place to talk it through—such as with family or friends.

The US Bureau of Labor Statistics reports that from May 2021 to May 2022, there were a total of 72 million people who changed jobs.[2] This number is increasing annually as job transience and short-term gigs become more common. This trend began during the pandemic, but it seems that this is becoming the norm. One downside of short-term jobs is not having enough time to grieve the previous job and celebrate the new job. This means that you might be pulling the negative baggage from your old job into your new job, instead of leaving it back where it needs to be.

I appreciated these suggestions from Eggcellent Work[3] for transitioning to a new job:

- Give yourself time. It takes between 3 and 12 months to feel comfortable at a new job, yet 33 percent of new hires quit within the first 6 months.
- Be patient with yourself. You will make mistakes; forgive yourself, learn from them, and move on.
- Celebrate little victories. As you feel yourself becoming more competent, take pride in yourself.
- Utilize resources. Ask questions. Connect with your managers. Attend trainings. In other words—create a foundation that will help you succeed.
- Find out your manager's expectations. There is nothing more disheartening than thinking you are doing a good job only to find out you were aiming at the wrong target. So check in with your manager frequently about what they would like.

TAKEAWAY

Strong emotions are your body's way of asking you to fix a problem. Pay attention! If you have tried to fix the problem in your office and it's not getting better, don't ignore your body's emotional warnings, because those feelings will squish out in other places.

I told one of my clients to picture their conflict like a small balloon that they were trying to squish and hide with their hands. The tighter they squeezed it, the more the balloon squished out in between their fingers. And conflict always finds a way to squish out. Like insomnia, yelling at your family, or getting snappy with your friends. If your gut is tied in knots, listen to it. This is not a healthy place for you.

36

WHAT ARE YOU WILLING TO DO?

When I have a free Saturday morning, I always face the same dilemma: *Do I clean or do I play?*

If I clean, I would probably find my sink underneath my dishes. If I clean, the house will feel more comfortable, and I will probably enjoy the rest of my day more. If I clean, I will stay on top of the mess before it eats me alive. If I clean, I can take pictures of my house later and post them on Facebook, Instagram, TikTok, whatever.

If I play, I will know that I'm truly living my life. If I play, maybe the mental rest I allow myself will give me strength for the rest of the week. If I play, I will enjoy myself. If I play, I will spend time doing something wonderfully fun, and bonding and memory building with my family, or shopping with Alison or Shahalie or my mom.

I know that you all face this same dilemma. Seriously, we are trying to colonize Mars, but we don't have a robot to put away our dishes?

There is no right answer. But different Saturdays bring different responsibilities and different opportunities. Sometimes it's better to clean, sometimes it's better to play. My friends and family will be supportive of both decisions. My friends and family can offer suggestions, but the choice is mine because not one of them has lived the week that I have, and they do not know how I need to prepare for next week. I will listen to their suggestions, but ultimately, I have to make the decision that is right for me. Both choices have different consequences for me and those around me. Both come with joy as well as guilt.

You are facing a similar choice right now: *Do I stay or do I go? Do I fight or do I ignore?* Nobody can make that decision for you. There is probably not a single right answer. Rather you are now faced with a few choices with their own unique challenges and opportunities. Let's look at both the potential outcomes of both choices. You should finish reading this chapter feeling more informed and empowered about making your decision.

IF YOU STAY

If you decide to stay in your current workplace, are you willing to do what you have to for it to be comfortable? Are you willing to take the time to "clean house"? What does a "comfortable workplace" look like for you? How will you know?

Are you willing to have conversations with problematic people? Are you willing to speak with a supervisor or a neutral if things don't get better? Are you willing and able to protect yourself if it is an abusive situation?

What Are You Willing to Do If You Stay?

Many negotiations can lead to effective *If, Then* clauses. For instance, I mediated a case between two men with drastically different working styles. One employee, let's call him Oladeji, had very high standards. He was also critical of everyone else who didn't have the same standards. His coworker, let's call him Pablo, had lower standards but prided himself on being easy to get along with. Pablo was flustered in his working relationship with Oladeji—they just couldn't seem to connect. Pablo, who was always friendly with Oladeji, couldn't understand why Oladeji was so critical. Finally, Pablo stopped talking to Oladeji, and Oladeji asked for a mediation.

Oladeji stated that he was responsible for the quality of the reports. Poor reports reflected poorly on him. He said that he continuously tried to talk to Pablo about it—every chance he got. Pablo continued to brush him off, instead asking irrelevant questions like what movie he had seen lately. Pablo's work product was deteriorating, and it had gotten to the point where Pablo seemed so lazy he didn't even want to review his findings with Oladeji.

Pablo stated that he wanted to have an effective working relationship with Oladeji, one where they could easily discuss reports. Pablo stated he had made multiple attempts at developing rapport with Oladeji, he had tried team-building techniques. His efforts were shunned, even ignored. Oladeji was becoming increasingly rude. Pablo began to put off speaking to Oladeji as long as possible, avoiding him at all lengths, and his reports were becoming late. Pablo decided that he would be better off doing his job without Oladeji and stopped involving him in the creation of the reports.

Clearly, what happened here is that Pablo and Oladeji had made false assumptions about the other's behavior. Instead of being curious or discussing it, both had continued viewing the other through their own erroneous filter.

To improve this relationship, we can use the same tips from the Robbers Cave Experiment earlier (with the 22 boys who were at odds with each other[1]). For them to work together, they had to realize that a) they both shared a common goal of desiring an effective relationship, b) both wanted to produce effective reports, and c) they needed to find a way to work together.

I worked with them to attack the problem: the communication pattern. Both Oladeji and Pablo were now on the same side of the table, creatively attacking a common problem together with If, Then solutions:

- Oladeji proposed that *if* Pablo came to him early enough to help prepare the reports, *then* Oladeji would work collaboratively instead of being critical.
- Pablo decided that *if* Oladeji would present ideas as suggestions instead of judgments, *then* Pablo would be willing to listen to his suggestions.

In order for this negotiation to yield a positive outcome, the two parties needed to feel heard. Oladeji and Pablo each also needed to feel like they had received something before they were willing to give something. Remember, both sides have probably been preaching to their own personal choir about what a jerk his coworker was. In order to save face, both guys needed to be able to go back to their friends and family and state what they had gotten out of the deal.

If you decide you want to stay in your current workplace, what are you willing to do to stay there? Are you willing to apologize for anything? If you want someone else's behavior to change, are you willing to change your behavior? To give them a second chance? Would you agree to contribute to a positive work environment by trying to say positive things about your coworkers?

Before you make your decision, write down a list of what you are willing to do and what you are not willing to do, including your If, Then requirements. "If Zander goes to anger management, then I would be willing to stay." "If Lesley starts proofreading her projects, then I would be willing to stay on the project with her." "If Ishiko stops swearing and turns his music down, then I will stop saying mean things about him to our coworkers."

Remember, Specific is Terrific! If you are ambiguous about what you want, you will get ambiguity. If you are specific about what you want, chances are much higher that you will get what you want. "If I am respected, then I will stay" is not a powerful statement. "If they listen attentively without interruption the next time I present my idea in our staff meeting, then I will continue to be involved in this project and reevaluate in another six months." Bam! That is a powerful statement right there!

The reason you are taking the time to write a list now is to make sure you are really getting what you want. Sometimes when people negotiate, they make bad decisions. They react out of fear, anger, bitterness, intimidation, or a need to intimidate and end up with a deal that is out of sync with their real desires. To avoid this, take some time to write down what you really want and what you are willing to do to get there. Your job is where you spend half of your waking life after all, so it's worth your time to make sure you are getting what you want from your job. And if you don't take the time to decide what you want and you end up with a bad outcome, who do you really have to blame? #realitysoldhere

If the answer is that you are not willing to do any of these things, then you might not really want to stay. Or you might need to see a little movement from the other person first, before you are willing to do anything. If you would be willing to make a few changes, take some time to consider what those might be.

What If Nothing Changes?

Are you willing to stay if nothing changes? If other people in the office won't change, if your manager is not willing to do anything, and if none of the policies can change, what will you do? Are you able to make any changes that could make the situation more comfortable? You still have options. You could ask to change your work description, your work location, or your work hours. You could ask if you could work with headphones or if you could have a partner who could act as a buffer. You could begin standing up for yourself more so that the conflict is not eating at you. You could choose to stand up for yourself less and decide that you like your job enough that this is something you are choosing to tolerate.

IF YOU GO

If you decide to leave your current employment, you are going to have different but still difficult questions. Like the earlier example where I could decide to play or clean house, you are now deciding to go outside and "play in a new sandbox." Which means that you haven't been able to clean anything up. Are you willing to leave those relationships undone? Are you going to feel comfortable with that six months from now? Every conflict you face is a learning experience, and it might be that you need to learn something from this conflict to deal with your next job.

What Else in Your Life Will Be Affected?

If you decide to go, think through what you can do to lessen the negative impact on your work, your family, and yourself. Many employers request that you provide a two-week notice. Are you willing to provide this notice and then continue to work in that office for another two weeks? What are some ways that you can make your exit smoother? You can ask your manager to keep your decision quiet until you decide to tell your coworkers. You may choose to have a final exit interview where you explain your reason for leaving.

You can lessen the impact on your family by giving them a schedule. Sit down with them and explain your reasons. Tell them specific ways that you would appreciate their support. For instance, you might ask for help updating your résumé, looking for jobs, and practicing for an interview. This transition might be easier for you if you talk through the specifics of it, or it might be too difficult to talk about, or it might vary day to day. You might want to have a party once you settle into your next job. You might ask your family for a night to yourself to think through this decision and make sure it is the right one for you.

If you have children, make sure to talk through this decision with them. Transitions can be a scary time for children. Explain your reasons, something like, "This was making me too distracted when I came home, and I want to be able to focus on you and your sister." Explain to them what the next few weeks will look like. Finally, paint a picture for them about how things will be different when it settles down in a few months. This might be a good time to talk to them about someone they are having a difficult time with and how they are handling it. In an ideal world, find time to sit down individually for a few minutes with your children. They might have fears or questions that they are uncomfortable voicing in front of their siblings. Or they might be a teenager like mine where their only question is, "But will you be able to afford to buy me new shoes?"

If you decide to leave, think through how to make that transition easy on yourself. You will probably have coworkers asking you why. What are you going to tell them? You might decide to share that it was due to the working situation, but you might decide instead to tell them about a new job, more time with the family, or that it was just time to go. If you decide to tell your coworkers the real reason, it might apply more pressure on them to change the situation. If the situation changes, they could always call you back to work there. Let me add, I have yet to see that happen, but I keep hoping. Call me if you succeed at this. What I have seen happen is people storming out of their office, furious, and saying unkind things about their coworkers. Then regretting it weeks later when they were unable to reconnect with their coworkers or get a recommendation letter. You shouldn't have to lie to your coworkers, but remember whatever you decide to say can never be unsaid.

TAKEAWAY

Most of this book has been focused on what you want the other person in conflict to do. But let's face it—nobody wants to be the first one to end a conflict! So if you are willing to take the first step, this can be the key to resolving conflict. It might be hard to take that first step, but it is definitely worth trying to stay in this situation to see if you can work through the problem.

37

SO YOU STAY . . . WHAT NEXT?

FIRST, STRENGTHEN YOURSELF

Resolving a conflict takes a lot more mental strength than people realize. This is actually why most people get into a conflict: It's easier. Think about it: When your coworker tells you that the report is going to be delayed, is it easy to pause, be understanding, and say, "Okay, thank you for letting me know, does that mean we will likely have to work late in order to meet our deadline?" Or is it easier to say, "Whatever, guess you're working late." It's easier to be snippy, right? To push the difficult situation back on them?

It takes strength to handle difficult situations, so the first step to resolving a difficult situation is to strengthen yourself.

To prepare for a difficult conversation, you will need to strengthen yourself physically and mentally. Conflict is a draining experience mentally, physically, emotionally, and socially. Most people downplay the effect this can have on your body, and so they are not prepared for it. Help yourself prepare for a difficult conversation the same way you would for a marathon. When someone is training for a marathon, we expect that they will need to get more sleep, make time to train, eat healthily, attend to self-care, and prepare mentally. Going through an escalated, protracted conflict takes an incredible physical toll on your body. Don't think so? Look at the rates of sick days, employee turnover, depression, and so on that result from someone in a conflict-ridden office.

When people are training for a marathon, they take steps to prepare themselves physically and emotionally.[1] Katie Barrett's half-marathon training tells her trainees to focus on eating whole foods that won't mess with their moods or thoughts. They arrange their schedule to be able to get enough sleep. They prepare their friends and family for the time and emotional expense that they will be devoting to the training. They prepare themselves mentally as well. They begin to visualize going through the process. They picture themselves in the hard moment, and pushing through. And they picture the end result—the pride they will feel. This is everything that we have to do to prepare for a difficult conversation. Just with fewer blisters.

Prepare for what you're facing. Strengthen yourself. You cannot get where you want to go if you are not strong enough to make it there. You cannot get to a resolution if you are too emotionally drained and you bail halfway through.

You have come too far to only go this far.

Prepare Yourself Physically

- *Move.* Physically get up and move. Prolonged conflict creates and releases cortisol—the long-term stress hormone—into our bloodstream. This hormone can have negative consequences on our sleep, our metabolism, our emotions, and our view of self and others. One of the best ways to counteract cortisol is by working it out of our bodies. Go for a jog, lift weights, play catch with your friends/kiddos/grand-kiddos, practice aikido, do a silly dance class. Do something that raises your heart rate enough that your body releases cortisol and produces myokines (hope molecules). This usually will also help you get a deeper rest, which is crucial during this time.
- *Rest.* You will need more sleep. Working on conflict taxes your brain, which eats up 25 percent of your energy. Try to work in an extra hour of rest.
- *Eat real food.* Don't snack, or binge, or fast. Eat foods that will help you to think clearly and quickly. Eat whole, unprocessed or minimally processed foods that will help you to have stable energy levels and clear thoughts. I know, you have every right to eat that bag of chips—look at what you are dealing with! But you

know what? You have a chance to make a change here, and you don't want to regret letting it pass you by. If you blow the opportunity to resolve this conflict, the only person you can blame is yourself. The reason why this is important is that processed foods cause mood swings—hormonal highs and sugar crashes. And this is too important of a decision to base it on a Snickers high.

Yup. This is super counterintuitive. I get that. I remember after one big fight with my hubby, I ate an entire bag of Ghirardelli's milk chocolate chips. And they were amazing. But I felt like junk afterward. My energy spiked and then crashed. I couldn't think as clearly. I knew I was frustrated, but I couldn't process why. I didn't have the energy to have a clear conversation with him about why I was upset. I wasted a whole day in that fight because of a chocolate chip hangover. Don't be like me; be better. Only eat five chocolate chips.

Prepare Yourself Mentally

- *Find a mantra.* Every good runner has a mantra that gets them through the hard parts; you deserve one too. When you are prepping for that difficult conversation, there will be times when you want to bail, or run out of the room, or slap the person in the face with rotten fish. But you won't. Because you have a mantra. What is your why? Think about that for a second. You know that something is wrong and you are taking the steps to do something about it. So when this becomes hard and you wonder why you are doing this, tell yourself that reason.

  I researched this study from the Himalayan Yoga Institute. The institute said that the verbal word is more powerful than the written word because you are releasing that thought into the universe, for your body and other bodies to hear it. That you are creating a positive energy that your body can feel. Different beliefs would say it aligns your chakras, or it affirms your faith. A psychologist might say hearing your mantra spoken confidently helps your brain to feel at peace with your decision. The institute conducted a study in 2012. During a hockey season, certain players were instructed to find and chant a mantra before playing, while others were instructed to begin playing. And the players who chanted a mantra performed much better—more confident and able to visualize their success.[2] Interesting idea, right? That saying your mantra out loud to the mirror or while driving to work can help your brain believe it. Let's all try it and report back to each other.

Here are some examples of a mantra. These are suggestions to get you thinking, and then create your own.

- "I deserve to be treated with respect."
- "I will work in a peaceful office."
- "I will not let this conflict steal my attention from my family when I get home."
- "This is wrong, and from now on I will stand up for what is right."
- "I am taking control of my future."
- "I deserve peace."

- *Visualize*. Seeing is believing, and if your brain sees you resolving this conflict, then it is going to work hard to make that happen. What does that look like? I mean, really, what is going to be different when this is resolved?

  - "I won't cringe when I see her name in an email."
  - "I will be interested in her stories."
  - "I will be able to disagree with him *and* we will both feel respected."
  - "We can sit in a team meeting and laugh together."
  - "We will have a healthy conversation, and I will walk away feeling heard."
  - "I will be proud of how I spoke to him, listened to his concerns, and shared my own."

  To get through a difficult situation without freaking out, our subconscious needs to have a picture of the goal. With details—time, place, sound, smells. Your brain needs to feel like it is in the moment of that goal. Then it can endure difficult situations.

  Your turn! Visualize the end goal. Write down what "success" looks like, one month later.

- *Select your goal (or goals)*. Now that you are rested, eating well, and have identified your mantra, let's find your true goal. This goal shouldn't be a *position* statement: "I will take 50 percent of the company!" Instead, phrase your goal as an *interest* statement: "I need to make sure that I can continue to meet payroll, offer a competitive benefit package, and provide dynamic jobs for my employees." A position statement is inflexible and limits your options, "I will work only until 4:00 p.m." An interest statement gets at your true goal, "I need to work enough hours to make the money to cover my bills, but I also need to make sure that I can leave work in time to pick up my daughter from school and get her to practice." Orienting your eventual conversation towards goals and interests can open up many more options for you than hanging on to a fixed position—perhaps now you can consider a 4:00 to 10:00 p.m. schedule, or telecommuting, or a shared office space.

Relationships are often derailed because people have not identified their true goals.

Why? Because they aren't sexy. (The goals, I mean. The goals aren't sexy. I'm sure the people are . . . I feel like I should stop here and get back on track.) Clear, collaborative goals aren't sexy because they don't make headlines or inspiring speeches or get clicks or ratings. When was the last time Thor raised his hammer and shouted to the sky, "I will calmly and confidently state my interests in a way that you can hear them, and I will also seek to understand your interests. And then we shall work together to create a new world and we will be friends!"?

No! Thor shouts, "I will destroy my enemies!" We are taught that goals should be conquering, vengeance, win-at-all-costs. This is such a destructive mentality. And it doesn't just destroy the other person, it destroys our own chance at peace, relationships, and growth.

So, pause and write down your short-term position, your version of: "I will be happy only if he is fired," or "I will quit unless I get my raise." Your one rule—write this in a positive, affirming statement. Positive statements are much more motivating to our brain than negatives. The carrot is more effective than the stick.

And now, write down the true goal: "I need to have a peaceful office environment," or "I need to know that I have financial stability." Write down your true goals for resolving this conflict.

Why are you doing this mental and physical preparation? Why not just go in guns-a-blazin' and take what you want? Or why not just duck-and-cover and avoid the whole thing?

The reason can be explained by Maslow's Hierarchy of Needs. Maslow stated that before we can reach our long-term, personal achievement needs, we have to satisfy our short-term, urgent needs. The urgent here supersedes the important. This means that if you don't strengthen yourself physically, you will go into this conflict able to make only a short-term decision. Instead of being able to have a difficult conversation, you might storm out, or scream, "I quit!" These moves might satisfy your short-term self's needs for vengeance or self-protection, but they won't satisfy your long-term needs. And if you plan on being around for more than a couple of days, at some point the long-term self is going to ask to be satisfied too.

Maslow[3] stated that our short-term needs are immediate physical and mental needs: Am I cold? Am I hungry? Am I safe? As those needs are met, we can move up the scale. Am I being respected? Am I validated in my job? As we move further up the scale we begin to satisfy our long-term needs: Am I making a difference? Am I doing work

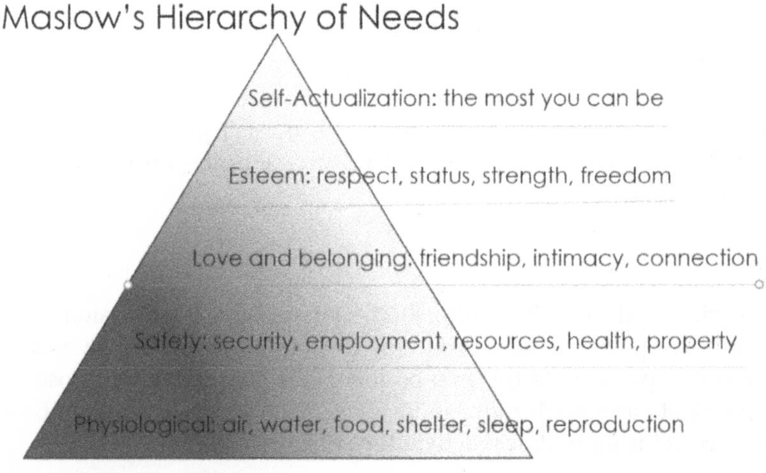

Maslow's Hierarchy of Needs

that I am proud of? Am I being treated in a way that I deserve? Am I acting in a way that is in line with my values? The way this relates to conflict resolution is by understanding that we need to take care of our physical needs first. After that we can begin taking care of our deeper needs for respect and validation in our office.

SECOND, CHOOSE YOUR PROCESS

Let's look at a continuum of options available to you. (Most offices will have a version of these options, perhaps under a different title. If not, perhaps you can suggest adding these options or developing them yourself.) Remember, you might be able to use your employee assistance program insurance to pay for third-party help.

This visual helps demonstrate some different conflict resolution options. We looked at this earlier to help understand that you can design your own process. Look at it again and think about where on the continuum you want to be. How much help do you want and how much power are you willing to give up?

Avoidance
Passive-aggression
Conversation
Negotiation
Conciliation
Workshop
Facilitated discussion
Facilitation
Mediation
Ombuds
Climate assessment
Individual or team coaching
Investigation
Arbitration
Early neutral evaluation
Law enforcement
Litigation

You will need to decide if you want to handle this on your own, bring in a neutral party, or if you want someone else making a decision for you in a more formal arrangement.

Solo

- *Avoidance*. You decide to avoid the problem and not mention it to anyone.
- *Passive-aggressive*. You take jabs at the other person, bad-mouth them, take sick days, or quit due to the conflict, but never address it directly.
- *Revenge*. Revenge is any time you are willing to hurt yourself in order to hurt the other person.[4]
- *Apology*. An apology is any time you rank the person higher than your need to be right.[5] Show them that you understand by sacrificing: "I won't do that again." Show them that you mean it by being able to express what they are feeling.
- *Negotiation*. You let the person know there is something you would like to discuss, and you arrange to sit down and hash it out yourselves.
- *Conciliation*. You are encouraged by someone else to resolve the situation through a conversation, with one of the primary purposes being to stop people from being angry.

With a Neutral

- *Workshop*. A neutral guides both/all of you through questions that help you to find out what the conflict is and brainstorm some possible solutions.
- *Facilitated discussion*. A neutral listens to your conversation about the conflict and ensures that everyone is able to speak, summarizing afterward what the key points were.
- *Facilitation*. A neutral creates a roundtable conversation, where everyone has a chance to speak. The neutral summarizes the interests and the suggested solutions that could satisfy those interests.
- *Ombuds*. An ombuds is often part of a company and helps someone to identify their interests and goals, and discusses options for resolution. Typically, the ombuds works with people individually, instead of joint conversations.

- *Mediation.* A guided discussion in which a neutral helps people to state their interests, hear the other side's interests, and negotiate an agreement together.
- *Climate assessment.* A series of surveys and/or interviews conducted by an off-site neutral, aimed at uncovering systemic issues. Some assessments will also include suggestions for next steps, generated by the staff or the neutral.
- *Individual or team coaching.* A neutral or a communication-trained HR employee works with an individual or a team for a finite period of time on a specific issue, such as a communication roadblock or improving team skills.
- *Investigation.* An HR representative, an ombuds, or a neutral reviews the situation to determine if a wrong has been committed.

Formal

- *Arbitration.* You present your case, often with time to explain your interests, before a panel of arbitrators who provide you a binding decision.
- *Early neutral evaluation.* You meet with a judge or an expert outside of the court to determine what they think happened and what the next steps should be.
- *Law enforcement.* When a situation escalates quickly and law enforcement forcibly de-escalates or removes an employee from a company.
- *Litigation.* You—typically an attorney working on your behalf—present your case before a judge who will consider the facts and give a binding decision on right/wrong and the next legal steps.

The main thing I hope you are picking up from all of this is that there are a variety of processes on the resolution spectrum, and most will involve talking to the other person. Note that as you move through this continuum, you begin to give up control in how the conflict will be resolved, and you also give up your opportunity to change.

Let's look at that conflict resolution continuum again and move through a decision tree to help you decide what to do next:

Are you involved in a work conflict?

No: That's great, go get some chocolate chips and celebrate.
Yes: Do you need this to be resolved?

No: Practice *avoidance* without being passive-aggressive.
Yes: Can you talk to this person?

Yes: Try *negotiation*.
No: Does your office have someone in HR who you can talk to?

Yes: Speak to HR and see if they can arrange a meeting.
No: If the conflict is with only one person, try having a *conversation* with the person. A conversation is where both people try to explain their interests and listen to the other's interests in a respectful manner.

Are multiple people involved?

No: Have a *conversation* with the person, or see if they would try *coaching*.
Yes: Arrange for a *facilitated discussion*. Is this an ongoing issue?

Yes: Set up a series of roundtable *discussions* with different *moderators*. A roundtable discussion allows everyone to have a chance to speak, and then the moderator summarizes and moves to the next issue.

Is this a company-wide, systemic issue?

Yes: Request a *climate assessment*. A climate assessment is led by a neutral, who uses interviews and surveys to gather information about a specific department or the company. These can be general or focused on a specific topic.
No: Would you like to resolve this issue and develop an agreement together that can prevent this from reoccurring?

Yes: Try *mediation*.
No: Try a formal approach. Do you need someone to determine who was right and who was wrong?

Yes: Try *arbitration*.
No: Try *early neutral evaluation*.

Are there potential legal or criminal implications? Do you need a judgment against the other person? Are you owed a lot of money?

Yes: Try *litigation*.

None of these situations seem to apply to you? Okay, time to pull out the secret menu. The secret weapon that only those who are true of heart and honestly desire to move on from conflict get to see: Ask the person out to coffee.

THIRD, INVITE THE OTHER PERSON

Now that you have made the decision to resolve the conflict and have chosen the best process, how do you invite the other person to resolve it?

Let's face it, this is often the biggest hurdle. You can design the perfect process and outline all of your goals, but you . . .

1. wilt when it comes to actually talking to the other person; or
2. explode at them and destroy any chance of having a real conversation.

Most people learn these two approaches to a difficult conversation. And they are both wrong.

Through bad habits passed down through generations, through movies, through social media trolls and mob mentalities, and from the passive-aggressive chapter of this book, we know two methods: *hard negotiation* and *soft negotiation*.[6]

Hard Negotiation

When people enter a negotiation, they want to appear tough, not letting anyone get the drop on them. They want to walk into a room and command respect. They don't have time to mess around with this kumbaya stuff. They are hard negotiators. They are unyielding. They often feel a calmness as their brain clicks into high gear. It feels as if time has slowed down and they can think faster than everyone. They have adopted a position and are going to stick to it, golldarnit. These are often people with a fight response. They were taught by their parents or society to be proud and stand up for themselves. They are going to walk into that negotiation room, state what they want, and not give an inch.

Soft Negotiation

When soft negotiators enter a difficult conversation, they might as well be jumping into the Indy 500. Things feel fast, terrifying, out of control. They know they will have to react to things getting in their space. If they are a flighter in conflict (y'know, of fight, flight, freeze), their pulse is quickened and they feel fidgety. If they freeze in conflict, things feel slow, like their brain is churning molasses. If they are someone who is genetically programmed to be a fighter, but they only learned the skills of soft negotiation, then conflict is going to be one confusing mess. They will have the instincts to attack but the learned habit to hide. This is often the case for someone who has been taught their whole life the need to "behave like a lady" or "fight like a man," but their programming is telling them to behave differently. Imagine having a leader personality, and then being told that you are supposed to be a soft negotiator, sit in the corner, don't speak until you are spoken to, don't rock the boat. Everything would feel topsy-turvy, confusing. Soft negotiators might have been taught that conflict is wrong, shameful, and to be avoided. They were taught that arguing is destructive and causes pain. They will walk grudgingly into that negotiation room and give up whatever is necessary to get quickly out of that room. Soft negotiators know how to be a great team player and support others, but they typically don't have the skills to stand up for their own interests. Ken Sande in *The Peacemaker* discusses how soft negotiators often think they are doing the right thing by just being nice and easy to get along with and sacrificing their own desires. Eventually they begin to realize that nothing is changing, they are becoming resentful, and this might not be the best long-term decision. That there needs to be a third option.[7]

Firm Negotiation

There is a third option. Not available in stores, not available around most dinner tables, and definitely not available in a theater near you. This is a style called *firm negotiation*. It is not aggressive and destructive like hard negotiation. It is not self-effacing like soft negotiation. Rather, it represents the middle ground. A firm negotiator knows her interests and wants to hear the other's interests. A firm negotiator will not budge on things that are important to her, and she is ready to work hard to find a solution that will satisfy both of them. A firm negotiator is ready to attack the problem.

Firm negotiation invitations. When you are ready to invite the other person to discuss the conflict, be a firm negotiator. Don't go in *guns a blazin'* and demand they speak to you. Don't go in downplaying your concerns, already losing the argument. Instead approach the other person, confident that you will be able to explain your interests, ready to listen to their interests, and excited to tackle this puzzle and find an answer together.

DON'T

- You don't want the other person to feel attacked in front of a group of people.
- You also don't want to approach them in some place that could be unsafe for you, such as a parking garage.
- Don't imply that either one of you has done something wrong.
- Don't suggest what the outcome is going to be.

DO

- Approach the other person in a semi-private space, such as a conference room or an empty lobby, that is also a safe space with others nearby if needed.
- State the problem. Let them know that things aren't working and could be improved.
- Make it clear the behavior not the person is at fault. "Our different communication styles are making it difficult for us to hear each other." This is much easier to work with than implying that there is something wrong with either of you.
- Suggest a process. "What if we meet up for lunch and figure this out?"
- Give them ownership. Ask them to agree to a detail. "If that sounds okay, just let me know a time or a place." "If you can think of a better time to talk, I'm pretty open this week, just let me know."

- Give them time and space. No matter how great a job you did presenting the concept, it is usually a lot to take in. This means it is hard to agree to in the moment. If you force an answer now, the answer could easily be no because they are feeling caged in. Instead give them a window. "Could you email me later when you think of a time?" This gives them space to think about it. You are not being a threatening, hard negotiator. But you are also not wimping out and saying, "If it's okay with you . . ." Handle this conversation as a firm negotiator, giving the other person time to hear your interests and figure out their own.[8]

FOURTH, RESOLVE THE CONFLICT

"Thanks a lot, Clare," you're thinking as you read this section's title, "I'll just resolve the conflict. Why didn't I think of that?"

I promise I will give you some tips.

Don't worry; you're not alone here. People have been fighting since, well, since Cain and Abel. And many of them have resolved those fights too. That means we have lots of good experience to build on.

I'm about to give you the secrets of the mediator league about how to resolve the conflict. Here's hoping they don't pull my special decoder ring.

This is what a mediator would do if your office hired one. You might want to try some of these skills yourself. And, of course, if you end up hiring a mediator, then you will know what to expect.

SONAR

Mediation is a five-step process for communicating with each other and moving toward resolution: Statement, Opening, Negotiation, Agreement, Resolution.[9]

SONAR uses sound to communicate, send and receive information, understand what already exists, and assess and feel comfortable with the situation around us (*statement* and *opening*).

- *Statement*. Where you describe what you want from the conversation at hand, explaining what the problem is and how you both should state what you want and figure out together how to achieve that.

- *Opening*. This is the segment of our program where each side will take a turn, outlining in a few minutes what you think the problem is and what you want. During the opening phase, you begin your attempts to see where the other person is coming from.

SONAR provides information about clear paths and potential roadblocks to explore and paints a picture of potential destinations (*negotiation*).

- *Negotiation*. The purpose of the back-and-forth negotiation phase is to work together to come up with a solution that satisfies both of your interests.

SONAR discovers hidden gems (*agreement* and *resolution*).

- *Agreement*. When you decide what is the best ending to your current conflict, you've reached an agreement.
- *Resolution*. When you decide what you will do going forward—work in the same department, transfer, try to be friends—you've come to resolution.

Getting Down and Dirty

We had an aboveground pool in the backyard. The filter broke while we were out of town for a week. We came back to a bright green mucky pool. I replaced the filter and was expecting to see some improvement the next morning. No change, pretty sure there were now frogs living in there. Second day, the pool water was getting so murky that I spotted the Loch Ness Monster. By the third day I found the problem. (Yes, fine, it took me three whole days. I'm a mediator, not a mechanic.) The filter was on the top of the water, and the first few inches of the water were indeed getting filtered. But the gross stuff was underneath, undisturbed, and it wasn't getting cleaned out. It was growing.

What did I do? I grabbed my brush and started stirring the sludge around. It was difficult. We hadn't been swimming in these waters for a while and things had gone unnoticed that we hadn't dealt with. The water looked 10 times worse than when I had started. I remember my son looking at it and saying, "I will never go in that pool again—it is going to dye my skin green and turn me into a frog." (He was 10 years old and had his first "girlfriend," so he cared about those things.)

It took two weeks of stirring and filtering and chemical-ing, but we got back our crystal clear water. The pool was saved and we lived happily ever after.

This picture sits vividly in my head. Partially because it was really gross. But mostly because this is what fixing relationships often feels like. We can work on the surface stuff, the top few inches, and we can survive with that. But if we really want things to get better, we need to dredge up the gunk at the bottom. And things might look worse before they get better. And it doesn't happen right away. We need to spend some time filtering those thoughts as they come up—pulling out the assumptions and the expectations and the hurts and the hate—and replacing them with clear thoughts. Not Pollyannaish, naive thoughts, just pulling out the past gunk that was damaging the relationship. Start with a fresh, clean slate that will allow you to see the person for who they really are.

TAKEAWAY

Let the other person know in a nonthreatening way that there is room for improvement. Ask if they would be willing to talk about it. If so, have them tell you when they are ready.

Part V

PREVENTING FUTURE CONFLICTS

Conflicts can be a positive experience, an opportunity for improvement. But wouldn't it be great if you could just improve your office culture without needing to go through an actual conflict? This section discusses how to do that: Prevent conflict before it starts.

38

STICK IN THE MUD

> Insanity is repeating the same mistakes and expecting different results.[1]

In the last section we worked hard to identify the conflict and figure out how to end it. Hopefully you have had a conversation with the troublesome other and taken steps to resolve the conflict.

But there are some conflicts that are just dandelions; they seem to keep coming back. Even if a problem is resolved, the same behaviors may lead you right back to the same problem.

When conversing with the other person at the other end of your conflict, there are some tactics that will help resolve a conflict and prevent it from coming back. Like Relationship Weed-'n'-Feed.

CLEANING OUR YARD

Allow me to digress a bit. My husband and I bought an abandoned Christmas tree farm years ago and began to clean it up. When we bought it, there was a gentle stream on one side. But then the rains began and this little stream flooded the whole back half of the property for six months out of the year. (The things you realize *after* you buy a place, huh?) We came up with a plan and developed a new path for the water. We had a clear destination and a route to get there.

The stick in the mud in our stream. Source: Author

My husband pulled out all of his toys and began pulling out trees and digging trenches and creating a lovely course for the stream to follow. The first year was gorgeous. We had this gentle meandering stream through peaceful meadows.

When we were next to the stream, we were too close to see that the ground was pushing up. There was actually a deep root that was pulling the mud to the side of the stream.

The stick in the mud.

The second year. The stick began to pull mud to the side. As this mud was pulled down, the walls deteriorated. Eventually our beautiful stream was sucked into its original path. Meaning once again our property was a flooded shambles.

Now it is important to note that my husband and I did a great job at the first two steps: We developed clear goals and we resolved the original conflict. Where we failed was taking the time to prevent this conflict from returning.

That stupid stick in the mud.

If we had taken the time to pull out that dang stick in the mud, then we would have prevented the return of the flood.

OUR OWN STICKS

I tell this story in many of my trainings. For me, it is a perfect example of reoccurring conflicts.

I see so many people who have done deep soul-searching work in step 1, strengthening themselves mentally and physically to tackle a conflict. Then they spend hours negotiating and are able to resolve a difficult conflict. But they haven't done the final step of removing those final sticks.

And why would you? There is a honeymoon period when a conflict is resolved. The tension dissipates and you are able to see the joy in life again. You have the best of intentions and you can finally have peaceful dreams that everything will continue to improve. You and the other person are on the path to resolving the conflict, which feels great, but just being on the path isn't enough. You need to walk down it. Ken Sande describes this as both people realizing that they have a log in their eye and making a decision to pull it out. Which is a great start! But then you actually have to do the work of digging the dang thing out.[2]

Without tough work, even the best of intentions will always remain a dream. We would be dealing only with the surface of the conflict, without going deep enough to pull out the conflict by the roots.

Without taking the time to pull out your sticks, you will never be able to find a sustainable resolution to your conflicts. The mud will come falling in and will pull you back into your old habits, which will pull you right back into your old conflicts.

The stick in the mud is our bad habit.

We have great intentions after a conflict to treat the other person with respect and really listen with attention. But there has to be some additional work where you examine why you lost that respect in the first place. You need to step back from this honeymoon period and be realistic about your filters and bad habits. Have you been disrespectful because there is just something about this person that you simply do not respect? Well, then you need to deal with that. If not, no matter how great your goal and your resolution process was, the disrespect stick will pull you right back into your conflict. *We can summarize this chapter by saying bad habits don't gently fade away, they need to be forcibly yanked out.*

So how can you remove these sticks? The hardest part is seeing them. We often have a blind spot to our own sticks because it might require seeing fault in ourselves. As an example, if you have spoken disrespectfully to another person, be honest with yourself about why you do not respect them. You might not be able to change it any time soon, but owning up to it will at least allow you to see that stick and eventually pull it out before it causes you any more trouble.

1. Place a sticky note on your wall for the first month after a conflict is resolved that says, "Find the sticks." This will help you be aware that the sticks exist and you are purposefully trying to find them. (Get it? Cuz it's a *stick*-y note.)
2. When you pull a stick out, a hole will be left. Purposefully fill this hole with something useful. If you pull out disrespectful habits, be intentional about filling that hole in your brain with positive habits. "Instead of judging her clothes every time I see her, I am going to notice she is actually a great boss." I remember going to a Catholic mass with a friend of mine and wondering why the bread was eaten before drinking the wine. The wine is supposed to represent cleansing us and getting rid of bad stuff. And the bread is supposed to represent filling us with the good, new stuff. I don't know about you, but normally I want the bad stuff out of a cup before I put the new good stuff in it. But my friend explained that once you have something good and new, it is easier to let go of the old and bad. This always stuck with me. In other words, if I start to focus on a good quality about my coworker first, it is easier for me to stop focusing on their bad qualities.
3. Acknowledge this is an opportunity for growth. The Chinese character for crisis[3] means a crucial juncture, implying that there is a choice when facing conflict—to fall right back down your own slippery slope or to use this self-knowledge to improve yourself.
4. If you keep slipping into the same bad habit, ask for help. Tell others that you are working on this and ask them to point out your stick in the mud when they see it. This requires courage, bravery, and humility. To be truly radical, you can even include this as part of resolving your conflict. This means that both you and the other person in conflict acknowledge you have had negative sticks in the mud toward each other and give yourselves grace for the month ahead to notice and pull out your sticks, *and* being brave enough to point out the other person's stick towards

> you ("hey, you just snapped at me—I think we found your stick in the mud!"), *and* being willing to listen when someone points out your own stick in the mud.

Heavy, right?

Set a goal to resolve a conflict once and for all. To make sure you don't end up back in the same conflict, address the habits and situations that got you into that conflict in the first place.

Why is this so transformational? You are taking responsibility for your part in a conflict, and you are acknowledging you are not perfect, *and* you are changing your life to prevent this conflict from attacking you again.

TAKEAWAY

Change the behaviors that led to the conflict. Once you take responsibility for your contribution to the conflict, then you have begun to resolve it. Once you deal with and change those behaviors, you are pulling conflict out by the roots. Sometimes the easiest way to do this is by seeing the good in others—and ourselves—first. When we are focusing on the good, it is easier to let go of the bad.

39

STRAIGHT, NO CHASER

Recently, my husband didn't take out the garbage. Shouldn't be a big deal, right? But I was tired, already feeling like I needed help handling my workload for the evening, and was looking for a reason to lay into him.

And I did.

I told him I thought he was lazy. I know, I know—I didn't use any of the techniques I have discussed in this book. I should have handled it a thousand different ways. But I was tired and I didn't. For this one: Do as I write, not as I do.

But telling him he was lazy felt hollow—it wasn't quite satisfying enough. I felt silly, like I was just whining about something petty and not upset about something legitimate. It didn't seem like he was taking me as seriously as I wanted him to. So, I amped up my attack. Not only was he lazy, I decided, but he was taking advantage of my kind nature by letting me do everything around the house. And that proves how inconsiderate he was. Just last week he made a huge mess and he left all his dishes in the sink—what did he think was going to happen with those? Some Keebler elf was going to come in and clean them? No! He clearly just left them for me, without a second thought, as if I was just the housemaid. (Have I mentioned how much my husband loves it when I use him for examples in this book to illustrate conflict theory?)

FIGHTING DIRTY

I escalated this fight by doing three things:

1. Attack ("You're lazy!")
2. Add ("And you're inconsiderate!")
3. Ammo ("Last week you also did something, and I'm bringing it up again!")

What I had done was dilute my original message. If you are drinking something and you don't like it, sometimes you will add in a chaser to distract you from the nasty flavor. Which is what I had done. I could have just said the one harsh thing, but I watered my message to the point that he couldn't find it anymore. I had thrown a lot of confusing chasers at him, instead of telling him straight how I felt and what I needed.

Arguments are actually much more powerful delivered *straight, no chaser*. If I had stuck to my original complaint about wishing he would take out the garbage then my argument would have been powerful and probably successful. The garbage would have been taken out, and I wouldn't have just hurt someone I cared about. But because I added in the chasers (attack, add, ammo), my message was diluted so much that it was lost. Needless to say, we got in an argument and the garbage was not taken out. The Straight, No Chaser message had a chance at success. If we can have a conversation that just sticks to our Straight, No Chaser message, we have a much higher chance of it being heard. This is a great way to have a chance at actually resolving conflicts, instead of making them worse. Doug Noll[1] explains that we take our original message and add on other complaints and issues and people, and this escalates and dilutes the message beyond recognition. (Hmm, this sounds like how they draft a bill in Congress. Thought for another day.)

Let's look at this a different and better way—with chocolate.

CARAMEL M&MS

Picture yourself eating a caramel M&M. If you haven't tried them, go get a bag, they are worth it. Okay, you're back? All right, caramel M&Ms have three different layers, the same type of layers we move through in conflict. First, pick up one of those lovely morsels and examine it. It has the tough outer candy shell in a bold color, right?

If you had never tried one before, you could easily assume that the entire candy was that tough hard candy shell, like a jawbreaker. Now bite into it. You'll realize there is another chocolatey layer underneath that tough exterior and it's wonderful. Finally, you'll get to the ooey-gooey-goodness at the center: the sweet caramel.

Tough Outer Shell

When I attacked my husband—he really puts up with a lot; please give him kudos if you ever meet him—I essentially threw a communication dart at him. Hard. Right in the face. I wanted him to see how tough and bold I was.

The outside shell was all of the additional stuff I had added on to my complaint, the chasers. The outside shell was the attack, the add, and the ammo. That made my argument feel strong. It made me feel like I was justified to complain. Maybe him forgetting to take out the garbage wasn't worth complaining about, but once I added on all of that ammo of the additional flaws and past events, then I felt like I had every right to be upset. I kept adding in more frustrations until my complaints felt big enough to justify my feelings.

And when I threw that attack at him, he retaliated. (I guess I can't blame him.) He was upset and began defending himself against that irrelevant ammo I had added on.

But that ammo wasn't what I was upset about. I completely diluted and derailed what I wanted to talk about by adding on this additional information. We were now arguing about the dishes he left in the sink (at least soak them though, seriously; food that has dried on dishes just takes twice as long to clean!) instead of talking about the garbage. I, all by myself, sabotaged this conversation.

Sweet Chocolate

If we look under that outer, tough candy shell, we get to the chocolate layer. If I pull out all of those additional chasers, then I could have asked him my straight request. The chocolate layer just states simply what I want: "Could you take out the garbage?"

If I had asked him this way, and he looked at me and saw how tired I was, I betcha he would have said yes. Can you imagine how much better that would have been? I wouldn't have said all of those hurtful things, he wouldn't have responded back with hurtful things. We could have had a simple conversation.

This is the beauty of the *straight, no chaser* approach. It is better for everyone involved. It is obviously nicer for my husband, since he is not being attacked. But the key here is that it is also better for me because I have a higher chance of actually getting the garbage out.

There is one more piece to discuss though. Caramel M&Ms have three layers, right?

1. *Tough position: the outer shell.* The hard candy shell is the chaser, the ammo, the tough act that I am attacking with. It has bold, bright colors to get attention and look tough.
2. *The interest: the chocolate.* The chocolate layer is what I actually want. It isn't tough. It doesn't have bold colors to get attention. It just simply makes a request. This is my real desire.
3. *The value: the caramel.* The caramel inside is my value, what I am hoping for, what I am afraid of, why it matters to me.

Valuable Caramel

The value is what fuels my interest, and if that interest isn't met, then it also fuels the attack. My value sounds like, "I am tired and I would really like a break from getting stuff done tonight. I need to know that you are here for me and I can count on you for help when I am tired." "I am feeling overwhelmed." "This house is your responsibility too, and I would like to feel like we are both invested in taking care of it." "I have had a hard day and just can't face everything on my plate." "I am just feeling alone and could really use a partner to stand by me tonight." "Help."

When you order a drink straight without a chaser, it is because you want to taste the true flavor of the drink.

When you give someone a straight request, it is because you want them to hear the true flavor of your request. "I need to know I can count on you."

This sounds like a simple concept, but adding chasers to our complaints is a habit deeply ingrained in most of us. It takes time to feel confident and comfortable in just making a simple request, without feeling the need to add to it. In keeping requests straight, no chaser will help to have smoother conversations at work, strengthen your relationships, or help you to get what you really want. Stand behind your simple request, and there is a much better chance it will be heard.

TAKEAWAY

A straight, no chaser request pulls off that distracting ammo and allows people to hear your actual message. This is also similar to Bill Eddy's BIFF method, of framing a difficult conversation as Brief, Informative, Friendly, and Firm.

Remember the KISS method, and Keep It Simple, Silly.

THE CARAMEL M&MS WORKSHEET

There are three layers that we go through in conflict:

Positions (the tough, bold, outer shell)
Interests (the sweeter inside)
Values (the sweet, amorphous filling)

Position: What do I really want out of this conflict?

Example: I want more flexibility.
I want:

Interests: Why do I want this?

Example: I want flexibility to spend more time with my family.
I want this because:

Values: Why does this matter to me?

Example: This matters to me because my need is family time (or acceptance, or feeling loved, or respected, or honesty, etc.).
This matters to me because my need is:

40

THE ROAD TO RELATIONSHIP IS PAVED WITH GOOD INTENTIONS

Another prevention technique: Change the relationships you have with your coworkers.

I've gotta be honest here: This step takes some major character growth on your part. Conquer this step, and I will gladly give you 50 good karma points. Or a gold star in Heaven. Or I can send you some brownies—everybody believes in brownies, right?

Think about a close relationship you have—a spouse, a parent, a friend. Now imagine that relationship without any bumps. You always agree on everything. There are not any funny misunderstandings or middle-of-the-night disagreements. Your relationship would be flat. Frankly, it would be boring. You wouldn't be learning anything new about the other person or yourself. Relationships need some conflict to identify boundaries. "All polishing is done by friction," says Mary Parker Follett.

It would be like putting two flat edges of a puzzle piece together—there is nothing to hold them together. Conflict helps us to see each other's strengths and weaknesses. We push and pull, and eventually find the bumps and grooves, and then we are two puzzle pieces that have figured out how we lock together. The more those conflicts push and pull on us, and we fit into each other's strengths and weaknesses, the stronger that bond is.

Now these conflicts have become an opportunity to find out about each other's strengths and values.

THE COFFEE CONFLICT

Say you notice the office fridge is out of creamer, and you ask the new guy to grab some.

When we discussed this example earlier in the book, he brings in almond creamer. You wanted cow's milk half-and-half. We all know what a disaster this could be.

This is a bump in the road, the entrance to a conflict. You could berate him for not asking you what you wanted; he could yell back that you should have been clearer.

Or . . .

What if we flipped the script and instead used the presenting conflict as an opportunity to deepen a relationship? What if, rather than assuming the worst about someone, our default assumption becomes that the other person had good intentions?

Then the conversation could go: "Oh, interesting. Why did you buy almond creamer?"

Now we can have a conversation—you find out he is a vegan; he finds out you are doing a keto/high-fat diet.

Because you assumed the other person may have had good intentions and gave him the benefit of the doubt, you are now beginning to form a relationship. *The value that you get from that new relationship likely outweighs the value you would have received from feeling right.*[1]

Good assumptions form strong relationships. Good intentions in a relationship mean that you are trying your best to explain your point of view and what you need *and* doing your best to listen to their point of view and what they need. *And* working with them to find a solution that will make you both proceed happily ever after.

Remember earlier we discussed *firm negotiation*? That instead of weak/soft negotiating or aggressive/hard negotiating, there is a middle path called firm negotiation in which you state what you want and listen to what the other person wants?

This is the same concept and helps develops *firm relationships*. Assume that the other person has amazing interests *and* that you have amazing interests, and you will protect both.

HOW INTERESTING; I WONDER WHY?

Approach conflict with curiosity.

Whenever you hit a bump in the road, find out why. Not to judge, but out of curiosity. He bought almond creamer? How interesting; I wonder why? She always is quiet during meetings? How interesting; I wonder why?

Let this be your new mantra when faced with a disagreement: *How interesting; I wonder why?* These five words can transform conflicts into relationships. Approaching a vexing interaction with curiosity shows that you respect the other person enough to find out more about them and their perspective.

Okay—let's pause for a moment and be real. Do you care that much why he got almond creamer? Probably not. But while you are sitting there stewing that you don't have your deliciously creamy half-and-half to put in your rich, dark French roast, you have to make a choice: bitterness or curiosity? Bitterness is the natural choice. Our instincts tell us to be upset when we have been wronged. Our brain is looking out for us and is infuriated that we do not have the correct creamer!

But that brain is looking out only for our short-term self. Our brain doesn't know yet that we are going to have to work with this new guy for years. It can be miserable, and this could be the beginning of that misery. Or it could be a lot of fun, and that fun working relationship could begin right here. Remind yourself: you both have amazing interests and speak truth to that power.

One of the main mantras I tell my clients in toxic environments is that it takes five words to reclaim your office. You might have to fake that curiosity at first, and yes, you will be biting your tongue. But limiting yourself to only these five words will slowly transform a vengeful, guarded office into one of trust. Practice saying these five words until they become an instinct, so that the next time your coworker does something that reminds you of Darth Vader, you can ask yourself: *How interesting; I wonder why?*

TAKEAWAY

Assumptions are dangerous, and they prevent creativity and collaborative solutions. Instead, approach conversations with curiosity, realizing that you actually, strangely enough, do not know everything. Listen with curiosity, as if you assume they have good intentions and you want to find out why. This allows you to get to know others and create relationships. When faced with an unexpected reaction, get in the habit of asking, "How interesting; I wonder why?"

41

SO, YOU GO . . . CHANGING THE DEVIL YOU KNOW FOR THE ANGEL YOU DON'T

Marika walked out of the boss's office. The red on her face let us all know: She had been fired. She walked to her office and began throwing her stuff in bags. She picked up a framed picture on the wall and "accidentally" dropped it on the floor. As it shattered, she looked at us and said, "Oops. But not my problem." As she threw things violently into her poor, innocent bags, she began muttering, "Have fun here, everyone. Hope you put in 12 years just like I did only to have them turn on a dime and decide they don't need you. Who cares about loyalty anymore? Not these jerkhats. I could have been working anywhere but I gave my time to this company. Why? So, they could throw it down the toilet."

EXIT GRACEFULLY

There were actually much more colorful words, but my computer keeps autocorrecting those.

What can we learn from Marika's exciting departure?

It is important to exit gracefully.

I know, I know. The dramatic exits on TV are so tempting. Taking a baseball bat to your obnoxious printer might feel so good in the moment. Slashing the boss's tires. Telling your coworkers some of the secrets you've been holding in. Feels so good for a split second. But I think your long-term self would be pretty disappointed.

Two different parts of your brain are responsible for short-term and long-term decisions. Your prefrontal cortex is the part of your brain that can access memories and think logically about the future. It is used when planning complex cognitive behavior going forward. This is the part of the brain you want to be using when making big decisions, because it is going to consider what you really desire long term. The instinctual, reactive part of your brain is the amygdala, as we discussed in The Hulk chapter. The amygdala is responsible for triage, for getting you out of painful or dangerous situations immediately. When you are making an important decision, you do not want to be controlled by your amygdala, because then you will be operating from a place of fear or revenge.

There are three problems. (1) When we feel that we are under attack, our amygdala often takes over. This is the fight-flight-freeze response. So, when we are triggered, it is difficult to make wise long-term decisions. Our amygdala does not think about future consequences. It also does not feel guilt or remorse. Meaning we can make some really poor decisions and not feel bad about it. (2) When our anxiety increases, and we are operating from our amygdala, our creativity decreases. So, when we are stressed or upset, it is harder for us to think of solutions. It becomes difficult to brainstorm and find a solution that everyone involved would be happy with.[1] (3) When there is a dramatic moment, and you allow the amygdala to take over, then your brain learns that habit. Which means the next time you are in a dramatic situation, the affectively influenced memory center of the brain says, "Things are tough, but I know what to do. Relinquish all rational thought and just let the amygdala be in charge." And this habit becomes more deeply ingrained every time you take this path. Meaning, the more you give in and let your amygdala be in control, the easier it will be. And the harder it will be going forward to have a rational response.[2]

All of this is to say: When you are upset and thinking how good it would feel to make a big dramatic exit, make sure that you are not operating from your amygdala. Your short-term self might love it, but your long-term self is going to give you detention.

In this world where everything is recorded and placed online, you can't afford an outburst. You can't destroy any chance you have of working for the company of your choice or getting a good recommendation. It just isn't worth it. Plus, you will always look like you were actually the bad guy in the conflict.

So exit with grace. With kindness. Even if it takes all of the goodwill you have been storing.

PLANNING MY EXIT WORKSHEET

The Sticks in the Mud
What habits are keeping me in this conflict?
What changes do I need to make in how I see the other person?

Straight, No Chaser
The main message I want the other person to hear:
I have been diluting my message by adding in this ammo (other people, other issues):

Exit Interview
What I will tell my coworkers about my leaving:
What I will tell my managers about this conflict:
What I will tell coworkers at my new office about this conflict:

WHAT TO LOOK FOR IN A NEW OFFICE

What you are looking for in your new office will vary from person to person. As an example, here is my brief checklist when looking for a new office:

- It should take no longer than 30 seconds to get there.
- I should get summers off.
- I need to be able to stay in sweatpants all day.
- I want unlimited, really good coffee.
- All of my coworkers need to be fun and agree with everything I do.

So, clearly, I need to work by myself in my living room. Yes, that was essentially living in quarantine.

Okay, maybe the items on my sample list aren't completely realistic. Unless you become an aspiring author? Start your own company? Professional cat lady?

If you still have to work in an office around other people, here are some things you might want to look for during your initial search and interview phase:[3]

- Everyone speaks. During the interview or a walk around the office, does it feel like one person speaks over the others, or that one person feels inhibited in speaking up?
- Humor. Humor is a great indicator of a healthy office. Inside jokes that are funny. Open laughter, not about someone or behind their back, but just genuinely enjoying each other.
- Flexibility. Obviously if you are going to be an airplane flagger, you need to be there when the plane is landing. But for a lot of jobs, the schedule could change along with your life. Ask about the option to push your schedule back or forward fifteen minutes as day care or school bus times change.
- Dispute resolution options. Hopefully I have made it clear that conflicts are going to happen. If not, I failed miserably in writing this book! Knowing that conflicts will come up, find out what options you have for dealing with them. Can you talk to someone in HR? Will they provide a protected time for you to talk with a coworker? Is there any ongoing coaching or training on communication and a desire to continually improve the office? Do you have the option to identify trends and prevent a conflict when it feels like there is tension?
- Focus on projects rather than tasks. This means that the manager outlines a general need but then trusts the employees to figure out the specifics.
- Meeting formats. Another great barometer is to ask people to describe a typical meeting. Is one person at the front of the room reading off policy changes, or is it a roundtable where everyone's input is requested?

DEATH RUMBLINGS

Even if you are sick of your current office and have made the decision to go, it can still feel bittersweet. Many people are caught off guard by a rush of emotion as they leave a company. Whenever you go through any loss, your mind needs a minute to deal with the change. It is funny, because you can be so happy about the move, and suddenly these feelings of sadness or loss or even anger come bubbling up.

"Oh no! Am I making the wrong move?"

For most people, these unwelcome and out-of-place emotions are your brain's way of saying good-bye to all of the hopes you had for that office. Maybe you used to think that if you just stayed a bit longer you would be respected. Or your project would work out. Or you would be friends with your department. Or you could tough it out until your retirement plan was fully vested.

This is known as the death rumblings phase. It is when things are coming to an end and you become nostalgic about your experience. Imagine your teenage daughter is about to move out and go to college and you remember all of the fun moments you shared, forgetting all of the times that she drove you through the roof.

The funny way that our subconscious works is that if we think about something and picture it, even if it is in the future, our brains still recognize it as being an experience we went through. Our brains need to take time to mourn and say good-bye to that reality. Allow your brain this space, normalize it. No, you are not going crazy. No, if this was an unhealthy environment, you are not making a mistake. It is just your body's way of officially saying good-bye. Give your brain space to hold those future memories, acknowledge what would have been nice, and then say good-bye and good riddance!

GRASSROOTS GRUMBLINGS

The beginning of a relationship is also ripe for conflict. Getting used to a new culture, what jokes are appropriate, what the communication standard is, how casual people are with each other: These things all take time to figure out. There will be missteps along the way. There will be miscommunications and misunderstandings. It is simply part of getting to know anything new.

This phase is the opposite of death rumblings. At the end of a relationship, people experience death rumblings when they remember wistfully the good times that were experienced (or hoped for).

This phase, grassroots grumblings, describes the concerns at the beginning of a relationship that you might have made a mistake. This is common. Without any positive history to fall back on, any small misunderstanding can be taken out of context. You might interpret it as a huge red flag, indicative of lots of crazy workers, instead of just realizing it was a coworker trying to get to know you by making a joke that fell flat.

During this phase, acknowledge what is happening. There will be an awkward grassroots grumblings phase. It doesn't mean you made a mistake; it probably just means you are figuring out a new culture.

TAKEAWAY

Unfortunately, there is not an easy way out. Even if you decide to leave your office, there is still work to do. Plan out your exit so that you can leave gracefully. This also allows you to move to your new office without holding on to baggage from your previous experience.

You know how in an airplane the flight attendants tell you to look for the closest exit, and they let you know that the best exit might be behind you? What this means to us is that the best way for us to coordinate our exit might be to look behind us: Focus on what went wrong with our previous workplace to decide how best to move forward.[4]

42

GOING FORWARD

Hopefully reading through this book has helped you to grow. Not horizontal growth, like me with my brownies. I hope you have experienced mental growth, emotional growth.

Whether you decided to stay in your current position or go to a new one, this book has helped you to learn a lot about communicating with other people in all of their strangeness.

Here's what else you should be prepared for as you move forward.

SHARED VISION

When you are able to communicate clearly with your coworkers you will find suddenly that you are all experiencing something wonderful: a shared vision. That's right. As you are able to clearly communicate your ideas about a project and listen to a coworker's ideas, those ideas meld to form something better. Suddenly you will find you are on the same page with someone you used to think didn't even speak the same language. Strange, huh? A little bit wonderful too? John Ford describes this moment as when a clam and a piece of sand came into contact and were initially frustrated by each other, but then they were able to work together to create a beautiful pearl.

PEACE BY YOUR PIECE

Another thing you have likely discovered through reading this book is that usually we all play a part in the conflict. It is rare to find a conflict where one person is 100 percent to blame, which means that you, gasp, might have had something to do with it. Even if your part was avoiding the conflict, or being unapproachable to discuss the conflict, hopefully you have walked away from this with more understanding. Understanding your part in a conflict not only helps you understand past conflicts, it also is the best medicine for warding off future conflicts. This is called identifying your contribution, and it is incredibly empowering. Obviously, it's not fun to face your mistakes, but this gives you control over your conflicts. It helps you to realize what changes you could make to avoid the conflict in the future.[1]

RETHINK YOUR THINK

There is a wonderful concept called *neuroplasticity*. It is one of those overly complicated words experts use to explain things. Here's what it essentially means: You can change your brain. You can change how you view the world, how you choose to interact with the world, and even how you unconsciously react to situations.[2]

Perhaps traditionally you have been a People Pleaser, or have a strong flight response, or felt like everyone was against you. Maybe there are a few people in your office you have disliked for years.

Now that you have resolved the immediate conflict in your office, you are in a critical period. Your ideas are in flux. Are you going to let your old habits take over and pull you back into the same conflict? Or, are you going to change how you think? This does not happen accidentally. You have to hold your thoughts captive before they run away from you. If you find yourself spiraling into your old negative thoughts, "Oh, he's such a jerk, he has it out for everyone, I don't even want to try talking to him," corral those thoughts. Tell them they are not welcome anymore. Remind yourself that you have gotten to know him, and he's actually not such a jerk after all. Remind yourself that you have gotten past those conflict chains and you are free to talk to him whenever you like. This is *pulling out the sticks in the mud* before they derail all of your hard work.

Remember the Christmas story about the Grinch (which has been redone approximately 17 times)? Grinch was a mean one, no doubt about it. But then he became kind and he went down into Whoville. What would have happened if all of those Whos had treated him like his old self? His mean self? His stinky self? What if they still wouldn't touch him with a 39½-foot pole? I bet that not only would the Grinch have gone back to his old ways, but he would have gotten even worse.

People are just like that dear old Grinch. If we open ourselves up to kindness after a conflict, we are counting on those around us to treat us kindly. If you have worked through a conflict with a coworker, they are also counting on you to treat them in a new way: with kindness. They are observing what you do to see if things really have changed. Are you listening to them with respect and sharing your ideas? Then maybe go celebrate with a glass of wine, or a beer, or a chai. They will begin to build up trust and respect if you show them that you have begun to respect them.

This takes intentionality. There are a lot of old habits and deeply ingrained ways of thinking that will try to pull you back. Habits are comfortable and take less work than retraining our brain. Don't fall for it. You have learned so much. You have control now. Don't waste all of your hard work. Give yourself a few weeks of intentionally banishing those thoughts and eventually you will find your brain has changed. You have pulled out all of the sticks in your muddy brain and have started to form new paths. It won't be an effort to think kindly about your coworkers—it will be your new norm.

There are three key steps to making these changes:[3]

1. *Research:* Intentionally understand the motivation behind these habits.
2. *Revise:* Revise your opinion of the person and catch yourself when you slip into bad habits of seeing them through negative filters.
3. *Reimagine:* Intentionally change your opinion of the other person and choose how you would rather perceive them.

Neuroplasticity is pretty dang cool, huh?

Look at you. You read a simple book, and your brain went and changed and you didn't even know it. Time to celebrate.

GREEN GRASS IS NO ACCIDENT

It is so easy to notice things that are better. Nicer homes, cleaner house, obedient kids, better car. But this is the catch: You can have six-pack abs or a pepperoni pizza habit; you can't have both. If you want the pizza, give up the abs. If you want the abs, give up the pizza. You make changes, you give up the things. Do the work; enjoy the results.

Same dang thing is true of offices. Calm and peaceful offices do not just happen. They take work and acknowledging our weaknesses. We have to be aware of our hang-ups. We have to be willing to talk to people when things get wonky. We have to choose to let go and give grace when people deserve it, and we have to stand up for our own interests because we deserve it. But peaceful workplaces are worth it.

And infectious. The more you model effective communication, the more it will ripple throughout your office. You might be changing your old office, or creating a brand-new wonderful culture at your new office. Maybe next you will write your own book on how satisfying it is to work in a collaborative office. Maybe these 20 different personalities can even merge into teams that have all pushed and pulled on each other and figured out how they fit like a perfect puzzle.

You have done the work.

Go enjoy the results.

CONCLUSION

As you are trying to decide what action to take, I hope you have learned three things:

> Talking is your magic wand.
>
> Tackle this conflict—everyone has conflict, but not everyone has these amazing skills you just learned to resolve conflict. Use them!
>
> Conflict is like a brownie—it doesn't get better with age.

There are no easy answers when it comes to conflict, but there are answers. The first answer is understanding what behavior you are dealing with. The next answer is developing your own plan for moving through your difficult conflict. If you stay in your office, use the suggestions in this book to be able to clearly state your own interests and identify others' interests. If you go, use this book as a guide for setting a good communication foundation at your next place, to prevent conflicts before they even start.

We spend about one-third of our lives working. Stop just trying to survive it. Make that time enjoyable by developing relationships with your coworkers, standing up for your interests, designing work tasks that you enjoy, and improving your office processes.

"When people don't express themselves, they die one piece at a time. You'd be shocked at how many adults are really dead inside—walking through their days with no idea who they are."[1]

This book began by discussing how communication theories were based on Deborah Tannen's work, saying that men have a report style and that women have a rapport style of communication. My hope is that by now you have unencumbered yourself of any limiting styles. Instead, choose your response for each situation. Pick a tool from whichever bucket fits your situation. Design a style that allows you to share your interests and be heard and that allows the other person to share their interests. Then you both use that information to resolve the dispute and go boldly into a beautiful new future. So shed the report or rapport style of talk and create your own resolve style.

You've worked hard to get to this job. You were made for this job. Now make it the job that you want.

When you think about your day as you are driving home from work, it shouldn't drag you down. When you are replaying the day with your family, you can be proud. When you think about getting up the next morning, you can look forward to seeing your coworkers. You are bringing an amazing set of values to the office, and I hope through these conflict conversations you have been able to rise above the dregs of it and find some amazing values in your coworkers as well. It is possible to be excited about the work that you do and to feel a sense of achievement. I hope you're excited about this new level of growth and possibility.

Since I wrote this book, I am excited to say that my friends who inspired this book have found their way through the conflict maze. Cheryl went to school in the evenings, leveled up, and moved into a more supportive position. Leroy, Willy, and Becky had difficult conversations with their coworkers that resulted in much healthier office cultures. Shahalie decided that this was not a supportive environment and opened her own business. They assessed where they were and what they needed, put in the time discussing and listening with their coworkers, and emerged with a sense of self-respect and pride. They were all in the middle of the conflict maze, but they navigated through it like a pro.

You deserve this. You have the tools. You have a plan. You have the support. Rise above the fear and the nastiness of conflict, and enjoy the growth and the bonding and the adventure of it. Get ready for a whole new work.

RESOLVE-ANY-CONFLICT BROWNIES

INGREDIENTS

- 1 cup butter, softened
- 1½ cups white sugar
- 1½ cups brown sugar
- 4 eggs
- 1½ tablespoons vanilla
- 1½ cups flour
- 1 cup cocoa powder
- ½ teaspoon salt
- 1½ cups semi-sweet chocolate chunks or chips

INSTRUCTIONS

1. Preheat oven to 350 degrees.
2. In a large mixing bowl, cream together butter, sugar, and brown sugar for 3–4 minutes or until light and fluffy. Add eggs one at a time, mixing well after each addition. Add vanilla.
3. Pour flour, cocoa, salt, and chocolate chips on top of wet ingredients and mix just the dry ingredients together with a fork. Stir the wet and dry ingredients together just long enough to say, "We disagree, how interesting, I wonder why?"—or whatever your mantra is.

4. Pour into greased 9" × 13" pan; spread evenly.
5. Bake for 28–36 minutes.
6. Let cool for at least 30 minutes before digging in. These take a long time to set up.

Good, right?

RESOURCES

If you have tried using the self-help steps in this book and things haven't improved, you might benefit from connecting with a professional resource. Here are a few suggestions.

LEGAL AID SOCIETIES

A legal aid society serves financially challenged people who need legal help. These are typically funded by the local bar association or government. The purpose is to provide suggestions to help people quickly move through their conflict. Find one near you at www.lsc.gov.

LOCAL COMMUNITY MEDIATION CENTERS/DISPUTE RESOLUTION CENTER

A community mediation center is mostly staffed by volunteers. They are trained mediators who are donating their time or who are trying to gain mediation experience. These are typically free/low-cost, court-funded centers. They also offer trainings to benefit the community. Find one at www.nafcm.org.

SMALL CLAIMS COURT

If the conflict has become a legal, monetary matter, then you might need to go to court. Small claims court is typically for cases that are lower in value (typically $5,000 for business and $10,000 for individuals, but it varies by state). You may choose to hire an attorney or be self-represented. You will have to pay to file a case in small claims court, but you may request to have the filing fees and the attorney fees be repaid if you win the case. Many cases that are filed in small claims court are mandated to mediation. If mediation is successful, the case is withdrawn. If not successful, then the case continues to small claims court.

EMPLOYEE ASSISTANCE PROGRAMS (EAPS)

Many insurance companies also include EAP mental health and dispute resolution benefits. Your HR office should be able to give you details about what assistance your program includes. These benefits can typically be used for a mediator to resolve a dispute, or a therapist or a coach to clarify your goals in a difficult situation. Speak to your HR office or call your insurance company for more details.

ODR.COM

ODR.com has a variety of solutions explorers and triage options for people to explore different processes. This lets employees investigate different ideas and walk away empowered to choose their own process.

NOTES

AUTHOR'S NOTE

1. Kinsey Gorman, Carol. 2016. "Is Your Communication Style Dictated by Your Gender?" *Forbes*. Accessed April 14, 2022. https://www.forbes.com/sites/carolkinseygoman/2016/03/31/is-your-communication-style-dictated-by-your-gender/?sh=5cfacdaaeb9d

2. Goldsmith, Joan, and Bennis, Warren. 1997. *Learning to Lead: A Workbook on Becoming a Leader* (People Skills for Professionals). Nicholas Brealey Publishing.

3. Tannen, Deborah. 1990. *You Just Don't Understand: Women and Men in Conversation*. Ballantine Books.

4. Cummings, Mark. 2011. *Marital Conflict and Children: An Emotional Security Perspective* (The Guilford Series on Social and Emotional Development). New York: Guilford Press.

INTRODUCTION

1. Slaikeu, Karl, and Hasson, Ralph. 1998. "The Preferred Method for Cost Control." *Controlling the Costs of Conflict: How to Design a System for Your Organization*. San Francisco: Jossey-Bass.

2. Slaikeu, Karl, and Hasson, Ralph. 1998. "Weighing Costs and Risks of Each Method." *Controlling the Costs of Conflict: How to Design a System for Your Organization*. San Francisco: Jossey-Bass.

3. Ford, John. 2014. *Peace at Work: The HR Manager's Guide to Workplace Mediation*. John Ford Press.

4. Ford, John. 2014. *Peace at Work: The HR Manager's Guide to Workplace Mediation*. John Ford Press.

5. Edmondson, Donald. 2018. "The Science Behind Behavior Change." Columbia University Irving Medical Center. Accessed April 14, 2022. https://www.cuimc.columbia.edu/news/science-behind-behavior-change

CHAPTER 1

1. Schein, Edgar. 2004. *Organizational Culture and Leadership*, 3rd ed. San Francisco: Jossey-Bass.

2. Schein, Edgar. 2004. *Organizational Culture and Leadership*, 3rd ed. San Francisco: Jossey-Bass.

3. Schein, Edgar. 2004. *Organizational Culture and Leadership*, 3rd ed. San Francisco: Jossey-Bass.

4. Fowler, Clare. 2013. "Workplace Conflict: A Phenomenological Study of the Types, Processes, and Consequences of Small Business Conflict" (PhD diss., Pepperdine University). Communication, scarcity, and confusion were the three top causes of conflict in the dissertation findings. https://pqdtopen.proquest.com/doc/1346686186.html?FMT=ABS

5. Fowler, Clare. 2013. "Workplace Conflict: A Phenomenological Study of the Types, Processes, and Consequences of Small Business Conflict" (PhD diss., Pepperdine University). Communication, scarcity, and confusion were the three top causes of conflict in the dissertation findings. https://pqdtopen.proquest.com/doc/1346686186.html?FMT=ABS

6. Fowler, Clare. 2013. "Workplace Conflict: A Phenomenological Study of the Types, Processes, and Consequences of Small Business Conflict" (PhD diss., Pepperdine University). Communication, scarcity, and confusion were the three top causes of conflict in the dissertation findings. https://pqdtopen.proquest.com/doc/1346686186.html?FMT=ABS

7. Moore, Christopher. 2003. *The Mediation Process: Practical Strategies for Resolving Conflict*, 3rd ed. San Francisco: Jossey-Bass.

CHAPTER 2

1. Holt, Jennifer L., and James DeVore, Cynthia. 2005, vol 29(2), 165–96. "Culture, Gender, Organizational Role, and Styles of Conflict Resolution: A Meta-analysis." *International Journal of Intercultural Relations*.

2. Eagly, Alice H., and Karau, Steven J. 2002, vol 109(3), 573–98. *Role Congruity Theory of Prejudice toward Female Leaders*. Psychological Review: American Psychological Association.

3. Zander, Rosamund Stone, and Zander, Benjamin. 2000. *The Art of Possibility: Transforming Professional and Personal Life.* Boston: Harvard Business School Press.

4. Sande, Ken. 1997. *The Peacemaker: A Biblical Guide to Resolving Personal Conflict*. Grand Rapids: Baker Books.

5. Brown, Brené. 2021. *Atlas of the Heart: Mapping Meaningful Connection and the Language of Human Experience*. New York: Random House.

6. Sande, Ken. 1997. *The Peacemaker: A Biblical Guide to Resolving Personal Conflict*. Grand Rapids: Baker Books.

7. Caron, Christina. 2021. "When Your Job Harms Your Mental Health." *New York Times*. Accessed April 14, 2022. https://www.nytimes.com/2021/06/02/well/mind/job-work-mental-health.html

8. SHRM. "Managing Workplace Conflict." Society for Human Resource Management. Accessed February 12, 2022. https://www.shrm.org/resourcesandtools/tools-and-samples/toolkits/pages/managingworkplaceconflict.aspx

9. Brown, Brené. 2021. *Atlas of the Heart: Mapping Meaningful Connection and the Language of Human Experience.* New York: Random House.

10. Baez, Sandra; Garcia, Adolfo; and Ibanez, Augustin. 2018. "How Does Social Context Influence Our Brain and Behavior?" *Frontiers for Young Minds*. Accessed March 13, 2022. https://kids.frontiersin.org/articles/10.3389/frym.2018.00003

11. Tugend, Alina. 2011. *Better by Mistake: The Unexpected Benefits of Being Wrong*. New York: Penguin.

12. Cloke, Kenneth. 2001. *Mediating Dangerously: The Frontiers of Conflict Resolution*. San Francisco: Jossey-Bass.

13. Cloke, Kenneth. 2001. *Mediating Dangerously: The Frontiers of Conflict Resolution*. San Francisco: Jossey-Bass.

14. Fisher, Roger; Ury, William; and Patton, Bruce. 2011. *Getting to Yes: Negotiating Agreement without Giving In*, 3rd ed. New York: Penguin Books.

15. Heon, Francois, and Davis, Albie. 2014. *The Essential Mary Parker Follett: Ideas We Need Today*. Published by Heon and Davis.

16. Brown, Brené. 2021. *Atlas of the Heart: Mapping Meaningful Connection and the Language of Human Experience*. New York: Random House.

17. Ibid.

18. Kocijan, Vid; Horvat, Marina; and Majdic, Gregor. 2017. "Robust Sex Differences in Jigsaw Puzzle Solving—Are Boys Really Better in Most Visuospatial Tasks?" *Frontiers in Behavioral Neuroscience* 11, 194. https://doi.org/10.3389/fnbeh.2017.00194

19. Tannen, Deborah. 1990. *You Just Don't Understand: Women and Men in Conversation*. Ballantine Books.

20. Denson, Thomas; O'Dean, Siobhan M.; Blake, Khandis R.; and Beames, Joanne. 2018. "Aggression in Women: Behavior, Brain, and Hormones." *Frontiers in Behavioral Neuroscience*. Accessed April 10, 2022. https://www.frontiersin.org/articles/10.3389/fnbeh.2018.00081/full

21. Ibid.

22. Kret, M. E., and De Gelder, B. 2012. "A Review on Sex Differences in Processing Emotional Signals." *Neuropsychologia* 50(7): 1211–21. Accessed April 10, 2022. 10.1016/j.neuropsychologia.2011.12.022. PMID 22245006. S2CID 11695245.

23. Ruppanner, Leah. 2019. "Women Are Not Better at Multitasking. They Just Do More Work, Studies Show." Science Alert. Accessed March 22, 2023. https://www.sciencealert.com/women-aren-t-better-multitaskers-than-men-they-re-just-doing-more-work

24. Mestre, M. V.; Samper, P.; Frías, M. D.; and Tur, A. M. May 2009. "Are Women More Empathetic than Men? A Longitudinal Study in Adolescence." *Span J Psychol* 12(1):76–83. doi: 10.1017/s1138741600001499. PMID: 19476221.

25. Deng, Yaling; Chang, Lei; Yang, Meng; and Huo, Meng. 2016. "Gender Differences in Emotional Response: Inconsistency between Experience and Expressivity." Published June 30, 2016. Accessed April 6, 2022. https://doi.org/10.1371/journal.pone.0158666

26. Brown, Brené. 2021. *Atlas of the Heart: Mapping Meaningful Connection and the Language of Human Experience.* New York: Random House.

27. Dana, Daniel. 2001. *Conflict Resolution*. New York: McGraw-Hill. Published in connection with the Mediation Training Institute based at Eckerd College, St. Petersburg, Florida.

CHAPTER 3

1. Cain, Áine. 2016. "12 Signs Your Coworkers Think You're Dumb." *Business Insider*. Accessed April 15, 2022. https://www.businessinsider.com/more-signs-your-coworkers-think-you-are-stupid-2016-10

2. Note: There is a separate chapter on neurodiversity in the workplace.

3. Cain, Áine. 2016. "12 Signs Your Coworkers Think You're Dumb." *Business Insider*. Accessed April 15, 2022. https://www.businessinsider.com/more-signs-your-coworkers-think-you-are-stupid-2016-10

4. Stone, Douglas; Heen, Sheila; and Patton, Bruce. 2010. *Difficult Conversations: How to Discuss What Matters Most.* New York: Penguin Books.

5. Tannen, Deborah. 2017. "The Truth about How Much Women Talk—and Whether Men Listen." *Time*. Accessed April 15, 2022. https://time.com/4837536/do-women-really-talk-more/

6. Johns, Ashley. 2021. "Uncertainty Reduction Theory." Study.com. Accessed April 15, 2022. https://study.com/academy/lesson/uncertainty-reduction-definition-theory-examples.html

CHAPTER 4

1. Cain, Áine. 2016. "12 Signs Your Coworkers Think You're Dumb." *Business Insider*. Accessed April 15, 2022. https://www.businessinsider.com/more-signs-your-coworkers-think-you-are-stupid-2016-10

2. Noll, Douglas. 2000. "Conflict Escalation: A Five-Phase Model." Mediate.com. Accessed April 15, 2022. https://www.mediate.com/articles/noll2.cfm/

3. Sivanathan, Niro. "TED Talk Blog." Rising Sun Consultants. Accessed April 15, 2022. https://risingsunconsultants.com/blog/ted-talk-niro-sivanathan-the-counterintuitive-way-to-be-more-persuasive/

4. This book is going to include studies that illustrate historical responses to conflict, which were often categorized as feminine or masculine. I recommend reading through both, regardless of gender, to choose which response you want to use for each situation.

CHAPTER 5

1. Fowler, Clare. 2013. "Workplace Conflict: A Phenomenological Study of the Types, Processes, and Consequences of Small Business Conflict" (PhD diss., Pepperdine University). https://pqdtopen.proquest.com/doc/1346686186.html?FMT=ABS

2. Bancroft, Lundy. 2002. *Why Does He Do That? Inside the Minds of Angry and Controlling Men*. New York: Putnam's Sons. This book looks at different types of abuse. It is a great resource for determining if an abuser is really changing.

3. Fowler, Clare. 2013. "Workplace Conflict: A Phenomenological Study of the Types, Processes, and Consequences of Small Business Conflict" (PhD diss., Pepperdine University). https://pqdtopen.proquest.com/doc/1346686186.html?FMT=ABS

4. Brown, Brené. 2018. *Dare to Lead*. New York: Random House.

5. Eddy, Bill. 2021. "Who Are High Conflict People?" High Conflict Institute. Accessed April 16, 2022. https://www.highconflictinstitute.com/podcast-episodes/who-are-high-conflict-people

6. Orth, Taylor. 2021. "What Are America's Love Languages?" YouGov America. Accessed May 1, 2022. https://today.yougov.com/topics/lifestyle/articles-reports/2022/02/11/what-are-americans-love-languages

7. Neville Miller, Ann. 2011. "Men and Women's Communication Is Different—Sometimes." National Communication Association. Accessed April 16, 2022. https://www.natcom.org/communication-currents/men-and-women%E2%80%99s-communication-different%E2%80%94sometimes

8. Daley, Beth. 2017. "Act Tough and Hide Weakness: Research Reveals Pressure Young Men Are Under." The Conversation. Accessed April 16, 2022. https://theconversation.com/act-tough-and-hide-weakness-research-reveals-pressure-young-men-are-under-74898

9. Goldsmith, Joan. 2003. *The Art of Waking People Up*. Wiley & Sons.

10. Sandberg, Sheryl. 2022. "Sheryl Sandberg Requests More Women Leaders." DePaul Digication. Accessed May 1, 2022. https://depaul.digication.com/julia_nelsons_final_portfolio_wrd_103/Rhetorical_Analysis_Final_Draft

11. "The Confidence Gap." *The Atlantic*. Accessed May 1, 2022. https://www.theatlantic.com/magazine/archive/2014/05/the-confidence-gap/359815/

12. Bradshaw, Leslie. 2011. "Why Luck Has Nothing to Do with It." *Forbes*. Accessed January 21, 2022. https://www.forbes.com/sites/lesliebradshaw/2011/11/08/why-luck-has-nothing-to-do-with-it/?sh=24cb44e74f98

CHAPTER 6

1. "Brain Anatomy and How the Brain Works." Johns Hopkins Medicine. Accessed May 1, 2022. https://www.hopkinsmedicine.org/health/conditions-and-diseases/anatomy-of-the-brain

2. Dodgson, Lindsay. 2018. "Constantly Imagining the Worst Case Scenario Is Called 'Catastrophising.'" *Business Insider*. Accessed April 29, 2022. https://www.businessinsider.com/what-catastrophising-means-and-how-to-stop-it-2018-3#:~:text=By%20thinking%20catastrophically%2C%20we%20are,the%20worst%2C%22%20Blair%20said

3. *Vacuum* meaning empty space. Hopefully you don't actually hate your vacuum cleaner. Although I completely get it if you hate vacuuming; it sucks. Hehehe.

4. Harmon, Katherine. 2019. "The Brain Adapts in a Blink to Compensate for Missing Information." *Scientific American*. Accessed May 1, 2022. https://www.scientificamerican.com/article/brain-adapts-in-a-blink/#:~:text=A%20similar%20phenomenon%20called%20%22filling,falls%20in%20the%20blind%20spot

5. *Psychology Today* Staff. "Shyness." *Psychology Today*. Accessed May 1, 2022. https://www.psychologytoday.com/us/basics/shyness

6. Pazzanese, Christina. 2020. "Women Less Inclined to Self-Promote Than Men." *Harvard Gazette*. Accessed May 1, 2022. https://news.harvard

.edu/gazette/story/2020/02/men-better-than-women-at-self-promotion-on-job-leading-to-inequities/

7. Chamorro, Tomas. "Science and Tech to Help Predict Human Performance: Why Do So Many Incompetent Men Become Leaders." Dr. Tomas. Accessed May 1, 2022. https://drtomas.com/

CHAPTER 7

1. Tegan and Sara. 2014. *The Lego Movie*, WaterTower Music.

2. Hagan, Ekua. 2017. "How to Deal with People Who Just Won't Stop Talking." *Psychology Today*. Accessed May 1, 2022. https://www.psychologytoday.com/us/blog/fulfillment-any-age/201708/how-deal-people-who-just-wont-stop-talking

3. Nicholson, Bebe. 2019. Accessed May 1, 2022. Medium. https://medium.com/swlh/people-who-wont-stop-talking-and-what-we-can-do-about-it-b8d4a14d5de0#:~:text=Different%20reasons%20for%20talking%20too%20much&text=Other%20people%20are%20insecure%20and,at%20long%20last%2C%20is%20listening

4. Enke, Susanne; Ginzehauser, Catherine; Hepach, Robert; Karbach, Julia; and Saalbach, Henrik. "Differences in Cognitive Processing? The Role of Verbal Processes and Mental Effort in Bilingual and Monolingual Children's Planning Performance." Science Direct. Accessed May 3, 2022. https://www.sciencedirect.com/science/article/abs/pii/S0022096521001739

5. MacRae, Fiona. 2013. "Sorry to Interrupt, Dear, but Women Really Do Talk More Than Men (13,000 Words a Day More to Be Precise)." Science Correspondent. Accessed May 3, 2022. https://www.dailymail.co.uk/sciencetech/article-2281891/Women-really-talk-men-13-000-words-day-precise.html

CHAPTER 8

1. Olson, Lindsay. 2012. "How to Be a Team Player When You Work with a Slacker." *U.S. News and World Report*. Accessed May 3, 2022. https://money.usnews.com/money/blogs/outside-voices-careers/2012/10/11/how-to-be-a-team-player-when-you-work-with-a-slacker

2. Ford, John. 2014. *Peace at Work: The HR Manager's Guide to Workplace Mediation*. John Ford Press.

3. Andersen, Erika. 2013. "Why Some Employees Need to Be Fired." *Forbes*. Accessed May 3, 2022. https://www.forbes.com/sites/erikaandersen/2013/06/25/why-some-employees-need-to-be-fired/?sh=4d6f3b34ef4e

4. "How to Support Mental Health at Work." 2022. Mental Health. Accessed May 3, 2022. https://www.mentalhealth.org.uk/publications/how-support-mental-health-work

5. "Brain Anatomy and How the Brain Works." Johns Hopkins Medicine. Accessed May 1, 2022. https://www.hopkinsmedicine.org/health/conditions-and-diseases/anatomy-of-the-brain

6. Oxfam. "Why the Majority of the World's Poor Are Women." 2021. Oxfam International. Accessed May 3, 2022. https://www.oxfam.org/en/why-majority-worlds-poor-are-women

7. Kelly, Claire. 2018. "The 'Slacker-Striver' Reversal." Claire Kelly. Accessed May 3, 2022. https://clairekelly14.wordpress.com/2018/07/09/the-slacker-striver-reversal-bridesmaids-2011-and-trainwreck-2015/

CHAPTER 9

1. Mesku, Melissa. 2015. "The Problem with Being a People Pleaser." Medium. Accessed May 3, 2022. https://medium.com/the-ascent/the-problem-with-being-a-people-pleaser-6a9714c6c8a1

2. Gupta, Sanjana. 2021. "How to Recognize When You're Being Used." Very Well Mind. Accessed May 3, 2022. https://www.verywellmind.com/how-to-recognize-when-you-re-being-used-5207959

CHAPTER 10

1. Grones, Geraldine. 2019. "Addressing Inappropriate Work Behavior (and How to Address Them)." Human Resources Director. Accessed May 3, 2022. https://www.hcamag.com/us/specialization/workplace-health-and-safety/addressing-inappropriate-work-behavior-and-preventing-them/194847#:~:text=However%2C%20employees%20displaying%20inappropriate%20behavior,and%20employee%20turnover%20might%20occur

2. Anderson, Amy Rees. 2014. "If You Want to Improve, Stop Defending and Start Listening." *Forbes*. Accessed May 3, 2022. https://www.forbes.com/sites/amyanderson/2014/02/07/if-you-want-to-improve-stop-defending-and-start-listening/?sh=6fe411a67e57

3. Gottman, John, and Silver, Nan. 1999. *The Seven Principles for Making Marriage Work*. New York: Three Rivers Press.

4. Cohen, Jessie. 2017. We Work. Accessed May 4, 2022. https://www.wework.com/ideas/professional-development/management-leadership/what-type-a-employees-need-from-you

5. Reuell, Peter. 2016. "Resolving Conflict: Men vs. Women." *Harvard Gazette*. Accessed May 4, 2022. https://news.harvard.edu/gazette/story/2016/08/resolving-conflict-men-vs-women/

CHAPTER 11

1. Mata, Henrique. 2021. Management 3.0. Accessed May 4, 2022. https://management30.com/blog/micromanagement/

2. Mata, Henrique. 2021. Management 3.0. Accessed May 4, 2022. https://management30.com/blog/micromanagement/

3. Gallo, Amy. 2011. "Stop Being Micromanaged." *Harvard Business Review*. Accessed May 4, 2022. https://hbr.org/2011/09/stop-being-micromanaged#:~:text=Principles%20to%20Remember,is%20apprised%20of%20your%20progress

4. White, Richard, Jr. 2010. *Public Personnel Management*, 39, no. 1 (Spring 2010). "The Micromanagement Disease: Symptoms, Diagnosis, and Cure." International Personnel Management Association.

5. Fowler, Clare. "Mental Health and Mediation." Panel discussion at the Online Dispute Resolution Conference in Dublin, Ireland, May 5, 2022.

6. Tannen, Deborah. 1990. *You Just Don't Understand: Women and Men in Conversation*. Ballantine Books.

CHAPTER 12

1. Daum, Kevin. "5 Signs That a Charismatic Leader Is Manipulating You." Inc. Accessed May 4, 2022. https://www.inc.com/kevin-daum/5-signs-that-a-charismatic-leader-is-manipulating-you.html

2. Daum, Kevin. "5 Signs That a Charismatic Leader Is Manipulating You." Inc. Accessed May 4, 2022. https://www.inc.com/kevin-daum/5-signs-that-a-charismatic-leader-is-manipulating-you.html

3. Hall, Nick. 2021. "9 Traits of a Narcissist: Behaviour to Watch For." Man of Many. Accessed May 4, 2022. https://manofmany.com/lifestyle/sex-dating/signs-you-are-dating-a-narcissist

4. Grensing-Prophal, Lin. 2020. "Praise in Public; Criticize in Private." HR Daily Advisor. May 4, 2022. https://hrdailyadvisor.blr.com/2020/11/13/praise-in-public-criticize-in-private/#:~:text=Most%20managers%20have%20probably%20heard,it%20one%2Don%2Done

5. Stack, Laura. 2003. "Employees Behaving Badly." Society for Human Resource Management. Accessed May 4, 2022. https://www.shrm.org/hr-today/news/hr-magazine/pages/1003stack.aspx

6. Stack, Laura. 2003. "Employees Behaving Badly." Society for Human Resource Management. Accessed May 4, 2022. https://www.shrm.org/hr-today/news/hr-magazine/pages/1003stack.aspx

7. Holland, Kimberly. 2017. "Amygdala Hijack: When Emotions Take Over." Healthline. Accessed May 4, 2022. https://www.healthline.com/health/stress/amygdala-hijack

8. Moore, Christopher. 2003. *The Mediation Process: Practical Strategies for Resolving Conflict*, 3rd ed. San Francisco: Jossey-Bass.

9. Raypole, Crystal. 2020. "Understanding the Cycle of Abuse." Healthline. Accessed May 4, 2022. https://www.healthline.com/health/relationships/cycle-of-abuse

10. Fowler, Clare. 2013. "Workplace Conflict: A Phenomenological Study of the Types, Processes, and Consequences of Small Business Conflict" (PhD diss., Pepperdine University). Dissertation findings report that 10 percent of workplace conflicts end in violence. https://pqdtopen.proquest.com/doc/1346686186.html?FMT=ABS

11. Cloke, Kenneth. Ken Cloke's lecture on Workplace Conflict at Pepperdine University, June 23, 2018.

12. Burton-Hughes, Liz. 2018. "How to Manage Anger in the Workplace." High Speed Training. Accessed May 4, 2022. https://www.highspeedtraining.co.uk/hub/how-to-manage-anger-in-the-workplace/

13. West, Mary. 2021. "What Is the Fight, Flight, or Freeze Response?" Medical News Today. Accessed May 4, 2022. https://www.medicalnewstoday.com/articles/fight-flight-or-freeze-response

14. Noll, Douglas. 2000. "Conflict Escalation: A Five Phase Model." Mediate.com. https://www.mediate.com//articles/noll2.cfm; and Jordan, Thomas. 2000. "Glasl's Nine-State Model of Conflict Escalation." Mediate.com. https://www.mediate.com/articles/jordan.cfm

15. Ford, John. 2014. *Peace at Work: The HR Manager's Guide to Workplace Mediation*. John Ford Press.

16. Cloke, Kenneth. 2001. *Mediating Dangerously: The Frontiers of Conflict Resolution*. San Francisco: Jossey-Bass. This book discusses the Princess Triangle, which states that in a conflict people choose three central roles: princess, prince, and dragon [sic].

17. Cloke, Kenneth. 2001. *Mediating Dangerously: The Frontiers of Conflict Resolution*. San Francisco: Jossey-Bass. This book discusses the Princess Triangle, stating that in a conflict people choose their role in relation to the princess/victim.

18. Bancroft, Lundy. 2002. *Why Does He Do That? Inside the Minds of Angry and Controlling Men*. New York: Putnam's Sons. This book looks at

different types of abuse. It is a great resource for determining if an abuser is really changing.

19. Eddy, Bill. 2014. *BIFF: Quick Responses to High-Conflict People, Their Personal Attacks, Hostile Email and Social Media Meltdowns*. Scottsdale, AZ: Unhooked Media, 55.

20. Cloke, Kenneth. 2001. *Mediating Dangerously: The Frontiers of Conflict Resolution*. San Francisco: Jossey-Bass. This book discusses the Princess Triangle, stating that in a conflict people choose their role in relation to the princess.

21. Indeed Editorial Team. 2021. "5 Signs You're in a Toxic Work Environment and How to Handle It." Indeed.com. Accessed May 4, 2022. https://www.indeed.com/career-advice/career-development/how-to-deal-with-a-toxic-work-environment

22. Break the Silence DV. 2019. "Reactive Abuse: What It Is and Why Abusers Rely on It." Break the Silence. Accessed May 4, 2022. https://breakthesilencedv.org/reactive-abuse-what-it-is-and-why-abusers-rely-on-it/

23. Jones, Alison. 2021. "'Be a Man': Why Some Men Respond Aggressively to Threats to Manhood." Science Daily. Accessed May 4, 2022. https://www.sciencedaily.com/releases/2021/01/210128155633.htm

24. O'Toole, Fintan. 2018. "'Being a Man Is Quite Scary': Readers Tell Us What Is Hard about Being Male in 2018." *Irish Times*. Accessed May 4, 2022. https://www.irishtimes.com/life-and-style/people/being-a-man-is-quite-scary-readers-tell-us-what-is-hard-about-being-male-in-2018-1.3700202

CHAPTER 13

1. SoP. 2017. "Prefrontal Cortex." The Science of Psychotherapy. Accessed May 4, 2022. https://www.thescienceofpsychotherapy.com/prefrontal-cortex/#:~:text=The%20prefrontal%20cortex%20(PFC)%20is,making%2C%20and%20moderating%20social%20behaviour

2. Eddy, Bill. 2014. *BIFF: Quick Responses to High-Conflict People, Their Personal Attacks, Hostile Email and Social Media Meltdowns*. Scottsdale, AZ: Unhooked Media, 55. Bill Eddy has additional books and resources available from the High Conflict Institute (https://www.highconflictinstitute.com).

3. Frothingham, Scott. 2019. "How Long Does It Take for a New Behavior to Become Automatic?" Healthline. Accessed May 4, 2022. https://www.healthline.com/health/how-long-does-it-take-to-form-a-habit

4. Eddy, Bill. 2021. "Who Are High Conflict People?" High Conflict Institute. Accessed April 16, 2022. https://www.highconflictinstitute.com/podcast-episodes/who-are-high-conflict-people

5. Eddy, Bill. 2020. "4 Red Flags of a High-Conflict Partner." *Psychology Today*. Accessed May 11, 2022. https://www.psychologytoday.com/us/blog/5-types-people-who-can-ruin-your-life/202012/4-red-flags-high-conflict-partner#:~:text=High%20conflict%20people%20(HCPs)%20tend,a%20description%20of%20conflict%20behavior

6. Somerset, Sarah. 2021. "4 Strategies to Manage High Conflict Personalities at Work." Finehaus. Accessed May 11, 2022. https://finehaus.com.au/association-governance/4-strategies-manage-high-conflict-personalities-work/

CHAPTER 14

1. Stone, Douglas; Heen, Sheila; and Patton, Bruce. 2010. *Difficult Conversations: How to Discuss What Matters Most*. New York: Penguin Books.

2. Gibbons, Serenity. 2020. "How to Defeat Busy Culture." *Harvard Business Review*. Accessed May 11, 2022. https://hbr.org/2020/09/how-to-defeat-busy-culture

3. Gibbons, Serenity. 2020. "How to Defeat Busy Culture." *Harvard Business Review*. Accessed May 11, 2022. https://hbr.org/2020/09/how-to-defeat-busy-culture

4. Gangle, Paul, and Gangle, Junie. 2014. "Personal Responsibility." Fernridge Faith Center. Accessed October 19, 2014. http://www.fernridgefaithcenter.org

5. "An Impossible Workload." Working America. Accessed August 1, 2022. https://www.workingamerica.org/fixmyjob/scheduling/impossible-workload

CHAPTER 15

1. Dean, William; Siegfried, W. R., and MacDonald, I. A. W. "The Fallacy, Fact, and Fate of Guiding Behavior in the Greater Honeyguide." *Conservation Biology* 4(1): 99–101. Accessed March 11, 2013. doi:10.1111/j.1523-1739.1990.tb00272.x

2. Mesiti, Pat. 2019. "What to Do When Someone Constantly Steals Your Glory." Mesiti. Accessed May 11, 2022. https://mesiti.com/what-to-do-when-someone-constantly-steals-your-glory/

3. Mesiti, Pat. 2019. "What to Do When Someone Constantly Steals Your Glory." Mesiti. Accessed May 11, 2022. https://mesiti.com/what-to-do-when-someone-constantly-steals-your-glory/

CHAPTER 16

1. Hall-Flavin, Daniel K. 2021. "What Is Passive-Aggressive Behavior? What Are the Signs?" Mayo Clinic. Accessed May 11, 2022. https://

www.mayoclinic.org/healthy-lifestyle/adult-health/expert-answers/passive-aggressive-behavior/faq-20057901#:~:text=Passive%2Daggressive%20behavior%20is%20a,what%20he%20or%20she%20does

2. Moore, Christopher. 2003. *The Mediation Process: Practical Strategies for Resolving Conflict*, 3rd ed. San Francisco: Jossey-Bass.

3. Hall-Flavin, Daniel K. 2021. "What Is Passive-Aggressive Behavior? What Are the Signs?" Mayo Clinic. Accessed May 11, 2022. https://www.mayoclinic.org/healthy-lifestyle/adult-health/expert-answers/passive-aggressive-behavior/faq-20057901#:~:text=Passive%2Daggressive%20behavior%20is%20a,what%20he%20or%20she%20does

4. Nikravan Hayes, Ladan. 2018. "Passive Aggressiveness: Why We Do It and How to Stop." Talkspace. Accessed May 11, 2022. https://www.talkspace.com/blog/passive-aggressiveness-how-to-stop/

5. Ford, John. 2014. *Peace at Work: The HR Manager's Guide to Workplace Mediation*. John Ford Press.

6. Nikravan Hayes, Ladan. 2018. "Passive Aggressiveness: Why We Do It and How to Stop." Talkspace. Accessed May 11, 2022. https://www.talkspace.com/blog/passive-aggressiveness-how-to-stop/

7. Nikravan Hayes, Ladan. 2018. "Passive Aggressiveness: Why We Do It and How to Stop." Talkspace. Accessed May 11, 2022. https://www.talkspace.com/blog/passive-aggressiveness-how-to-stop/

CHAPTER 17

1. Gallo, Amy. 2014. "How to Deal with a Mean Colleague." *Harvard Business Review*. Accessed May 12, 2022. https://hbr.org/2014/10/how-to-deal-with-a-mean-colleague?registration=success

2. Cloke, Kenneth. 2001. *Mediating Dangerously: The Frontiers of Conflict Resolution*. San Francisco: Jossey-Bass.

3. Gallo, Amy. 2014. "How to Deal with a Mean Colleague." *Harvard Business Review*. Accessed May 12, 2022. https://hbr.org/2014/10/how-to-deal-with-a-mean-colleague?registration=success

4. Gallo, Amy. 2014. "How to Deal with a Mean Colleague." *Harvard Business Review*. Accessed May 12, 2022. https://hbr.org/2014/10/how-to-deal-with-a-mean-colleague?registration=success

5. West, Mary. 2021. "What Is the Fight, Flight, or Freeze Response?" Medical News Today. Accessed May 12, 2022. https://www.medicalnewstoday.com/articles/fight-flight-or-freeze-response#:~:text=The%20fight%2C%20flight%2C%20or%20freeze%20response%20refers%20to%20involuntary%20physiological,escape%2C%20or%20hide%20from%20danger

6. Cloke, Kenneth. Ken Cloke's lecture on Workplace Conflict at Pepperdine University, June 23, 2018.

7. Brainerd, C. J.; Stein, L. M.; Silveira, R. A.; Rohenkohl, G.; and Reyna, V. F. 2008. "How Does Negative Emotion Cause False Memories?" National Library of Medicine. Accessed May 12, 2022. https://pubmed.ncbi.nlm.nih.gov/18947358/

8. Gallo, Amy. 2014. "How to Deal with a Mean Colleague." *Harvard Business Review*. Accessed May 12, 2022. https://hbr.org/2014/10/how-to-deal-with-a-mean-colleague?registration=success

9. Aurit, Michael. 2021. "Lecture on Family Mediation Training." Presented by Mediate.com, at Mediate.com/zoom, June 21, 2021.

10. Beebe, Steven. "Interview: Uncertainty Reduction Theory." Accessed May 12, 2022. https://www.mastersincommunications.com/research/interpersonal-communication/uncertainty-reduction-theory

11. Maltz, Maxwell. 2016. *Psycho-Cybernetics Deluxe Edition: The Original Text of the Classic Guide to a New Life*. New York: TarcherPerigee, 75.

CHAPTER 18

1. May, Christina. 2019. "Five Key Characteristics of Generational Family Business." Illumine8. Accessed May 12, 2022. https://www.illumine8.com/blog/five-key-characteristics-of-generational-family-businesses

2. May, Christina. 2019. "Five Key Characteristics of Generational Family Business." Illumine8. Accessed May 12, 2022. https://www.illumine8.com/blog/five-key-characteristics-of-generational-family-businesses

3. Barraza, Carlos. "What Is Family Business and Its Characteristics." Accessed May 12, 2022. https://barrazacarlos.com/what-is-family-business-characteristics/

CHAPTER 19

1. Watershed. 2022. "Interests versus Positions." Watershed Associates. Accessed May 12, 2022. https://www.watershedassociates.com/learning-center-item/interests-versus-positions.html#:~:text=Positions%20are%20surface%20statements%20of,someone%20takes%20a%20certain%20position

2. Watershed. 2022. "Interests versus Positions." Watershed Associates. Accessed May 12, 2022. https://www.watershedassociates.com/learning-center-item/interests-versus-positions.html#:~:text=Positions%20are%20surface%20statements%20of,someone%20takes%20a%20certain%20position

3. Torres, Monica. 2022. "The 7 Personalities of Bad Bosses Who Think They're Good Bosses." *Huffington Post*. Accessed May 12, 2022. https://www.huffpost.com/entry/bad-boss-personality-types_l_5ff486e9c5b6ec8ae0b63938

CHAPTER 20

1. Health Harvard. 2020. "Understanding the Stress Response." Harvard Health Publishing. Accessed May 12, 2022. https://www.health.harvard.edu/staying-healthy/understanding-the-stress-response

CHAPTER 21

1. Oxford Dictionary. Definition of "abuse." Accessed May 1, 2022. https://languages.oup.com/google-dictionary-en/

2. Reach Team. 2022. "6 Different Types of Abuse." From REACH Beyond Domestic Violence. Accessed May 1, 2022. https://reachma.org/blog/6-different-types-of-abuse/

3. Namie, Gary. 2021. "What Is Workplace Bullying?" WorkplaceBullying. Accessed May 1, 2022. https://workplacebullying.org/

4. "How to Prepare for Your Initial Whistleblower Claim." Hoyer Law Group. Accessed May 1, 2022. https://www.hoyerlawgroup.com/whistleblower-law/resources/preparing-your-whistleblower-claim/

5. NWC. 2020. "National Whistleblower Protection Act." Accessed May 1, 2022. https://www.whistleblowers.org/faq/whistleblower-protection-act-faq/#:~:text=The%20Whistleblower%20Protection%20Act%20protects,and%20specific%20danger%20to%20public

6. "The Concept of 'Just Cause' in Union Contracts." Massachusetts Nurses Association. Accessed May 1, 2022. https://www.massnurses.org/labor-action/labor-education-resources/grievances-101/just-cause

CHAPTER 22

1. Shore, Stephen. "Autism Is One Word Attempting to Describe Millions of Different Stories." Autism Speaks. Accessed May 12, 2022. https://www.autismspeaks.org/blog/autism-one-word-attempting-describe-millions-different-stories

2. I have been asked many questions on working with people on the special needs and neurodiversity spectrum, and I wanted to make sure to address it in this book. There is so much misinformation, contradictory information, and so many generalizations that could not apply to an entire group of people. I have tried to cover the most common questions that people ask, but this is still a poor substitute for simply talking to your coworker.

3. Long, Leslie, and Kearon, Dave. 2018. "Changing the Spectrum: Autism in the Workplace." Autism Speaks. Accessed May 12, 2022. https://www.autismspeaks.org/blog/changing-spectrum-autism-workplace

4. Long, Leslie, and Kearon, Dave. 2018. "Changing the Spectrum: Autism in the Workplace." Autism Speaks. Accessed May 12, 2022. https://www.autismspeaks.org/blog/changing-spectrum-autism-workplace

5. Baez, Sandra; Garcia, Adolfo; and Ibanez, Augustin. 2018. "How Does Social Context Influence Our Brain and Behavior?" Frontiers for Young Minds. Accessed March 13, 2022. https://kids.frontiersin.org/articles/10.3389/frym.2018.00003

6. Anxiety Centre blogs. Accessed May 12, 2022. https://www.anxietycentre.com/

7. Clay, Rebecca. 2017. "Women Outnumber Men in Psychology, but Not in the Field's Top Echelons." American Psychological Association. Accessed May 12, 2022. https://www.apa.org/monitor/2017/07-08/women-psychology

CHAPTER 23

1. Jolly, David. 2010. "France Telecom Needs 'Radical Change' after Suicide, Report Says." *New York Times*. Accessed May 12, 2022. https://www.nytimes.com/2010/03/09/technology/09telecom.html

2. Sinolak, Mark. 2022. Talk on Organizational Ombuds and Mental Health at the International Ombuds Association Conference, April 5, 2022.

3. Bernstein, Elizabeth. 2014. "Domestic Abusers Can Reform, Studies Show." *Wall Street Journal*. Accessed May 12, 2022. https://www.wsj.com/articles/domestic-abusers-can-reform-studies-show-1410822557

4. Bernstein, Elizabeth. 2014. "Domestic Abusers Can Reform, Studies Show." *Wall Street Journal*. Accessed May 12, 2022. https://www.wsj.com/articles/domestic-abusers-can-reform-studies-show-1410822557

5. Schulman, Sarah. 2017. *Conflict Is Not Abuse.* Arsenal Pulp Press.

6. Bancroft, Lundy. *Why Does He Do That? Inside the Minds of Angry and Controlling Men*. 2002. New York: Putnam's Sons. This book looks at different types of abuse. It is a great resource for determining if an abuser is really changing.

7. Bernstein, Elizabeth. 2014. "Domestic Abusers Can Reform, Studies Show." *Wall Street Journal*. Accessed May 12, 2022. https://www.wsj.com/articles/domestic-abusers-can-reform-studies-show-1410822557

CHAPTER 24

1. "How to Support Mental Health at Work." 2022. Mental Health. Accessed May 3, 2022. https://www.mentalhealth.org.uk/publications/how-support-mental-health-work

2. Graham, Katherine. 2013. Accessed May 1, 2022. http://www.mediate.com/articles/GrahamKbl20141004.cfm#. The Health and Occupation Research network (THOR), data request no: 2013-01-THOR-GP, Centre for Occupational and Environmental Health, University of Manchester, p. 96.

3. "How to Support Mental Health at Work." 2022. Mental Health. Accessed May 3, 2022. https://www.mentalhealth.org.uk/publications/how-support-mental-health-work

4. "How to Support Mental Health at Work." 2022. Mental Health. Accessed May 3, 2022. https://www.mentalhealth.org.uk/publications/how-support-mental-health-work

5. Medline authors. "How to Improve Mental Health." Medline Plus. Accessed May 12, 2022. https://medlineplus.gov/howtoimprovementalhealth.html

6. Fisher, Roger; Ury, William; and Patton, Bruce. 2011. *Getting to Yes: Negotiating Agreement without Giving In*, 3rd ed. New York: Penguin Books. "Attack the problem not the person" is one of four main tenets from this book.

CHAPTER 25

1. Skekoski, Mimi. *Anger and Your Vision*. HappyEyesight.com. Accessed October 20, 2018. https://www.happyeyesight.com/anger-and-your-vision/

2. Abraham, Micah. *Affected Hearing*. CalmClinic.com. Accessed October 15, 2018. https://www.calmclinic.com/anxiety/signs/affected-hearing

3. Cherry, Kendra. 2019. "How the Fight-or-Flight Response Works." Very Well Mind. Accessed May 12, 2022. https://www.verywellmind.com/what-is-the-fight-or-flight-response-2795194

4. "What Really Happens in Your Body When You Fight." Thelist.com. Accessed August 6, 2017. https://www.thelist.com/54883/really-happens-body-fight

5. Vazquez, Laurie. 2017. "What Fear Does to Your Brain and How to Stop It." Accessed August 6, 2017. https://bigthink.com/laurie-vazquez/what-fear-does-to-your-brain-and-how-to-stop-it

6. "What Really Happens in Your Body When You Fight." Thelist.com. Accessed August 6, 2017. https://www.thelist.com/54883/really-happens-body-fight

7. Dion, Lisa. "Fight-Flight-Freeze Comparison." Prepared collaboratively during a 2011 training.

8. Cloke, Kenneth. 2001. *Mediating Dangerously: The Frontiers of Conflict Resolution*. San Francisco: Jossey-Bass.

9. Cloke, Kenneth. 2001. *Mediating Dangerously: The Frontiers of Conflict Resolution*. San Francisco: Jossey-Bass.

10. Karpman, Stephen. *A Game-Free Life*. Drama Triangle Publications.

11. Brainerd, C. J.; Stein, L. M.; Silveira, R. A.; Rohenkohl, G.; and Reyna, V. F. 2008. "How Does Negative Emotion Cause False Memories?" National Library of Medicine. Accessed May 12, 2022. https://pubmed.ncbi.nlm.nih.gov/18947358/

CHAPTER 27

1. Sherif, Muzafer; Harvey, O. J.; White, B. J.; Hood, W. R.; and Sherif, Carolyn. 1998. *The Robbers Cave Experiment*. Middletown, CT: Wesleyan University Press.

2. LeVine, Robert; Brewer, Marilynn; and Campbell, Donald. 1972. *Ethnocentrism: Theories of Conflict, Ethnic Attitudes and Group Behavior*. New York: Wiley. There is an additional study, although with fewer participants and for a shorter period of time. Lufty Diab studied 18 boys from Beirut, made up of Christians and Muslims, divided into a Blue group and a Red group. Fighting ensued, not between the Christians and the Muslims, but between the Blues and the Reds. This was not a replica of the original study, but it did seem to reinforce the conclusions drawn from the Robbers Cave Experiment.

CHAPTER 28

1. Frank, Anne. 1949. *Anne Frank's Tales from the Secret Annex: A Collection of Her Short Stories, Fables, and Lesser-Known Writings*, revised edition (2003). New York: Bantam.

CHAPTER 29

1. Whitbourne, Susan Krauss. 2014. "Why We Fantasize about Other Partners." *Psychology Today*. Accessed May 12, 2022. https://www.psychologytoday.com/us/blog/fulfillment-any-age/201411/why-we-fantasize-about-other-partners

2. Caesar, Vance. 2008. "The Importance of Understanding Workplace Options." Doctoral Introduction Lecture, Pepperdine University, Culver City, California, August 11, 2008.

CHAPTER 30

1. Schein, Edgar H. 2010. *Organizational Culture and Leadership*, 4th ed. San Francisco: Jossey-Bass, 367.

2. Dana, Daniel. 2001. *Conflict Resolution: Mediation Tools for Everyday Worklife*. New York: McGraw-Hill. This resource examines how much time we spend in conflict at work and a way to break down the cost of that conflict.

3. Bolman, Lee, and Deal, Terrence. 2003. *Reframing Organizations: Artistry, Choice, and Leadership*, 7th ed. San Francisco: Jossey-Bass, 115.

CHAPTER 31

1. Scott, Vivian. 2010. *Conflict Resolution at Work for Dummies*. Indianapolis: Wiley, 250.

2. Ford, John. 2014. *Peace at Work: The HR Manager's Guide to Workplace Mediation*. John Ford Press.

3. Fowler, Clare. 2013. "Workplace Conflict: A Phenomenological Study of the Types, Processes, and Consequences of Small Business Conflict" (PhD diss., Pepperdine University). https://pqdtopen.proquest.com/doc/1346686186.html?FMT=ABS

4. "What Really Happens in Your Body When You Fight." Thelist.com. Accessed August 6, 2017. https://www.thelist.com/54883/really-happens-body-fight

5. Jessup, Ryan; Ritchie, Levi; and Homer, John. 2019. "Choose Quickly or Naught: Paralyzed by a Plethora of Options." American Psychological Association. Accessed June 22, 2022. https://www.apa.org/pubs/highlights/spotlight/issue-160

CHAPTER 32

1. Slaikeu, Karl, and Hasson, Ralph. 1998. "The Preferred Method for Cost Control." *Controlling the Costs of Conflict: How to Design a System for Your Organization*. San Francisco: Jossey-Bass.

2. Vozza, Stephanie. 2017. "These Are the Six Red Flags That You're Getting Bad Advice." *Fast Company*. Accessed June 22, 2022. https://www.fastcompany.com/40438756/these-are-the-six-red-flags-that-youre-getting-bad-advice

CHAPTER 33

1. Sangha, Forest. "The Island: An Anthology of the Buddha's Teachings on Nibbana." Accessed June 22, 2022. https://forestsangha.org/system/resources/W1siZiIsIjIwMjAvMTEvMjAvMmxyYXNvYmlodV9UaGVfSXNsYW5kX1dlYi5wZGYiXV0/The%20Island-Web.pdf?sha=aed10513643c52d8

2. Ferre, Sofia, and Benter, Neil. 2019. Daily Gospel. Accessed June 22, 2022. https://www.dlshsi.edu.ph/daily-lasallian-reflection-prayer/matthew-1815-20#:~:text=15%20%E2%80%9CIf%20your%20brother%20sins,of%20two%20or%20three%20witnesses

3. Little Simple. 2017. "Agathokakological." Accessed June 22, 2022. https://www.urbandictionary.com/define.php?term=agathokakological

4. Krath, Jeanine; Schürmann, Linda; and von Korflesch, Harald F. O. 2021. "Revealing the Theoretical Basis of Gamification: A Systematic Review and Analysis of Theory in Research on Gamification, Serious Games and Game-based Learning." Science Direct. Accessed June 22, 2022. https://www.sciencedirect.com/science/article/pii/S0747563221002867

5. Lessons and Guidelines. Quran Wiki. Accessed June 22, 2022. http://www.quran-wiki.com/ayat.php?sura=41&aya=34

6. Rabbi Jonathan Sachs. June 2010. "The Torah of Conflict Resolution." https://www.rabbisacks.org/covenant-conversation/chukat/the-torah-of-conflict-resolution/

CHAPTER 34

1. Sinolak, Mark. 2022. Talk on Organizational Ombuds and Mental Health at the International Ombuds Association Conference, April 5, 2022.

2. Fowler, Clare. 2013. "Workplace Conflict: A Phenomenological Study of the Types, Processes, and Consequences of Small Business Conflict" (PhD diss., Pepperdine University). https://pqdtopen.proquest.com/doc/1346686186.html?FMT=ABS

3. Zander, Rosamund Stone, and Zander, Benjamin. 2000. *The Art of Possibility: Transforming Professional and Personal Life*. Boston: Harvard Business School Press.

4. Slaikeu, Karl, and Hasson, Ralph. 1998. *Controlling the Costs of Conflict*. San Francisco: Jossey-Bass.

5. Dana, Daniel. 2001. *Conflict Resolution*. New York: McGraw-Hill. Published in connection with the Mediation Training Institute based at Eckerd College, St. Petersburg, Florida.

6. Schein, Edgar H. 2010. *Organizational Culture and Leadership*, 4th ed. San Francisco: Jossey-Bass, 299–360.

7. Martinez, Jan; Amsler, Lisa; and Smith, Stephanie. 2020. *Dispute Systems Design: Preventing, Managing, and Resolving Conflict*. Stanford, CA: Stanford University Press.

CHAPTER 35

1. Cloke, Kenneth. 2001. "Creating Organizational Cultures That Support Resolution." *Mediating Dangerously: The Frontiers of Conflict Resolution*. San Francisco: Jossey-Bass, 125.

2. USBL. 2022. "Job Openings and Labor Turnover Summary." Accessed July 10, 2022. https://www.bls.gov/news.release/jolts.nr0.htm

3. "New Job Adjustment Period." 2022. Eggcellent Work. Accessed July 10, 2022. https://eggcellentwork.com/new-job-adjustment-period/

CHAPTER 36

1. Sherif, Muzafer; Harvey, O. J., White, B. J., Hood, W. R., and Sherif, Carolyn. 1998. *The Robbers Cave Experiment*. Middletown, CT: Wesleyan University Press.

CHAPTER 37

1. Craggs, Tom. 2021. "25 Rules of Successful Marathon Training." *Runner's World*. Accessed July 10, 2022. https://www.runnersworld.com/uk/training/marathon/a36969929/successful-marathon-training-rules/

2. Yoga Institute. 2022. The Himalayan Yoga Institute. Accessed July 10, 2022. https://www.himalayanyogainstitute.com/transformational-power-mantra

3. Maslow, Abraham. 1943. "A Theory of Human Motivation." *Psychological Review*, 50(4): 370–96.

4. Cloke, Kenneth. Ken Cloke's lecture on Workplace Conflict at Pepperdine University, June 23, 2018.

5. Cloke, Kenneth. Ken Cloke's lecture on Workplace Conflict at Pepperdine University, June 23, 2018.

6. Stone, Douglas; Heen, Sheila; and Patton, Bruce. 2010. *Difficult Conversations: How to Discuss What Matters Most*. New York: Penguin Books.

7. Sande, Ken. 1997. *The Peacemaker: A Biblical Guide to Resolving Personal Conflict*. Grand Rapids: Baker Books, 206.

8. Moore, Christopher. 2003. *The Mediation Process: Practical Strategies for Resolving Conflict*, 3rd ed. San Francisco: Jossey-Bass.

9. Fowler, Clare. 2013. "Workplace Conflict: A Phenomenological Study of the Types, Processes, and Consequences of Small Business Conflict" (PhD diss., Pepperdine University). https://pqdtopen.proquest.com/doc/1346686186.html?FMT=ABS

CHAPTER 38

1. Quote investigator, research. https://quoteinvestigator.com/2017/03/23/same/

2. Sande, Ken. 1997. *The Peacemaker: A Biblical Guide to Resolving Personal Conflict*. Grand Rapids: Baker Books.

3. Conflict Character. Accessed September 17, 2018. http://www.pinyin.info/chinese/crisis.html

CHAPTER 39

1. Noll, Douglas. 2000. "Conflict Escalation: A Five-Phase Model." Mediate.com. Accessed April 15, 2022. https://www.mediate.com/articles/noll2.cfm/

CHAPTER 40

1. Ford, John. 2014. *Peace at Work: The HR Manager's Guide to Workplace Mediation*. John Ford Press, 29.

CHAPTER 41

1. SOP. 2017. "Prefrontal Cortex." The Science of Psychotherapy. Accessed July 11, 2022. https://www.thescienceofpsychotherapy.com/prefrontal-cortex/

2. McGaugh, James L.; Cahill, Larry; and Roozendaal, Benno. 1996. "Involvement of the Amygdala in Memory Storage: Interaction with Other Brain Systems." Proceedings of the National Academy of Sciences of the United States of America. Accessed July 11, 2022. https://www.pnas.org/doi/10.1073/pnas.93.24.13508

3. Ryan, Liz. 2018. "Ten Unmistakable Signs of a Healthy Workplace." *Forbes*. Accessed July 10, 2022. https://www.forbes.com/sites/lizryan/2018/05/19/ten-unmistakable-signs-of-a-healthy-workplace/?sh=251c3db15cad

4. Power of Positivity. 2020. "13 Ways a Bad Situation Can Help Transform Your Life." Accessed May 3, 2022. https://www.powerofpositivity.com/13-ways-a-bad-situation-can-help-transform-your-life/

CHAPTER 42

1. Stone, Douglas; Heen, Sheila; and Patton, Bruce. 2010. *Difficult Conversations: How to Discuss What Matters Most*. New York: Penguin Books.

2. Voss, Patrice; Thomas, Maryse; Cisneros-Franco, Miguel; and de Villers-Sidani, Etienne. 2017. "Dynamic Brains and the Changing Rules of Neuroplasticity: Implications for Learning and Recovery." Accessed July 10, 2022. https://www.frontiersin.org/articles/10.3389/fpsyg.2017.01657/

full#:~:text=Neuroplasticity%20can%20be%20viewed%20as,and%20in%20response%20to%20experience

3. Schmitz, Amy. 2022. "The Future of Dispute Resolution." Keynote lecture at the Association of Family Conciliation Courts, May 12, 2022.

CONCLUSION

1. Anderson, Laurie Halse. 2011. *Speak*. Square Fish.

INDEX

ABOUT MEDIATE.COM

Mediate.com has been helping mediators since 1996. With more than 15,000 articles, news items, blog postings, and videos, and more than 5 million visitor sessions each year, Mediate.com is the world's leading mediation website.

Mediate.com serves as a bridge between professionals offering mediation and people needing mediators. Mediate.com also offers resources for those seeking to resolve conflict, such as online calculators, tutorials, trainings, and directories.

ABOUT THE AUTHOR

Dr. Clare E. Fowler was initially introduced to conflict resolution in a peer mediation course in the third grade and has been studying it since. She received her master's degree and doctorate in workplace mediation from Pepperdine University. She is an adjunct professor at the University of Oregon School of Law and mediates workplace disputes. She is also the executive vice president at Mediate.com. She believes that people want to resolve their own conflict, they just need the right tools.

She enjoys spending time out in the Northwest with her family.

For article links, follow Clare on LinkedIn. For conflict soundbites, follow Clare's social media through Mediate.com.

Additional resources and articles available at clarefowler.com

ACR PRACTITIONER'S GUIDE SERIES
AN ACR/ROWMAN & LITTLEFIELD PARTNERSHIP PUBLICATION SERIES

ACR/Rowman & Littlefield Publication Editors:

Michael Lang, Institute for Reflective Practice, Sarasota, Florida, mlang@mediate.com

Susanne Terry, Institute for Reflective Practice, Danville, Vermont, sterry@highreachfarm.com

Cheryl Jamison, Belonging & Connectedness Consultant, Columbus, Georgia, cheryl.jamison26@gmail.com

Books in the ACR Practitioner's Guide Series are *field guides* for the benefit of practitioners actively engaged as third-party intervenors, scholars, educators, trainers, researchers, and participants in conflict resolution processes. Each book is a practical guide that illuminates thought processes that lead to action—the underlying rationale for practice decisions—rather than simply describing "what to do." Grounded in Reflective Practice principles, the books examine the application of theory and research in relation to practice choices and guide the reader/user in a deeper understanding of why we make particular choices in our work.

Titles in Series:

The Guide to Reflective Practice in Conflict Resolution by Michael D. Lang

More Justice, More Peace: When Peacemakers Are Advocates edited by Susanne Terry

Beyond Equity and Inclusion in Conflict Resolution: Recentering the Profession edited by S.Y. Bowland, Hasshan Batts, Beth Roy, and Mary Adams Trujillo

Self-Determination in Mediation: The Art and Science of Mirrors and Lights by Dan Simon and Tara West

Rising Above Office Conflict: A Light-Hearted Guide for the Heavy-Hearted Employee by Clare E. Fowler

Forthcoming:

Walk It Like You Talk It: An Action Guide for Practicing Conflict Resolution by Gloria Rhodes

About ACR

The Association for Conflict Resolution (ACR) is a professional organization enhancing the practice and public understanding of conflict resolution. An international professional association for mediators, arbitrators, educators, and other conflict resolution practitioners and researchers, ACR works in a wide range of settings throughout the United States and around the world. Our multicultural and multidisciplinary organization offers a broad umbrella under which all forms of dispute resolution practice find a home. Website: www.acrnet.org; Twitter: @ACRgroup.

Angelia Tolbert, president of Absolute Resolution Services, Inc., Little Rock, Arkansas

Maria Volpe, professor of sociology, director of the Dispute Resolution Program at John Jay College of Criminal Justice–City University of New York; director of the CUNY Dispute Resolution Center

Barbara Wilson is an independent family and workplace mediator in the south of England, including London, and is published in the UK, the United States, Denmark, and Australia.